© Richard A. Bloom

JONATHAN RAUCH, a senior fellow at the Brookings Institution in Washington, is the author of several books and many articles on public policy, culture, and government. A recipient of the 2005 National Magazine Award, he's a contributing editor of *The Atlantic*. He has also written for *The New Republic*, *The New York Times*, *The Wall Street Journal*, and *The Washington Post*, among many other publications. He lives with his husband in Washington, D.C.

Also by Jonathan Rauch

Political Realism: How Hacks, Machines, Big Money,
and Back-Room Deals Can Strengthen American Democracy

Kindly Inquisitors: The New Attacks on Free Thought

Denial: My 25 Years Without a Soul

Gay Marriage: Why It Is Good for Gays, Good for
Straights, and Good for America

Government's End: Why Washington Stopped Working

The Outnation: A Search for the Soul of Japan

Additional Praise for *The Happiness Curve*

"Rauch fills his book with reassuring research on why a midlife malaise is normal, as well as some sound lessons on how to cultivate happiness in general. With strong family relationships, a trust-filled community, and supportive friends, anyone should be able to ride out even their darkest years."   —*The Wall Street Journal*

"A refreshingly thoughtful, positive view of aging."

—*AARP Magazine*

"In a youth-obsessed culture, it may be difficult to convince some that life gets better after fifty. But by supplanting dated clichés with compelling scholarship, Rauch offers a fresh and reassuring vision of aging that supersedes superficial fixations."   —*The Washington Post*

"*The Happiness Curve* is about a midlife transition that empirical lifetime studies and 'big data' have demonstrated to be just as reliable a finding as was Stanley Hall's groundbreaking 1907 definition of 'adolescence.' In order to demonstrate that our psychological well-being declines until the fifth decade and then steadily improves, Rauch not only provides illustrative case histories—always scientifically suspect if reassuring—but also reviews authoritative lifespan studies, ranging from primatology to neurophysiology, from demography to frequency of mood-altering medication use. With maturity, gratitude becomes easier, and 'giving it away' becomes a source of joy, rather than a life sentence of 'letting go.' *The Happiness Curve* should be essential reading for everybody over forty."

—George E. Vaillant, MD,
professor of psychiatry at Harvard Medical School,
director of the Grant Study of Adult Development,
and author of *Triumphs of Experience*

"*The Happiness Curve* delivers on the promise of its title, with wise insights and practices to help you become the best you can be. Leave the midlife slump. Enter into an encore adulthood of powerful purpose."

—Richard J. Leider, international bestselling
author of *The Power of Purpose*,
Repacking Your Bags, and *Life Reimagined*

"When I was forty, I used to think that life begins at forty. How naïve I was in my callow youth! It's fifty, of course—no, make that sixty. In this warm, wise, and witty overview, Jonathan Rauch combines evidence and experience to show his fellow adults that the best is yet to come."

—Steven Pinker, bestselling author of
Enlightenment Now and *The Blank Slate*

"Do you wish to understand the arc of your life? And why you are likely to end up happier than you are right now? If so, *The Happiness Curve* is the place to start. And I write this as someone who can vouch that the upper part of the happiness life curve is very glorious indeed."

—Tyler Cowen, *New York Times* bestselling
author of *The Complacent Class* and *The Great Stagnation*

"What makes midlife so difficult for so many? Being human, as this illuminating and beautifully reasoned book explains. If it's hard to believe that happiness increases with age, Jonathan Rauch suggests, just wait. Or read this book."   —Ashton Applewhite, author of
This Chair Rocks: A Manifesto Against Ageism

"It's a great paradox of happiness: The decades when we experience our greatest worldly success are also when our happiness craters. Why are middle-aged people so miserable? Jonathan Rauch tackles the question

in this helpful, rigorous, and fun book. *The Happiness Curve* will make readers smarter—and perhaps even a little more joyful."
—Arthur C. Brooks, president of the American Enterprise Institute

"Jonathan Rauch has taken the midlife crisis and transformed it into the kinder, gentler happiness curve. He pierces the old, cliché-ridden landscape of broken marriages and red sports cars, and replaces it with a new and rich understanding of the natural life cycle. *The Happiness Curve* is a helpful travel guide through the middle and later years that will be passed from one generation to another with the reassuring message: 'it gets better.'"
—Ellen Goodman, Pulitzer Prize–winning journalist

"Anyone between age thirty-five and seventy must read this book. Armed with scientific rigor, compelling stories, and winsome self-revelation, Jonathan Rauch reveals the mystery of midlife."
—Barbara Bradley Hagerty, *New York Times* bestselling author of *Life Reimagined: The Science, Art, and Opportunity of Midlife*

"Rauch contrasts the happiness people experience in midlife with the happiness they expect, making an important scientific finding come to life with urgency and passion. Beautifully written and a must-read for those who are interested in the science of happiness and for anyone approaching the age of forty." —Martin Binder, professor of economics at Bard College Berlin

"This brilliant book is chock-full of unexpected findings, revelatory insights, and consoling wisdom about aging, happiness, and the stages of life. I would say that everyone in his or her forties should read it—it will be a soothing balm for those in the dark wood of middle age—but that's too

limiting: Really, every thinking adult should read this stimulating intellectual adventure story, which is also a genuinely helpful guidebook to life."
—Scott Stossel, author of *My Age of Anxiety: Fear, Hope, Dread, and the Search for Peace of Mind* and national editor of *The Atlantic*

"This is a book destined to be passed hand to hand as a balm for the travails of midlife. Required reading for anyone between the ages of thirty-five and fifty-five who wants to avoid needless suffering."
—Miles Kimball, professor of economics at University of Colorado Boulder

"Rauch's elegantly lucid and nuanced book, which smoothly summarizes the work of dozens of economists, scientists, and psychologists, begins by examining the work of 'happiness economists,' who use 'big data' to trace the arc of happiness. Filtering out variables such as health, wealth, and marital status, they found a consistent U-shaped pattern."
—*The Columbus Dispatch*

"Journalist Rauch (*Political Realism*) argues for a 'happiness curve' to life—a common, U-shaped path from youthful idealism, through middle age disappointment, to eventual happiness—in this inspired take on midlife crises. [Readers] will also take comfort from Rauch's personal investment in the subject—he has moved through the bottom of his own happiness curve and concludes his heartening self-help book by writing that it was 'worth the wait.'"
—*Publishers Weekly*

"This uplifting report offers hope and encouragement for aging readers doubting the longevity of bliss. Stimulating reading for those seeking enlightenment and joyfulness throughout middle age."
—*Kirkus Reviews*

"Psychologists agree that the midlife crisis is a myth. But why are so many middle-aged people so dissatisfied with their lives? Sifting through happiness studies and conducting his own interviews and surveys, Rauch discovers a pattern . . . This thoughtful study is sure to find an audience."

—*Booklist*

THE
HAPPINESS
CURVE

Why Life Gets Better After 50

Jonathan Rauch

PICADOR

A Thomas Dunne Book

St. Martin's Press

New York

picadorusa.com • instagram.com/picador
twitter.com/picadorusa • facebook.com/picadorusa

Picador® is a U.S. registered trademark and is used by Macmillan Publishing Group, LLC, under license from Pan Books Limited.

For book club information, please visit facebook.com/picadorbookclub or email marketing@picadorusa.com.

The Library of Congress has cataloged the Thomas Dunne Books edition as follows:

Names: Rauch, Jonathan, 1960– author.
Title: The happiness curve : why life gets better after 50 / Jonathan Rauch.
Description: First [edition]. | New York : Dunne Books, 2018. | Includes
    bibliographical references and index.
Identifiers: LCCN 2018005155 | ISBN 9781250078803 (hardcover)
Subjects: LCSH: Middle age—Psychological aspects. | Happiness. |
    Interpersonal relations.
Classification: LCC BF724.6 .R38 2018 | DDC 155.6—dc23
LC record available at https://lccn.loc.gov/2018005155

Picador Paperback ISBN 978-1-250-08091-2

Our books may be purchased in bulk for promotional, educational, or business use. Please contact your local bookseller or the Macmillan Corporate and Premium Sales Department at 1-800-221-7945, extension 5442, or by email at MacmillanSpecialMarkets@macmillan.com.

First published by Thomas Dunne Books, an imprint of St. Martin's Press

First Picador Edition: May 2019

10 9 8 7 6 5 4 3 2 1

For Oscar Rauch and Donald Richie
In loving memory

Contents

Thomas Cole painted *The Voyage of Life,* which was strongly influenced by Romanticism, in 1842. The series of allegorically Christian paintings portrays the four stages of human life, which are childhood, youth, manhood, and old age.

THE VOYAGE OF LIFE

Thomas Cole's journey—and mine

Karl is forty-five years old. He is a successful professional who works with a nonprofit organization in a major American city. He has a PhD, two kids, and an okay, though not perfect, marriage. He is friendly, personable, approachable. Mostly, he is pleased with the way his life has turned out. Middle height, brown hair, not someone you would notice on the street, except maybe for his partiality to skinny-brim fedoras. A nice guy.

Like a lot of people, he got off to an exciting start in his twenties. Finished graduate school. Moved to New York City, a whirlwind for a Midwestern boy. *Wild, free, energetic* are words he uses to recall that period. "Staying out all night. Getting laid left and right."

His thirties brought responsibility, then predictability. Graduate school ended, the search for a job began; he split painfully with a bohemian, fascinating, mercurial girlfriend. "It was the end of an era." His next girlfriend was more sober, solid. At age thirty-three, Karl had a good job at a government agency; at thirty-four, he married; at thirty-six, they had their first child, and a second followed when he was thirty-nine. After his twenties, responsibility was a jolt, but he adjusted well: "For a long time

I embraced it. It was kind of fun feeling like a grown-up doing the things I was supposed to do."

But then the complexion of his life began to change. Not the external circumstances: everything was going well. Something else seemed wrong. That story about being a grown-up, hitting all the marks: "After a while it ceases to be very persuasive, and you begin to say, 'Oh, man, all this is, it's fuckin' *work*.'"

Karl didn't have time for a midlife crisis; by the age of forty he had two young kids and a brand-new baby. "The circumstances sort of pushed off whatever reckoning I'd have to do." But only temporarily. "It felt like my life was for the most part either going to a job where I was increasingly unsatisfied, or it was going home and changing diapers and doing more work." He applied for higher-up, managerial jobs. Then he switched jobs altogether, leaving the government to launch a new project at a nonprofit. Giving up tenure at one of the world's few really secure employers was a risk, but he felt he needed change. "It's helped a bit. But quite frankly I think what I'd really love to do is take off to someplace in Europe for a while by myself." He won't run away, of course; he's not the type. "It's been more of a grabbing freedom at the margins."

Karl isn't depressed, at least not in any clinical or medical sense. He is a vibrant, fully functional individual who is, in many ways that count, living his dream. No, not depressed: dissatisfied. And dissatisfied about being dissatisfied. And, he says, *scared*.

For this book, I gave scores of people a questionnaire about their satisfaction in life, both in the present and at earlier ages. I asked them to rate their life satisfaction in each decade of life on a scale of zero to ten, and I also asked for a few words or phrases to describe each decade. Karl described his forties with the words *confused, searching, scared*.

I ask him: "Why 'scared'?" He pauses, draws breath. What he's going through makes no sense. If his life were rotten, he would understand. But he has the things he wanted. He has *more* than he wanted, or more than he thought he wanted. "Am I losing my mind? How am I going to get out of this? The feeling of being lost, for a type-A, overtly successful, highly intelligent human being—to find yourself completely at sea, and not knowing where port is, and whether you're going to get there . . ." He trails off.

I ask if he has considered going the medical route: therapy, medication? That might be necessary or valuable at some point, he replies, but it doesn't feel relevant now. Especially not the pharmaceutical route. I think I understand why: when I talk to Karl, I see no mental illness or instability or dysfunction. The disease model doesn't seem to fit.

"Whom do you talk to about all this?" Another pause. "I have one dear friend who I've brought it up with. Otherwise, nobody. You."

"Not your wife?"

"I don't know how much she would actually get it." Besides, he'd risk triggering alarm and disruption. "It would be a shitstorm."

"Friends?"

"It feels conceited to bring it up with them. I come from a pretty humble background in Pennsylvania. They'd just kind of look at me and say, 'Jesus, you've got it all. What are you bitching about?' I know people who've got cancer in their families." Midlife crisis "is almost a punch line. Who wants to bring it up and feel like you're walking into a joke? And it's also fundamentally so *irrational*. Am I hungry? No. I have fine clothes on my back; a beautiful office; way more freedom than almost anyone who has a job has. Beautiful home. Good health. *So what the hell am I complaining about?*"

In the sentence that begins, "I'm dissatisfied with my life right now because," there is nothing after the *because*.

Dominic is a little older than Karl: fifty, rather than forty-five. Other than that, the two have a lot in common. They work in related fields, travel in overlapping social circles, and are acquainted professionally. They share salt-of-the-earth backgrounds: Dominic grew up on a rural farm. They both had exciting, eventful twenties, though Dominic's were not as bohemian as Karl's. Dominic married young, then took degrees from two of the world's most prestigious institutions (one abroad), then worked in Congress.

Dominic's thirties, like Karl's, brought responsibility and predictability. He describes that period as goal-oriented, though unlike Karl he landed in a role he actively disliked. He established himself in a high-pressure business job, one which provided a handsome salary, but at the cost of seventy-hour workweeks. "I had a growing sense of disconnect between the goals that were in front of me and what I felt was inspiring or valuable to me. I was working very hard and was adept at what I was doing but didn't feel good about myself for doing it."

Things came to a head for Dominic soon after he turned forty. He realized he would not make partner without taking on assignments that were even less to his liking. So, much as Karl did in his early forties, he made a jump into the nonprofit world. "I loved the clients, I loved the colleagues; the cynicism that had built up in me completely dissipated." Professionally, he was in a good place.

Still, he felt discontent. "In my forties, my wife and I grappled with, *Well, things haven't turned out the way we expected*. I realized that my professional prospects—and so much of my identity was wrapped up in my work—likely aren't going to change. By any measure I was successful, and there weren't any particular ambitions I had that weren't being fulfilled. But I began to observe that I just had a friend win a MacArthur Award, and a friend who was confirmed as a federal judge. You start to see peers assume positions and you realize that my career pathway is not going to lead me to that kind of outcome. There was in the early forties some gnashing of teeth over that."

When I ask Dominic to characterize his forties, he uses the adjective *stressed* and rates his life satisfaction as relatively low. But when I ask him to characterize his life right now, at fifty, he uses the word *appreciative* and rates his life satisfaction at nine out of a possible ten.

"Why?" I ask.

"In the late forties there was kind of a reappreciation of what I had done and where I was." He found himself circling back to the values of his childhood on the farm, values centered on sturdy relationships and worthwhile work. "I came to appreciate that the life or the marriage or the employment are just such incredible assets. Try as I might have, I haven't fully screwed those up."

"Yes," I say. "But *why*? What brought about your rebirth of gratitude?"

"That's a good question. I think there's a spiritual dimension to it. A spiritual maturity. Less of a self-centered or self-absorbed outlook on life. I came to appreciate that the best is the enemy of the good. There was an awareness that the life I had didn't play out exactly as I imagined, but was still pretty good. I would describe it as a sense of feeling gratitude for where we're at.

"What's interesting is that by any objective measure things haven't changed all that much. We're dealing with a lot of the same issues. Our kids are facing some real challenges. I like my work, but there are aspects that don't speak to me as much as prior forms of employment. So it's not that I find myself in new external circumstances. I don't know if it's a combination of expecting less or appreciating more."

He reflects for a moment, then adds: "I guess I'm expecting less *and* appreciating more."

Dominic doesn't know precisely what changed to make him feel more grateful. He only knows that his nagging sense of disappointment is diminishing. The closest he comes to an explanation is to venture that, after years of defining accomplishment in the language of competition, achievement, and keeping score, he is opening up to new sources of satisfaction.

"Like what?" I ask.

The other day, he was home with his eleven-year-old daughter, working on his laptop and trying to focus on the task at hand, when she announced she wanted to paint his toenails. "I said, 'No, I don't want painted toenails.'" And then, after a moment, he heard himself, somewhat to his own surprise, change his mind. "So right now, I'm going around with a smiley face on my big toenail."

Like *that*.

In November 1828, almost two centuries before my conversations with Karl and Dominic, a young man of twenty-seven, on the cusp of a storied career as the founding father of American landscape painting, wrote to a friend about his own dissatisfaction. Having come out of nowhere from a working-class background, Thomas Cole was experiencing the first flush of lifelong success; he had already been elected a founding member of the National Academy of Design. But he wanted to be, he wrote, more than just a painter of leaves and pretty scenes. He hoped to make paintings that teach: "I still look forward with hope to the time when I shall be able to produce pictures that shall affect the mind of the beholder like the works of a great poet—that shall elevate the imagination and produce a happy moral effect."

In 1839, in his late thirties, Cole received a commission for a series of four paintings called *The Voyage of Life*. "I work at it 'con amore,'" he wrote, "and hope to make it the finest work I have executed." His hopes were not disappointed. First exhibited in 1840, *The Voyage of Life* was greeted with critical and public acclaim, proving to be Cole's most popular and durable work and more than fulfilling his ambition to tell elevating stories with art.

The paintings are imposingly large; including their frames, they are more than seven feet long and five feet high. That alone is enough to ensure they make an impression. They are also meticulously detailed. Inspect them up close and the trees seem to sprout real leaves, the rocks real crags. The palette is rich, almost phantasmagorical, and the contrasts bold.

Years before the magic of computer-generated graphics and video games, Cole created an immersive otherworld. In it, he tells a story.

The voyage begins, in the first painting, with *Childhood*. The scene here is all promise, all joy. From a craggy cave at the left of the picture, a river emerges. On it glides a gilded boat, whose passenger is a joyful baby, delighted at having materialized from the darkness of preexistence into an Eden of dawning sensation. Behind the child in the boat, holding the tiller and hovering within close reach, like an attentive parent, stands the traveler's guardian angel. Infancy, for Cole, is a time of untroubled security and innocent wonder. The prow of the boat is decorated with the figurehead of a golden angel, holding up before her an hourglass. The voyage, we are reminded, is through time.

The second painting, *Youth,* is the lightest, the airiest, the loveliest of the four, a scene of magical beauty and charm. The river is placid, the banks lush with grass and trees, the sky azure and cloudless. The infant is now a young man in the first blush of adulthood, his cheeks still smooth. Now he steers the boat himself, but his guardian angel stands behind him on the bank nearby, unseen but in easy hailing distance, gesturing ahead encouragingly.

Ahead—there, beckoning to the Voyager—is the proverbial castle in the sky, "a cloudy pile of Architecture," as Cole describes it (in his own commentary on the paintings), "an air-built Castle, that rises dome above dome in the far-off blue sky." The celestial Taj Mahal soars like a cumulus formation, and the Voyager reaches eagerly toward it. We, however, from our elevation above ground level, can see what the Voyager cannot. The river will turn away from the castle, bearing the boat sharply off toward rough waters and rocks faintly visible through trees in the distance. The way to the castle is not by river at all, but instead along a winding dirt path that disappears into hazy hills on the horizon: the road not taken. Perhaps the Voyager fails to notice the side road, or perhaps he pauses to wonder where it might lead; but his fate belongs to the river and the hourglass. "The gorgeous cloud-built palace," Cole says in his description, "whose glorious domes seem yet but half revealed to the eye, growing more and more lofty as we gaze, is emblematic of the daydreams of youth, its aspirations after glory and fame: and the dimly seen path would intimate that Youth, in its impetuous career, is forgetful that it is embarked on the Stream of Life, and that its current sweeps along with resistless force. . . ."

Youth is a masterpiece of both draftsmanship and storytelling, perhaps the greatest depiction in Western visual art of the boundless expectations of early adulthood (though it has a literary rival in Joseph Conrad's short story "Youth"). The air in the painting vibrates with hope and aspiration. In *Manhood,* the third of the four, the scene and story are very different. The Voyager is now (as Cole tells us) "a man of middle age," appearing to modern eyes to be perhaps in his early forties, bearded, and robust, but holding his hands clasped before him as if in supplication. The colors, the clouds, and the horizon all are dark. "Storm and cloud enshroud a rugged and dreary landscape. Bare, impending precipices rise in the lurid light. The swollen stream rushes furiously down a dark ravine, whirling and foaming in its wild career, and speeding toward the Ocean, which is dimly seen through the mist and falling rain. The boat is there plunging amid the turbulent waters." Its rudder has broken off; the Voyager cannot steer and must trust his fate to the guardian angel. But the angel, though still attentive, now looks on from behind and afar, gazing down through the clouds. The seraphic figure is out of the Voyager's sight and too distant to hail in any case. For all the Voyager can tell, he is on his own. His clasped hands pray for deliverance, but his eyes show fear.

"Trouble is characteristic of the period of Manhood," Cole tells us. "In childhood, there is no carking care: in youth, no despairing thought. It is only when experience has taught us the realities of the world, that we lift from our eyes the golden veil of early life; that we feel deep and abiding sorrow: and in the Picture, the gloomy, eclipse-like tone, the conflicting elements, the trees riven by tempest, are the allegory. . . ." At our elevation we can see calm oceanic waters beyond, but the Voyager can catch only fitful glimpses of peace, and the river bears him not there but toward implacable rapids and what appear to be the watery mists of a cataract.

The fourth and last painting of the series, *Old Age,* is also dark in hue, but its tone is again very different. The sky is dark but the storm is clearing; heavenly light breaks through. The boat, battered and broken, has lost both its figurehead and its helm; rudder and hourglass alike are gone. Neither marking time nor setting course is now necessary, for the boat has emerged from sharp crags at the mouth of the river into calm waters of a boundless ocean. The Voyager is balding and white-bearded, as battered as his vessel. He sits in the boat as the infant did, rather than standing like the youth and middle-aged man. His aspect, seen in left profile, is calm, expressing neither joy nor wonder nor fear; his hands are raised in a gesture of greeting—for before him, now nearby and in full view, the guardian angel beckons him heavenward. "Directed by the Guardian Spirit, who thus far has accompanied him *unseen,* the Voyager, now an old man, looks upward to an opening in the clouds, from whence a glorious light bursts forth; and angels are seen descending the cloudy steps, as if to welcome him to the Haven of Immortal Life. The stream of life has now reached the Ocean to which all life is tending."

These, then, are the ages of man. Life begins and ends with happiness, but with happiness of two very different kinds, the first joyful and excitable, the latter calm and resigned. The youth and old man both see hopeful apparitions, but whereas the youth sees castles in the sky, the elder sees a beckoning angel. The middle-aged man, by contrast, sees only savage rocks and turbulent waters.

Soon after Cole painted his splendid quadriptych, the paintings were purchased and locked in a private collection, much to the ambitious artist's disappointment. Eager to display them, in 1842 he painted a second set, almost identical to the first. They were exhibited repeatedly and to great effect. Cole, meanwhile, converted to Anglicanism and turned more explicitly to religious themes in his work. Alas, his life was fated to be short, ending with a case of pleurisy in 1848, when he was only forty-seven. His reputation, burnished both by his landscapes and his allegories, was such that a posthumous retrospective of his work in 1848 drew nearly half a million attendees in New York City, at the time equivalent to half the city's population. Later, the second *Voyage* set disappeared into private hands, eventually resurfacing to be displayed at a hospital, where it was poorly looked after. In 1916, an unnamed "eminent artist" called for all four paintings to be bought, relined, cleaned, reframed, "then properly established in some gallery by themselves, either at the Metropolitan Museum in New York or the National in Washington."

So they would be. In 1971 the National Gallery of Art, in Washington, D.C., acquired the 1842 *Voyage* set, there to be encountered by millions, one of whom was me.

It is winter of 1980. I am a college sophomore on break, spending a few days in Washington. Sightseeing with a friend, I am visiting the National Gallery for the first time. In a passageway between buildings, hung there temporarily while renovations are under way, Thomas Cole's four *Voyage* paintings loom into view. Like so many people, I'm stopped first by the sheer size of the paintings, then am captured by the immediacy of their storytelling. Only one other painting, a landscape by Rembrandt, would remain in my memory of that day. I linger a long time with Cole's vision. I wonder if their story will be my story.

The swaddled innocence of Cole's *Childhood* certainly rings true. So do the sky-high aspirations of *Youth*. Almost twenty years old myself, standing on the foothills of maturity, I want to make a mark on the world, though I have no settled ambitions. I've recently joined the college newspaper, having given up, for lack of talent, the notion of being a musician. I love reading and writing, so perhaps the future points that way? But it is hard to be a writer, and I imagine I am more likely to wind up as a lawyer, like my father, if only because that path is so well marked. I feel myself reaching upward for—well, for something, though I don't yet know what. *Youth* is a story about high hopes and great expectations, and mine are high enough and great enough. As for the calm of *Old Age,* it seems plausible, but too far in the future to interest me.

Manhood, too, seems far away, but in some respects all too close. Even at the young age of almost twenty, I was well aware that middle age can be difficult. My father was overworked and overstressed, my mother suffered from depression, and their marriage broke up when I was twelve, leaving my father to raise three kids on his own. One day, when I was fourteen or fifteen, I learned that my father, then in his mid-forties, had lost his anchor client and half his law practice. If there was a moment when I left the coddled world of Cole's *Childhood,* that was it. A few years later, gazing upon *Manhood,* I see my father in the skiff, beset by white water and rocks as he tries to raise a shattered family and rebuild a broken business, all on his own and with no tiller or guardian angel.

Manhood, I suppose, does not show the way *my* life will go. There are sure to be crises and difficulties, true. I will encounter disappointment and failure. Perhaps there will be challenges as daunting as my father's. But, at age twenty, I assume that *anywhere* will be better than here. As of now, I have no firm goals, no money, no love life (or prospect of one), no conspicuous talent, just my studies and a summer job. Not that day at the National Gallery, perhaps, but around that time, I make a vow to remember where I started and appreciate any blessings that come my way. I am certain I will accomplish something worthwhile by middle age, and, of course, I will feel thankful.

Twenty eventful years pass. I'm about to be forty and my accomplishments have exceeded my hopes. I'm seventeen years into a successful career as a journalist. Three years into my first successful romantic relationship. Yet, on a cold February day in Washington, D.C., I am writing a troubled diary entry.

I am counting blessings this morning, in a particular sense. I've been puzzled about the turbulent restlessness I've been carrying around all the time lately, the sense that my life is disappointing and that I am disappointing. I live too safely, I am not Mozart, I lack an audience, I am stuck at *National Journal,* etc., etc., all day long, though the volume gets louder and softer depending on my mood.

This morning, lying in bed, I did a little enumerating.

When I was twenty, I dreamed of being a writer or public intellectual, but assumed I would end up a lawyer. I thought I would be fortunate to be published just once in a major magazine. Today I have been published in many of the major publications and have routine access to them and have graced their covers. I have as friends and acquaintances many of the best nonfiction writers of my generation. I am anthologized in *The Norton Reader*!

When I was twenty, I loathed my body, and a girl who saw it remarked that I looked like I had just escaped from Auschwitz. I weighed probably 112 pounds, or 116. Today I weigh 136 or 138 and the difference is all muscle.

When I was twenty, I had no money of my own. Today I have $600,000, including this condo. It is possible that I'll be worth a million in a few years.

When I was twenty, I believed that romance and love and sex were impossible for me; I thought there was no one to kiss. Today I am in my fourth year with a man I love, and I have forgotten what it is like to be sexually tortured.

I tend to go around flaying myself for not working hard enough, not accomplishing what I might. I wonder why I seem not to digest, emotionally, what is obvious about the list I just wrote: accomplishing any one of those things in twenty years is unusual and worthy of pride. To accomplish all of them! And still to be young! It strikes me as a crime to be blasé about these changes. Why don't I walk around filled with fulfillment?

I'm puzzled. Just the previous month, I had visited my alma mater as a guest speaker, fulfilling yet another of the promissory notes I had written to myself at age twenty. "This trip has been great for my complexes," I wrote in my journal. "I am treated like a VIP and even with a certain amount of awe. People want to know How I Got Here. I still feel like young-little-aspiring-me, and suddenly I am on the other side of the mountain. I recall so vividly being here and dreaming of having even one article in a major publication. In truth, the place I always yearned to get to is: here."

Why don't I walk around bursting with fulfillment? I was entering the trough of the happiness curve.

I couldn't have known that in midlife it is perfectly natural to feel dissatisfied without having anything to be dissatisfied about. I couldn't have known I was entering an adjustment period that occurs not only in humans but in chimps and orangutans, too. In 2000, when I turned forty, evidence of what scholars call the U-shaped life-satisfaction curve had only just begun to surface. The first major study documenting the phenomenon was four years in the future.

To an extent, the evidence confirms what we all know: the middle years of adult life are often the most restless, stressed, and unhappy. Of course, midlife stress can come from the burdens of demanding jobs and jammed schedules and teenaged kids and aging parents. But here is where the evidence and the conventional wisdom part ways: the midlife dip in happiness shows up even after factoring out the stresses and strains and ups and downs of life. In fact, it shows up *especially* after factoring out the stresses and strains and ups and downs of life. The passage of time, by itself, affects how satisfied and grateful we feel—or, more precisely, how easy it is to feel satisfied and grateful. Young adulthood tends to be a period of natural excitement and, in the phrase Dickens made famous, great expectations, along with great uncertainty. Together, those feelings make for life satisfaction that can be high but also volatile and precarious. What comes next is a period of consolidation and achievement, but also of growing disappointment and declining optimism. The downturn is gradual, gentle, but cumulative, and it sinks into a trough, a frequently years-long slump when instead of savoring our accomplishments we question and reject them, feeling least fulfilled just when we have most cause for satisfaction. Under the surface, though, the trough is really a *turn*, a change of emotional direction. Almost imperceptibly, our values shift, our expectations recalibrate, our brains reorganize, all in ways that lead to an upturn in late middle age and then to surprising happiness in late adulthood.

Everything I just said is true on average, not for every person. As I will say often in this book, your mileage may vary. But the pattern applied to me, and with a vengeance. At age forty-five, I had published books, won journalism prizes, been republished in anthologies, done more speeches and media appearances than I could count: all the hallmarks of success in my chosen profession. My health was good, my finances solid; my relationship with the man I would eventually marry was strong and getting stronger. Objectively, I had nothing, as in zero, to complain about. Chase them away as I might, however, preoccupations pestered me about what I had *not* accomplished. Mornings were worst, before the day brought its distractions. As soon as my eyes snapped open, a voice in my head carped at me. *I'm wasting my life . . . I haven't done anything worthwhile in years . . . I need to move somewhere else, do something else, anything . . . How come I'm not on the Sunday talk shows? How come I'm not in charge of something, like a business?*

What especially puzzled me was that many of my buzzing self-condemnations were manifestly absurd. For example, appearing on Sunday talk shows and running a business were never things I had aspired to do. It was as if, having met so many of my own goals, some perverse organ of my brain was busy creating new, spurious ones. In the same fashion, try as I might, I could not suppress comparisons of myself with others. *How come I'm not doing what he or she is doing? Look where she is, and look where I am. Pathetic!* Dissatisfaction would alight on any convenient cause, real or invented. I began to think of it as a parasitic wasp that had lodged itself in my brain and was feeding on discontent it created.

Keenly aware of how elated and grateful the twenty-year-old me would have been to accomplish even part of what the forty-five-year-old me had done, I felt ashamed of my ingratitude and embarrassed by my dissatisfaction. I didn't tell my husband about it. I tried not to talk about it at all. "Prozac," said one of the few friends I did consult. But I felt dissatisfied, not depressed, and there is a difference. Getting out of bed, enjoying enjoyable things, working hard, or savoring music or making love or entertaining friends: all of those pleasures remained.

Of course, I was aware of the concept of midlife crisis, but in my case the concept did not seem to fit. A crisis, by definition, would be dramatic. It would come rapidly to a head, push other matters aside, and demand an urgent response. According to the stereotype, midlife crisis would impel me to behave disruptively or self-indulgently. None of those descriptions fit me. I fantasized about quitting my magazine job, *now, today,* without having made other plans or even having other ideas, but I never acted rashly. If anything, I was risk averse. Instead, I hunkered down. As months turned into years and forty became forty-five and then forty-six and forty-seven, I came to think that my dissatisfaction was the very opposite of a crisis.

I thought it was permanent. It was just something I would have to live with: the new normal.

Believing that I could soldier on and nothing dramatic would happen was reassuring in some respects, but it raised an unsettling prospect. What if I had become a chronically dissatisfied person? Gradually, my morale sank. It dawned upon me that I was becoming someone I didn't like. I began to feel defined by my ingratitude.

And then, seemingly as inexplicably as it had descended, the fog began to lift. The timing was strange, to say the least. When I was in my late forties, my mother died. My father, to whom I was much closer, contracted a vicious neurological syndrome, and he died, too. When I was fifty, my magazine job went away, a victim of the economic mayhem in America's newsrooms. I decided to launch a start-up, an idea market for writers, but it failed. So there I was, finally, in the rapids, being hurled against the crags of middle age. And yet that voice in my head became ever so slightly less loud and insistent, then noticeably so. My obsessive habit of comparing myself with others, always to my own disadvantage, diminished. The change was so subtle, so gradual, that I was hesitant to acknowledge it, for fear it would prove illusory or fleeting. Still, whatever part of me was busy inventing causes for dissatisfaction seemed to be quieting down.

I couldn't have known then what I know now. Like Cole's middle-aged Voyager, I was at the mercy of time.

That middle age can be hard is not news. Thomas Cole obviously knew it. Dante knew it in the early fourteenth century. Not coincidentally, his visit to hell begins in middle age:

> *Midway upon the journey of our life*
> *I found myself within a forest dark,*
> *For the straightforward pathway had been lost.*

Ah me! how hard a thing it is to say
What was this forest savage, rough, and stern,
Which in the very thought renews the fear.

Dante's metaphor is a dark forest, not so different from Cole's midlife rapids (likewise "savage, rough, and stern"). As brilliant as Cole and Dante both were, however, there is a lot they didn't know about age and happiness. In these pages, I retrace the route of Thomas Cole's Voyager, but with the aid of a map provided by recent discoveries in economics, psychology, and neurobiology. The book is about new light being cast on happiness by the dismal science, economics. It is about the frequently perverse behavior of life satisfaction, which has less to do with our material circumstances and accomplishments than we imagine. It is about the serendipity which led maverick economists to discover that age, independent of other things going on, makes contentment harder to come by in midlife. It is about the slow-motion emotional reboot which makes the years after midlife surprisingly satisfying, and why evolution might wire us to reboot. It is about the dawn of a whole new stage of adult development which is already starting to reshape the way we think about retirement, education, and human potential.

Along the way, I will introduce a young economist who discovered a negative feedback loop that manufactures midlife unhappiness without apparent cause. I'll introduce psychologists and neuroscientists who are bringing to light the surprising payoffs, personal and social, awaiting on the far side of the slump. I'll introduce a psychiatrist and a sociologist and others who are building a new science of wisdom and showing how aging equips us to be happier and kinder, even as our bodies get frailer. I'll introduce social thinkers and reformers who are exploring and mapping a whole new stage of adult development.

If what those and other researchers are learning is correct, some adjustments are in order. We need to understand why a lot of what we believe about aging and happiness is wrong. We need to understand why midlife dissatisfaction is, for the large majority of people, not a "crisis," but a natural and healthy transition. With that understanding, we can become smarter about coping with the happiness curve, in ways which I'll illustrate. Although we can't think our way around the trough, we can think our way *through* it.

We can help others through it, too. I spent years exploring the science of the happiness curve and the evidence on age and happiness, but I did not understand the story until I realized that it is not a story about me. Or about you. It is about *us*. The curve seems to be imprinted on us as a way to repurpose us for a changing role in society as we age, a role that is less about ambition and competition, and more about connection and compassion.

How to cope with the happiness curve is also a social story, because coping is not something we can do very well alone, in the privacy of our heads. We need society's help. Society needs to reeducate itself about middle age and old age, abandoning clichés about red sports cars and sad, cranky decrepitude. It needs to offer support and outreach rather than shame and isolation to those who are in the midlife trough.

If you are in the trough, or know someone who is, I have no magic cures (there are none), but I do have some practical suggestions, which you'll find in the last couple of chapters. I also have some heartening news:

First, midlife slump (not "crisis"!) is completely normal and natural. Like teething or adolescence, it is a healthy if sometimes painful transition, and it serves a purpose by equipping you for a new stage of life. You may feel dissatisfied, but you don't need to feel too worried about feeling dissatisfied.

Second, the post-midlife upturn is no mere transient change in mood: it is a change in our values and sources of satisfaction, a change in *who we are*. It often brings unexpected contentment that extends into old age and, yes, even into frailty and illness.

Third, by extending our life spans, modern medicine and public health have already added more than a decade to the upturn, and they will add more years in the future. We are in the process of adding perhaps two decades to the most satisfying and pro-social period of life. Some sociologists call this new stage of life *encore adulthood*. Whatever you call it, it is a gift the likes of which mankind has never known before.

Understanding and exploiting the gift require rethinking patterns of life that our parents and grandparents (and their parents and grandparents) took for granted and built into their worlds, and into ours. Fortunately, the knowledge we need is advancing quickly. It begins with the perverse logic, or illogic, of human happiness.

2

....

WHAT MAKES US HAPPY (AND DOESN'T)

The strange illogic of life satisfaction

Carol Graham has straight, glossy brown hair and a slender build that belies her age of more than fifty years. On most days she runs ten miles, and her go-ahead attitude toward life is reflected in her direct, plain-spoken style of conversation. Even on first meeting, you would not be surprised to learn she is an economist, though you might be surprised to learn what kind.

Graham and I are about the same age and first met in our early forties. We both work at the same think tank, and at some point we began hanging out. I was in the closet then about my midlife dissatisfaction, and was not about to reveal my vulnerability to a colleague. Still, over periodic lunches, our conversations grew more personal. I learned that her forties were not a smooth time. She had three children, a husband who traveled most of the time, and new administrative responsibilities in two places, both of them challenging. Then her mother came down with Alzheimer's, and her father with emphysema, and her marriage began to fail. After eighteen years together, she and her husband separated. "It was absolutely traumatic," she said. Something like low-level warfare broke out with her ex; making peace with him took seven years. I remember the frustration she expressed during that time, and she reports still having a touch of post-traumatic stress disorder from it. "I'm still programmed to wake up and think something awful could happen any minute." Through it all, however, she managed to do some of her best work, including a successful book: *Happiness Around the World: The Paradox of Happy Peasants and Miserable Millionaires* (published in 2010).

When I met her, I assumed that human happiness, including my own, reflects how well things are going, or at least *should* reflect how well things are going. Subjective wellbeing and objective wellbeing, perception and reality, ought to go hand in hand. That was why I felt so unentitled to my dissatisfaction and didn't tell Graham or anyone else about it. As she began to explain her work, however, it gradually dawned on me that my assumption was wrong. Thomas Cole's Voyager is at the mercy of a winding, capricious river, one whose course doubles back on itself and makes no apparent sense.

To understand the happiness curve, it's helpful to know that happiness isn't rational, predictable, or reliably tethered to our objective circumstances. That finding, which economics for many years did its best to ignore, has recently received important support from some peculiar discoveries by a new breed of economist, whose number includes Carol Graham.

Lima, Peru, was a place of extremes when Graham was born there in 1962. Her father was a prominent American doctor, her mother "as Peruvian as could be." The youngest of six children, she did not speak English until her family moved to the United States, when she was almost four. "I'm as Peruvian as I am American, in many ways," she told me on a spring day in her office in Washington. As a child, she saw extreme poverty and extreme wealth: "The contrasts were incredibly sharp." Her early interest in social inequality and economic development never waned.

Her twenties, like so many people's, were a time of adventure, discovery. She became a research assistant at the Brookings Institution after college, and loved it; earned a doctorate in development economics and political economy; wrote a dissertation on how Peru's poor coped with hyper-inflation. Eschewing the usual path toward a tenure-tracked academic job, she lived from fellowship to fellowship, collaborating with famous economists and traveling to places like China, Vietnam, and Mongolia to learn how to help the poor in countries undergoing rapid social and economic change. She tramped around slums and grappled firsthand with infant malnourishment. "I was doing exactly what I wanted to do. Sometimes it was scary. I remember getting on a plane to Africa thinking, *What the hell are you doing? The only thing you know about Africa is French.*" By her early thirties she was married, had had her first child, and was about to publish a book, *Safety Nets, Politics, and the Poor: Transitions to Market Economies.*

In the 1990s, in the wake of the North American Free Trade Agreement and other international trade negotiations, a backlash against globalization arose. Activists demanded that economists pay more attention to inequality, which economic development had often seemed to exacerbate. As it happened, Graham had a trove of data on the social and economic mobility of poor Peruvians. She found a surprisingly large amount of movement in and out of poverty—more in Peru than in the United States. That finding led her to a question, highly unorthodox in the economics of the time. "I thought: *You know, I wonder how these people* think *they've done? Everyone is saying globalization is bad for the poor, so why don't we ask the poor?*"

She did, using questions such as: "How do you compare your economic situation today with ten years ago?" Because she had data on how people had actually fared economically, she could compare objective outcomes with subjective satisfaction. The result was, to say the least, unexpected. "It turns out that, of the ones that had done the best, so they had the most movement up the income ladder, roughly half said their economic situation was *worse* than it was before." Equally strange, though at least consistent, was a reciprocal finding. "The people who didn't move up at all, who were primarily rural poor, who had had no income change—they said their situation was *better*, or the same."

Graham's first instinct was to doubt the findings. Maybe Peruvians were strange. Maybe Peru's circumstances were strange. So Graham got data for Russia. There, in the tumultuous 1990s, 70 percent of the people who had experienced the most upward mobility said their situation was worse than before, not better. More data, more countries—same pattern. In 2015, Graham looked at China between 1990 and 2005, a period of explosive economic growth. Life expectancy had reached more than seventy-five years, a leap from only sixty-seven years as recently as 1980. "Yet," she writes with two colleagues, Shaojie Zhou and Junyi Zhang, in a 2015 paper titled "Happiness and Health in China: The Paradox of Progress," "during the same period, life satisfaction levels in China demonstrated very different trends—in particular dropping precipitously in the initial stages of rapid growth and then recovering somewhat thereafter. The drops in life satisfaction were accompanied by increases in the suicide rate and in incidence of mental illness." In China, as in Russia and Peru, becoming better off economically seemed to make people less satisfied.

The same curious phenomenon also holds in industrial democracies. "All the evidence says that on average people are no happier today than people were fifty years ago," writes Richard Layard, a prominent British economist, in his 2005 book *Happiness: Lessons from a New Science*. "Yet at the same time average incomes have more than doubled. This paradox is equally true for the United States and Britain and Japan." In the United States, he notes, large increases in material wellbeing have neither increased the number of self-described "very happy" people nor substantially decreased the number who are "not very happy."

So, at both the individual level and the national level, how you feel about your life does not necessarily reflect how one might suppose you should feel, at least by the materialistic standards of *homo economicus*. More often, the relationship works backward (even after adjusting for the effects of noneconomic variables like demography and health). "People who are in very fast-growing economies are less happy than people in slower growing economies," Graham told me. "Rapid change makes people very unhappy." The result is what she calls the paradox of frustrated achievers and happy peasants.

In the 1990s, when Graham unearthed that paradox, her findings seemed bizarre. Conventional economics assumed, of course, that income gains will tend to make people happier, more satisfied, less socially restive. "I didn't know how to explain it," Graham said. "But I started poking around and found what was then this very, very minute literature on the economics of happiness." That was how she found her way to Richard Easterlin.

I called Easterlin one late-spring day and reached him in California, where he was a professor in the University of Southern California's economics department. Like a number of Nobel Prize–winning economists I have encountered, he was approachable and humble—though, unlike them, he had not won a Nobel Prize, which seemed unfair, considering that he had founded a new branch of economics.

For many years, if the modern discipline of economics had had a motto, it might well have been: look at what people do, not at what they say; at how they behave, not how they feel. Economics likes to think of itself as rigorously scientific, which means concerning itself with the hard facts of the real world. In any given month, you know how many cars people buy and how many new jobs are created. To a conventionally trained economist, knowing how people *feel* hardly seems of comparable importance, except inasmuch as consumer sentiment might drive demand up or down. Anyway, how can you be sure how people feel? You could ask them—but change the wording of a survey question, and you might get a different answer. Besides, people don't always understand their own true desires and feelings, and, even if they do, they might not give a straight answer. The better way to understand preferences and desires, and even to infer subjective states of mind, is by looking at *revealed* preferences. Americans might tell you they like hot dogs better than hamburgers, but the sales statistics don't lie, and those might show that Americans really prefer hamburgers. Every day, people reveal their priorities by trading goods and services to get more of whatever it is they value. In a properly functioning market, then, satisfaction should increase by definition.

In his mid-forties, Richard Easterlin found himself doing work on demography. He noticed that demographers paid a lot of attention to subjective testimony, as psychologists also do. To Easterlin, mainstream economics' rejection of what people said about their states of mind and wellbeing seemed "pretty ridiculous." One day around 1970, over lunch at an advanced-research center at Stanford University, a sociologist mentioned surveys of happiness. Easterlin thought it might be interesting to leaf through them.

The upshot was a paper he published in 1974, "Does Economic Growth Improve the Human Lot? Some Empirical Evidence." It posed some fundamental questions. "Are the wealthy members of society usually happier than the poor? What of rich versus poor countries—are the more developed nations typically happier? As a country's income grows during the course of economic development, does human happiness advance—does economic growth improve the human lot?" One might have thought that economics would have long since come to grips with such basic questions, but no. "The term 'happiness' is used intermittently, albeit loosely, in the literature of economics," Easterlin wrote. "To my knowledge, however, this is the first attempt to look at the actual evidence."

Easterlin gathered surveys from nineteen countries in which people were asked a couple of happiness questions. One question simply asked: "In general, how happy would you say that you are—very happy, fairly happy, or not very happy?" The other was called the Cantril Ladder question, named after Hadley Cantril, an American public-opinion researcher who was prominent in the middle of the last century. Cantril asked people to place their lives on an eleven-rung ladder, where, the poll said, "the top of the ladder represents the best possible life for you and the bottom represents the worst possible life for you." Although asking people about their happiness was simple, or perhaps *because* it was simple, "the approach has a certain amount of appeal," wrote Easterlin. "If one is interested in how happy people are—in their subjective satisfaction—why not let each person set his own standard and decide how closely he approaches it?"

Sifting the results, Easterlin came across an odd phenomenon. Within particular countries, "income and happiness are positively associated." Thus, for example, in the United States, people in the highest-income group were almost two times more likely than people in the lowest group to describe themselves as very happy. The correlation between economic status and happiness didn't seem surprising, and to one degree or another it held in every survey Easterlin looked at.

Obviously, if richer *people* were happier than poorer people, then richer *countries* should have been happier than poorer countries. It stood to reason. But it wasn't so! "The happiness differences between rich and poor countries that one might expect on the basis of within-country differences by economic status are not borne out by the international data," Easterlin wrote. Knowing how wealthy a country was, relative to other countries, did not tell you how relatively satisfied people were in that country.

Something else was puzzling. In the United States, which had the best data in those days, incomes had grown dramatically over time since the mid-1940s. To this day, the quarter decade or so after World War II is looked upon by economists as a golden age of shared prosperity. But "higher income was not systematically accompanied by greater happiness." So richer *people* were happier than poorer people, but getting richer didn't make a *country* happier.

What could explain such seemingly inconsistent results? Perhaps they only appeared inconsistent. Suppose, Easterlin hypothesized, happiness comes from judging our own standing relative to those around us. Then, wrote Easterlin, "An increase in the income of any one individual would increase his happiness, but increasing the income of everyone would leave happiness unchanged. Similarly, among countries, a richer country would not necessarily be a happier country." People, after all, for the most part do not spend a lot of energy comparing themselves with others in far-off lands. They compare themselves with their friends, colleagues, and compatriots. Easterlin used height as an analogy. Whether you feel tall depends on how tall the people around you are. If you grow but everyone in your comparison group grows by the same amount, you won't feel taller. And if others grow and you don't, you'll feel shorter, even though you haven't shrunk a millimeter. In fact, if everyone was frantically busy working to get richer, the result might be to put everyone in competition with everyone else, resulting in a society stuck on what happiness economists call a *hedonic treadmill.*

The Easterlin Paradox (as it came to be known) had the potential to revolutionize economics. It challenged the hegemony of revealed preferences and material metrics. If economists cared about making people better off, not just materially but in a deeper, life-savoring sense, then revealed preferences might be painting an incomplete or even misleading picture. To fill in the gaps, economists might need to resort to subjective measures. They might need to learn how people feel, and why. They might even need to rethink what economics is about.

Back in the real world, however, Easterlin's revolutionary paper did not revolutionize anything. Economists remained suspicious of survey data. What exactly (they demanded to know) does *happiness* mean, anyway? Leaving people to define it for themselves, as questions like the Cantril

Ladder do, allows different people to interpret the question differently. In any case, the profession's collective mind was not ready to take on board any idea with such challenging ramifications. Easterlin's findings hinted that happiness, far from smoothly tracking material wellbeing, is complicated and nonlinear. But even assuming that's true, exactly what was anyone supposed to do with the information? It was not as if people would stop trying to increase their paychecks, or companies would give up on making profits. If people are irrational or neurotic, that's a problem for psychologists, not economists.

Perhaps, then, it was not surprising that by and large, as Easterlin told me, his 1974 paper was ignored at the time, except insofar as it made for interesting cocktail conversation. From today's perspective, his now venerable work holds up remarkably well. But back then there were too many questions he couldn't answer. For a couple of decades the Easterlin Paradox remained a curiosity, until a successor generation got hold of it.

The most fundamental question posed by Easterlin proved the least troublesome. What is it people mean by happiness, and how do we know if different people mean the same thing? In the abstract, that question has challenged philosophers since biblical days, and it continues to provoke lively debates. In the 1980s and 1990s, however, surveys came pouring in from countries all over the world, in quantities far greater than were available to Richard Easterlin, and they showed remarkable consistency in the way people reported their happiness. The data demonstrated that ordinary people, unlike philosophers, knew what they were talking about when they talked about happiness. Researchers have since determined that people's assessments of their subjective wellbeing closely track the assessments made by friends and independent observers, and even correspond with electrical activity in the brain. "What's remarkable," Carol Graham told me, "is how consistent the standard patterns are in terms of the basic determinants of happiness. All the factors we know just keep showing up as very stable."

Something else also turned up consistently, a distinction upon which much else hinges. *Happiness* can mean a couple of things. It can mean my mood just at the moment: how cheerful, annoyed, or worried I feel. That very likely depends on whether I am drinking with friends on Friday after work, breathing bus fumes in a traffic jam, or missing a deadline. This kind of short-term state of mind is called *affective happiness*; it relates to *affect*, our momentary emotions. Researchers measure it by asking people questions like: "How often did you smile yesterday? How much stress are you feeling right now?"

The second meaning of happiness asks for a quite different kind of assessment: *How satisfied are you with your life? How does your life compare with the best possible life you could imagine for yourself?* Though there are many variations, a typical question is: "If you were to consider your life in general, how happy or unhappy would you say you are, on the whole?" Such questions ask you not to report your mood but to evaluate your life in its entirety, and they bear on what's appropriately called *evaluative happiness*— or, an equivalent term, *subjective wellbeing.*

Affective happiness and evaluative happiness bear some relation to each other (a consistently depressed mood is not good for life satisfaction), but less than you might suppose. It turned out, as the data came in, that people grasp intuitively the difference between the two concepts and have no trouble distinguishing between them. Ask people about their happiness yesterday—their mood, in other words—and they say they are happier on weekends. Ask them about their happiness with their lives, and such "weekend effects" disappear. In my own forties, my life satisfaction was low, and much lower than I thought it should be, but my *mood* was usually not a problem. That was part of the reason I did not believe I was a candidate for medical care. I did not have a mood disorder. I had a *contentment* disorder.

In his conversation with me, Easterlin went out of his way to empha-size the distinction between affective and evaluative happiness, and, be-ginning with his 1974 article, it was the latter that primarily concerned happiness economists like Graham. They wanted to know: *if money does not necessarily increase life satisfaction, what does?*

There, too, the results proved quite consistent—consistent enough so that, today, many researchers consider the basic tenets to be established as fact. In her 2011 book *The Pursuit of Happiness: An Economy of Wellbeing*, Graham, having by then spent her career sifting through data from coun-tries all over the world, wrote: "Everywhere that I have studied happiness some very simple patterns hold: a stable marriage, good health, and enough (but not too much) income are good for happiness. Unemployment, di-vorce, and economic instability are terrible for happiness—everywhere that happiness is studied."

We can unpack Graham's list. Start with money. It matters. What my father used to say—"I've been rich and I've been poor, and rich is better"—is true. Not knowing where your next meal is coming from, or how to put a roof over your head, is immiserating. The relationship between money and life satisfaction, however, is not linear. "Income matters to individual well-being, but after a certain point other things such as the incomes of others also start to matter," Graham wrote, in her 2015 article with Zhou and Zhang.

How do the "incomes of others" matter? The answer is not flattering to human generosity. Once people's income reaches a fairly comfortable level, they start comparing themselves with their neighbors and friends and setting their expectations accordingly. This is not good. "These stud-ies," Layard writes, assessing the literature, "provide clear evidence that a rise in other people's income hurts your happiness."

A striking, if slightly depressing, example comes from an experiment in Kenya, discussed in a 2015 paper whose title tells the story: "Your Gain Is My Pain: Negative Psychological Externalities of Cash Transfers." A non-profit organization called GiveDirectly randomly chose households in sixty poor Kenyan villages to receive a no-strings-attached, one-time grant of either about $400 or $1,500. Either sum was a large windfall; these were places where the typical household's wealth was under $400. Analyzing the results, Johannes Haushofer and James Reisinger of Princeton University, along with Jeremy Shapiro of the Busara Center for Behavioral Economics in Nairobi, found that the life satisfaction of grantees increased, as one would certainly hope. The rub was that the increased life satisfaction of those who did receive windfalls was more than offset by a large *decrease* in life satisfaction on the part of those who did not receive windfalls. "The magnitude of this [negative spillover] effect," write the scholars, "is noteworthy, as this is more than four times the magnitude of the effect of a change in own wealth by the same amount." In other words, my dollar gain causes you four times as much dissatisfaction as it brings me in satisfaction, at least if we are poor Kenyan villagers. (Fortunately or not, depending on your point of view, most of the positive effects of the windfalls and all of the negative effects wore off after about a year, as villagers adjusted to the new status quo.)

We can add another wrinkle: because happiness is subjective, perception can matter as much as reality. Suppose some mischievous demon, not in a poor African village but in an advanced economy, decided to exacerbate the happiness gap between rich and poor by publishing everyone's tax returns online in an easily searchable format. Norway did just that in 2001. In 2016, a Microsoft researcher named Ricardo Perez-Truglia looked at Norwegians' happiness before and after 2001, using some clever statistical controls to isolate the likely effects of transparency. Again, the results, if unsurprising, are unflattering. First, he found that huge numbers of people went online to find out what their friends and acquaintances were earning. So energetically did people snoop that they performed a fifth as many income searches as YouTube searches. Second, once people learned their place in the pecking order, happiness inequality soared after years of stability. The happiness gap between rich and poor increased by 29 percent; the life-satisfaction gap increased by 21 percent. "These findings suggest that the change in disclosure had a large effect on the wellbeing of Norwegians," Perez-Truglia writes dryly.

Note that what changed in Norway was not the actual degree of inequality in society; what changed was what people knew (or thought they knew) about inequality. Our subjective wellbeing depends not on our absolute material wellbeing, nor even on where we stand relative to others, but on where we *think* we stand. (What others think of us also matters. Exploiting that fact, in 2014 the authorities stopped allowing Norwegians to search the tax records anonymously. As soon as people realized their curiosity might be noticed by friends and neighbors, they reduced their tax snooping by almost 90 percent and redirected their energies to finding out who was snooping on them.)

So Easterlin's original conjecture appears to have been borne out: beyond a certain point, increases in the gross national product will not reliably increase gross national happiness, especially if inequality—real or perceived—also rises. It is not enough for a society as a whole to grow wealthier. In fact, if gains in social wealth are unequally spread, economic growth could increase frustration and anger—even if the wealth of the middle class is growing in absolute terms. As income dispersion grows, the rungs on the income ladder get further apart, and the person on the rung above me pulls further ahead, which I resent; the person above me, looking at the next rung above her, likewise sees herself falling behind. An increase in the *visibility* of inequality would compound the effect, as the Norwegians discovered.

In the United States, both phenomena are on display. Inequality has grown, and the visibility of inequality may have grown even more: as sociologists have noted, the economic elite has increasingly pulled away into its own world, with separate schools and neighborhoods and distinctive lifestyles and tastes. If you're, say, a middle-class teacher or a working-class taxi driver in San Francisco, and if every morning you watch as millionaires who look like teenagers queue on Van Ness Avenue for the Google bus, the status gap probably feels even bigger than the income gap. Rising inequality, both real and perceived, thus poisons economic growth, even for many who are doing okay but watching others do much better. That seems to be happening in America right now.

Here's the most fundamental finding of happiness economics: the factors that most determine our happiness are social, not material. Humans are ultra-social creatures, after all. It would not be so surprising, then, if (beyond a certain point) we care about money not so much because of what it buys as because of where it ranks us among our peers. As another of my father's sayings had it, "Money is applause."

So what else is in the mix? Mostly things you might expect. Richard Layard, in his book, identifies seven big factors: "our family relationships, our financial situation, our work, our community and friends, our health, our personal freedom, and our personal values. Except for health and income, they are all concerned with the quality of our relationships."

John F. Helliwell, another prominent figure in happiness economics, has reached a similar conclusion. Helliwell calls himself "Aristotle's research assistant," because Aristotle was an early and great student of what happiness means and how to achieve it. In his teachings, Aristotle emphasized the difference between moment-to-moment pleasure or pain and the deeper satisfaction of a life well lived, which is more important to wellbeing. Deeper satisfaction comes not from feeling good, he taught, but from doing good: from cultivating and maintaining virtuous habits that balance one's own life and create and deepen ties with others.

Aristotle's insights have held up remarkably well. Helliwell and colleagues regularly mine a vast data set called the World Values Survey, which asks people in more than 150 countries about their satisfaction with life and provides much other information about them and their social and economic environments. When Helliwell and other researchers crunch the data, they find that six factors account for three-fourths of reported wellbeing:

- **social support:** having someone to count on in times of trouble
- **generosity:** people are happier when they do generous things and live among generous people
- **trust:** corruption and dishonesty are bad for life satisfaction
- **freedom:** feeling that you have sufficient freedom to make important life decisions
- **income per capita**
- **healthy life expectancy**

If you look at that list, you will notice, again, that of the six factors, four have to do with social interaction. Of the bunch, social support is the most important, and together the social four—"relational goods," as the term of art would have it—comprise the bulk of what makes us happy. As the 2015 *World Happiness Report* notes, the strong link between life satisfaction and being connected to others "appears in almost all empirical analyses of life satisfaction data irrespective of geographical and time differences." Psychological experiments reach the same conclusion. If required to choose, the experiments show, you would be better off with less health but more social ties than the other way around. Income also matters—but, as we have seen, not in a terribly reliable way, especially if other people are doing as well or better than you materially. In fact, when Stefano Bartolini and Francesco Sarracino, two Italian economists, looked at data from twenty-seven (mostly developed) countries, they found that growth in national income correlates with life satisfaction only over a very short time span, about a couple of years; after that, people adjust to their gains. Over longer spans, any effect of economic growth on happiness vanishes altogether. By contrast, increases in group membership and in other measures of social connectedness are associated with only mild increases in satisfaction over the short term, but large increases over longer spans. So the effects of connectedness are cumulative and durable. Instead of making you earn more just to stay satisfied, as building income seems to do, building trust and relationships and other forms of social support puts wellbeing in the bank.

On the other side of the coin, social connectedness can go a long way toward alleviating the misery caused by a financial crisis. Countries with high levels of trust and mutual support fared far better through the Great Recession, where life satisfaction was concerned, than did countries with weak social ties. A sense of pulling together in times of need can buffer even severe social or economic setbacks, as many Americans and Britons who lived through World War II can remember. The truest form of wealth is social, not material.

The most intimate and, for many of us, most important form of social connectedness is marriage. Your husband or wife is your doctor and nurse and counselor and therapist of first resort; your spouse is your partner in raising children and meeting the challenges of life; marrying roughly doubles the size of your networks of kin and acquaintance, and establishes around you the most important of all forms of connectedness, the family. (All of which is why gay people fought so hard for the right to marry.) No wonder, then, that marriage is on average very good for happiness, especially at first, and divorce is dreadful. According to one estimate, the amount of money needed to "compensate," statistically speaking, for a lost marriage is on the order of an extra $100,000 a year.

In 2010, at the age of fifty, as soon as it became legal near where we live, I married Michael. By that time we had been together for more than a decade, and we needed no "piece of paper from the government" (as some skeptics have called marriage) to prove the value of our relationship. Nonetheless, and although our marriage at that point was recognized in only a few states, I can tell you that it was worth at least $100,000, not only because it brought us closer together but because it wove us, as a couple, more tightly into our community.

In the last few years, I have also learned firsthand that what the data say about social capital and life satisfaction is true. I live in a town house community in a northern Virginia suburb. Our street mixes middle-class and working-class residents—natives and immigrants of many ethnicities. Our cul-de-sac is nondescript physically and adjoined by ugly strip developments. Home values are modest. Yet Ardley Court is the wealthiest place I have ever lived. On a summer evening, you'll see young and old gathering impromptu on lawns and decks, sharing drinks and food as adults chat and children circulate like free electrons. People watch each other's kids and houses, which may explain why crime has been close to nonexistent. Property prices do not remotely reflect the value of coming home on a Friday and getting hugs from the neighborhood kids and licks from the neighborhood dogs and catching up on how everyone is doing.

Unemployment, of course, is a financial problem for most people who get hit by it, and so it counts as an economic factor in happiness. But—again—the bigger story is about social connectedness and status. Jobs pay the bills, yes, but they also enrich our social networks, provide us with a sense of vocation, and enhance our standing as breadwinners and community members. No wonder that, statistically speaking, the happiness cost of unemployment has been calculated at the equivalent of about $60,000 a year, more than the median wage in the United States: not as large as marital breakup, but large.

What about parenthood and happiness? That gets complicated. Parenting is a core human endeavor. Although I made my peace with not having kids, I still recall how, many years ago, when I asked my father why he had had children, he simply said, "Because it's the only game in town." Well, it isn't the *only* game, but it is a big one. You don't know how much of both love and anger you are capable of feeling until you're a parent, an ancient truism which modern scholarship bears out. But the economist Angus Deaton and the psychologist Arthur Stone, after looking at data on 1.7 million Americans, have found that the higher emotional amplitude of parents "does not carry through to their life evaluations, which are on average lower than those without children." Having parented successfully in the past may rank as a satisfying accomplishment retrospectively; but the bulk of research finds that being a parent, while it is happening, does not increase life satisfaction and may reduce it. New parents, especially, confront very high stress. One study in Germany found more than two-thirds of parents reporting drops in life satisfaction—often sharp drops—during the two years after their kids were born. "One of the dark stories that people don't talk about is the toll that young children take on a marriage," one of my friends told me, explaining why the birth of her two children was a particularly difficult period. Her marriage survived, and now, with both kids grown, she said, "I've got two great kids. I enjoy spending time with them. I feel like I won child-raising." Those who look to parenthood as a solution to their discontent will typically find that the rewards, though real, are some years in the future.

One other factor turns out not to matter as much as you might expect: gender. The 2015 *World Happiness Report* finds that women's life evaluations are on average slightly higher than men's, but that the differences are very small. My own interviews and surveys for this book led me to the same conclusion.

Had I known at forty about the paradoxes of happiness, I would have been less puzzled by my failure to appreciate my résumé. I was not comparing my forty-year-old self to my twenty-year-old self, as the twenty-year-old version of me had assumed I would. I was comparing myself to other fortysomethings in my peer group, many of whom also had sustained relationships (often longer), accumulated wealth (often more), and achieved professional status (often higher). True, I was better off than most of humanity, but most of humanity was not my comparison group. Unfortunately, the self-critical voices that pestered me about wasting my life insisted on comparing upward, which is the worst thing you can do. As Richard Layard writes, "One secret of happiness is to ignore comparisons with people who are more successful than you are: always compare downwards, not upwards."

Unfortunately, that advice, while sound, is difficult to follow; how difficult depends on not just our attitude, but also our age.

After her own difficult, sometimes traumatic, yet still productive forties, Carol Graham turned a corner. The wilderness years of happiness economics ended; her discipline began to catch on in the academic mainstream, and the news media loved it. "I can't disentangle being in my fifties from having my research take off," she told me. "I get incredible satisfaction from thinking this approach has gotten some traction. It's changing the way people think. Young scholars are picking it up and doing much cooler things than I would have thought of." She also enjoys having teenage kids: playing guitar with them, running races together.

"And," I asked, "have you changed as a person?" She reflected for a moment. Her teenaged son, she said, falls head over heels when he's in a relationship, then is devastated when it breaks up. "As you get older, your ability to benchmark a bad experience against other things you've navigated just puts it all in a very different perspective. You do get wiser. There are things that would have bothered me before." Negative comments about her work, for instance. "If that had happened to me in my forties, I would have thought, *Oh, this is terrible*. Now I couldn't care less. I just feel like I can write what I want to write, but don't feel I have anything to prove anymore. I think it's very much internal. I don't care about how others judge me."

She has rounded the bend in the happiness curve—the curve she helped discover. In 2001, she and another development economist, Stefano

Pettinato, published a book titled *Happiness and Hardship: Opportunity and Insecurity in New Market Economies.* They included a chart showing that in Latin America life satisfaction declines from the twenties to about age forty-eight, then increases. "Studies in advanced industrial economies find a similar relationship," they wrote, "although the low point on the happiness curve usually occurs either slightly earlier or slightly later, depending on the country." After another few sentences, they moved on to the next point. The pattern seemed like a curiosity, a digression from more important subjects. It mostly seemed like a curiosity to others who had noticed it, too. But not to everyone.

3

....

A TIMELY DISCOVERY

How unsuspecting economists (and apes)
found the happiness curve

No one went looking for a happiness curve, because no one expected to find one.

The idea of a difficult emotional passage in midlife, followed by growing tranquility in older age, is not new, as any visitor to the National Gallery's Thomas Cole exhibit will attest. But the idea of a midlife crisis as such, something unique and specific that happens to people in middle age, is surprisingly new. The phrase itself dates back only to 1965, when a Canadian-born psychoanalyst named Elliott Jaques coined it for an article titled "Death and the Midlife Crisis," published in the *International Journal of Psychoanalysis*. Perhaps not surprisingly, Jaques was then in his late forties.

"I first became aware of this period as a critical stage in development," Jaques wrote in the article, "when I noticed a marked tendency towards crisis in the creative work of great men in their middle and late thirties." With the peculiar combination of shrewd insight and reckless conjecture which is so characteristic of the psychoanalytic method, Jaques expanded his observation into a general theory. "The midlife crisis," he wrote, "is a reaction which not only occurs in creative genius, but manifests itself in some form in everyone."

A reaction to what? Beginning in the middle thirties, Jaques hypothesized, the fact of death, heretofore abstract and distant, becomes concrete and personal. "The individual has stopped growing up, and has begun to grow old. A new set of external circumstances has to be met. The first phase of adult life has been lived. Family and occupation have become established (or ought to have become established unless the individual's adjustment has gone seriously awry); parents have grown old, and children are at the threshold of adulthood." The implications of one's impending end can no longer be suppressed or evaded. This, he wrote, "is the central and crucial feature of the midlife phase."

What followed was a fusillade of Freudian jargon that was already going out of style in the 1960s. ("The inner world is unconsciously felt to contain the persecuting and annihilating devoured and destroyed bad breast, the ego itself feeling in bits.") What it boiled down to, though, was that in middle age we are forced to resign ourselves to all that we cannot be or do. "Important things that the individual would have liked to achieve, would have desired to become, would have longed to have, will not be realized. The awareness of on-coming frustration is especially intense."

More than half a century later, a lot of scientific water has flowed under the bridge, and there is a lot to say about what Jaques got right and wrong, a topic I'll come back to in later chapters. Suffice to say, for now, that the popular culture seized upon Jaques's basic concept, or at any rate his pithy phrase, and ran with it, quickly transforming it into a cliché.

But psychologists could not find evidence that he was right. Sure, some people have difficulties in midlife; but that is hardly an interesting finding. When psychologists went looking for something special about the middle years, they came back empty-handed. "Objectively, scholars don't find anything very different going on," Elaine Wethington, a sociologist and professor of human development at Cornell University, told me. In 2000, in an article titled "Expecting Stress: Americans and the 'Midlife Crisis'" (published in the journal *Motivation and Emotion*), she found that about a quarter of people she randomly surveyed reported having "personal turmoil and sudden changes in personal goals and lifestyle, brought about by the realization of aging, physical decline, or entrapment in unwelcome, restrictive roles." (Women and men were equally likely to report a midlife crisis.) Yet, she noted, "Epidemiological study of psychological distress in adulthood does not suggest that midlife is a time of out-of-the-ordinary distress, for either men or women." People often *said* they experienced a midlife crisis, but Wethington suspected that that's because they often go through difficult stuff in and around their forties. "There are people who believe that the midlife crisis exists," she said. "It's a term that makes sense to them in respect to their biographies. They perceive that somewhere in a very long range of midlife, they indeed had a crisis." And so the idea of midlife crisis, regardless of its scientific validity, might be useful to people as a way to think about their lives. "If we believe it is real, it is real and has consequences," Wethington told me. But it's more like folk wisdom or a social convention than solid science.

Others in psychology have little patience for the idea of a distinctive crisis in midlife. "For the most part we didn't see evidence of it in the data," Carol Ryff, the director of the Institute on Aging at the University of Wisconsin, told me. In any case, like many psychologists, she sees little point in generalizing about the whole of life or all of humanity, because what are much more interesting and important are the courses and contours of particular people's lives. "In the final analysis, you're not talking about real people when you tell these big, generic stories," she said. "This is an arena where everybody would be helped a lot by not thinking of this or that as something that happens to everybody or doesn't happen to everybody. It's better to think in a textured way about *for whom,* and *under what conditions.*"

That fits with psychologists' job description, which is to study the emotions and development of individuals—usually in small groups, and often in laboratory conditions or controlled environments. In small groups and particular cases, the effects of individuals' circumstances and personalities determine how people are doing. Isolating the effect of just one statistical cause of happiness or unhappiness seems beside the point, because humans aren't statistics and overall risk factors tell us little about our own lives. Midlife *stressors* are real, of course. Ask anyone who is caring for her parents and her kids at the same time. But that is not the same as a predictable, definable syndrome linked to age. And so, by the early 2000s, mainstream psychology had decided that the notion of a midlife crisis was unsupported and uninteresting. The profession moved on.

To this day, a lot of people assume that's the end of the story. "The Midlife Crisis Is a Total Myth," read one headline in 2011, over an article by Robin Nixon on the website Live Science. "Worried About a Midlife Crisis? Don't. There's No Such Thing," ran another headline, in 2015, above an article on *Psychology Today*'s website by Susan Krauss Whitbourne, a respected psychologist. In her article, Whitbourne made a set of seemingly final assertions: that there are "virtually no data to support the assertion that the midlife crisis is a universal experience" (which is true); that it's usually not a crisis anyway (which is also true); and that she herself, in a study of nearly five hundred people in their thirties, forties, fifties, and sixties (a fairly big sample by the standards of psychology), had found no evidence of midlife crises.

But there turns out to be a different way of thinking about midlife and happiness, which needed to be discovered by a different kind of thinker.

When I first met Andrew Oswald, in 2015, he was sixty-one years old. He was a bit above average height, balding and graying, but with a slender, athletic build honed by daily two-hour walks. His bearing was erect, his manner reserved, his voice soft, his conversation sharply analytical. He described himself as a "buttoned-up Englishman," and I could see what he meant. Although we met on a late spring day in his office at the University of Warwick, a campus where formality was neither expected nor observed, he wore a dark blue suit with purple and orange stripes, set off by a cream-colored necktie, brown shoes, and a skinny-brim fedora hat. He likes dressing up, he told me. The office contained several chairs, many books, and a whiteboard covered with scrawled equations—apparently for show, since Oswald assured me he does all his work at home. Breaking the otherwise predominant impression of Vulcan reserve was the laughter with which he periodically punctuated his sentences.

Oswald was born in Bristol, England, in 1953. His father was a formidable academic psychiatrist who moved the family to Edinburgh and Australia and set high expectations for his son. Oswald exceeded them, marrying his first girlfriend, obtaining an Oxford doctorate, writing a dissertation that became mildly famous, and having two children, all while still in his twenties. "I was driven, to put it at its mildest," he recalled.

In the 1970s, Oswald was fascinated by the miserable economy he saw around him in pre-Thatcher Britain, and by the toll it took on ordinary people. "I came into economics because of the tremendous unemployment and inflation and turbulence in Britain in that era," he said, adding, with a laugh, "I decided to solve that." At the time, strange though it seems now, British economists were debating whether unemployment was really a serious problem for the unemployed. Maybe it was often voluntary, the result of people preferring leisure to work. Or maybe it just wasn't so bad. "The Right, with a capital R, argued then, and have always argued, that people more or less chose unemployment because they had low skills and they were offered benefits and that was the rational thing for them to do," Oswald said. "This issue has been central to economics for more than a hundred years: whether you should think of unemployment as an equilibrium or as an absolute human disaster." Oswald thought it was probably an absolute human disaster, a suspicion which steered him to the field of labor economics, the study of jobs and wages—but with an emphasis, in Oswald's case, on how jobs and wages affect subjective wellbeing. His first published paper, in 1979, was about "relative concern," the phenomenon—at that point much less well known than it is today—of evaluating one's own income based on others'. Trade unions, he noticed, were obsessed with relative income: keeping their members on par with or ahead of others. "It just seemed to me intuitively obvious that this is what drove humans."

In those days, his interest in subjective factors marked him and his work as eccentric. He didn't care. He told himself what he still tells young scholars: "If everyone likes your work, you can be sure it's not important. I had a really obdurate streak. I was pretty sure I knew what mattered."

Also unusual then, though not today, was his belief that data trumps theory. "I'd grown up in the Oxford tradition, where implicitly we were left with the view that we didn't need data." He had been trained to suppose that clever economists did mathematics rather than grubby empirical work, a view he now calls a "dangerous and awful thing." Armed with equations, the young Oswald arrived for a fellowship at Princeton University, presented his mathematical models, and was greeted frostily. "They said, 'This is fine, Andrew, but where's the evidence?' This was hugely educational and painful. *What do you mean, where's the evidence?*" Discombobulated, Oswald reassembled himself. "I realized that *really* clever people used evidence." He became a "big-data" guy years before the term existed.

Perhaps it was inevitable that a scholar attracted to big data, contrarian stories, and subjective wellbeing would find happiness economics irresistible. "I was concerned about how unemployment had affected people. We discovered data sets, *huge* data sets, where people were asked about their happiness. It seemed natural to try to understand the patterns." At that point, Easterlin's pioneering work was still mostly forgotten, but the profession's complete lack of interest in subjective wellbeing only made the topic more enticing. "I knew no one would like it, and I thought there was a good chance it would never be published. But it seemed fascinating to me. The issues were obviously of first-order importance. We're trying to understand *human happiness*. What's the role of economic factors and other factors? It's possibly the most important question in all of social science."

As Joshua Wolf Shenk has observed in his book *Powers of Two: How Relationships Drive Creativity,* a lot of the greatest creativity is the result of creative dyads, partnerships in which two very different people complement each other and become a sort of super-thinker or super-creator. John Lennon and Paul McCartney, of the Beatles, are an iconic example; or Steve Jobs and Steve Wozniak, the founders of Apple Computer; or Thomas Jefferson and James Madison, whose political partnership married the ideas of individual freedom and constitutional order. Though each member of the dyad was exceptionally talented, their combination sparked a chemical reaction that created something fantastic.

Around the time he discovered big data sets on happiness, Oswald met his own creativity reagent: David Blanchflower. "He's a genius," Oswald said. "A genius with data."

At 10 a.m. one June morning, not long after meeting Andrew Oswald, I arrived at Dartmouth College's economics department, made my way along a creaky hallway, and encountered Oswald's opposite number—and *opposite* seemed an understatement. Beckoning me into his office, Blanchflower, then sixty-three, was a big-boned, heavyset man with graying, tousled brown hair, and thick hands that swallowed mine whole when we shook. He had a room-filling, boundingly jovial personality. That day he was dressed in summer mode, wearing a floral print shirt (torn near the tail and not wholly tucked in), along with khaki shorts and sandals; but he seemed to be the sort of person who is often in summer mode, regardless of the season. Conspicuous in his cluttered office was a sofa, where he reclined for a good portion of our interview. Even more conspicuous were three side-by-side computer screens on his desk.

Before I could ask my first question, Danny, as he's called, launched our interview by announcing that half an hour before I arrived he had opened a data set which he had never before examined. He had run some quick analyses and found the typical U-shaped relationship between life satisfaction and age. "Pretty cool, eh?" he said, as I squinted over his shoulder at rows of digits on the monitor. "I'd literally never looked at it. But there it is!"

This particular data set contained a collection of thirty-seven countries, most of them developed countries like the United States and Denmark, but with a sprinkling of other places like China, Latvia, and Turkey. "This is a really strange bunch of countries," Blanchflower said, which is why he had not bothered with it before. The data came from a survey in which people were asked, "If you were to consider your life in general, how happy or unhappy would you say you are, on the whole?"

I asked him to show me how he crunched the numbers. "There are only twelve hundred observations for the U.S.," he said, peering at the data. Not enough for meaningful results. So he selected the countries in Western Europe. The man's fingers almost literally blurred over the keyboard as he bounced his cursor from screen to screen, pulled up data tabs, specified equation variables, ran regressions. At every point, he accompanied himself with imprecations: *"Where is that bloody thing?"*; *"Oh, come on, Danny!"* ("Talking to myself," he mumbled. "Best way to do it!") It occurred to me that he was probably doing in a few minutes what might take some analysts hours. Sure enough, a U-shaped curve popped out, its bottom in the early to middle fifties. Then we looked at Eastern Europe; a U again, with the bottom later in middle age, and not as much of a rise afterward as in Western Europe. ("Eastern Europeans are all miserable.") Next up: developing countries and another U, this time bottoming in the early fifties. He added and removed various statistical controls, or used none at all, but the story rarely changed. Then, clearly enjoying himself, and perhaps also relishing my hopeless struggle to keep up with him in my notes, he started in on stress and anxiety, pulling up a British data set with 305,000 people. It showed that U.K. life satisfaction forms a U shape bottoming at age forty-nine, while anxiety and stress peak at about the same age.

"There are hundreds and hundreds of data files I've looked at," he said, when we came up for air. "Hundreds of them. Basically, I do what you've just seen. You get these kinds of plots. I know these people who say you don't see them. But how hard was that to see?"

Blanchflower wasn't always a genius with data. His youth, in Brighton, on the south coast of England, was haphazard. No one in the family had attended university, and young Danny did not seem likely to be the first. When he was thirteen, his parents were called in to school because he was at the bottom of the bottom class. In high school, he got more interested and did well enough to be asked to take the exams for Oxford, but instead he went to Leicester University, a middle-tier British institution, where he majored in economics, didn't work hard, and performed more than adequately with little effort. There followed a period when he was "a bit of a hippie," doing odd jobs—working as a bouncer in California and as a roadie for a rock band, among other things—and then quitting them when he had earned a little money to travel, at one point trekking overland to Afghanistan. "I kind of went sideways for a while," he said.

But along the way he discovered an affinity for economics, and particularly for statistics. Finding himself in a dead-end job teaching basic economics at the British equivalent of a community college, he had a "light-bulb-flashing moment" ("It was like, Holy shit, I didn't know I was that smart!") and, at twenty-eight, went off to do a master's degree in economics. At that point, he made up for lost time, completing the master's and then, in under two years, a PhD. This was in 1970s Britain, where strikes and unemployment left many talented young people out in the cold.

His dissertation, like Andrew Oswald's, was on unions and wages, and his inclination, like Oswald's, was to listen to data and pay attention to the everyday world. "I call it the economics of walking around," he told me. "I liked the economics. But I really wanted to try to understand youth unemployment."

Perhaps it was inevitable, then, that he and Oswald would meet, which they did in the mid-1980s, somewhere in London. They soon agreed to collaborate, not knowing that they would go on to write more papers together than they have bothered to count. "He and I have probably written hundreds of papers together," Blanchflower said. "We're complete complements. I do the data, he writes the first draft." A lot of their work was on wages and labor markets, including one paper in 1988 in which the two of them, seemingly goading each other to new heights of contrarianism, give the academic equivalent of the middle finger to conventional economics by announcing, "This paper contains no mathematical model . . . nor any econometric analysis." That in-your-face disclaimer caused consternation among economists who saw it, which Blanchflower and Oswald relished. "We were sticking it up everyone's nose in 1988." By the late 1980s, the two of them and another like-minded economist, Andrew Clark, were holed up together at Dartmouth, creating a little pod of activity that focused on Richard Easterlin's nearly forgotten subject of happiness.

Oswald got interested in happiness first, then tried to interest Blanchflower, who initially was indifferent. "He was trying to persuade me there was something in the happiness data. I said: 'Yeah, yeah.' But when you look at it, you find the same unbelievable stability in the happiness data as in the wage data." To a big-data guy, stable, recurring patterns are a sign that something is going on. So in 1993 Oswald and Andrew Clark and a few others organized a conference on happiness economics. "We advertised it hugely, all over the school," Oswald recalled. "Put out a hundred chairs. Essentially nobody came." The few speakers who turned up gave papers only vaguely related to happiness, if at all.

The profession's indifference, of course, only made the subject more appealing to the contrarian duo, who dived obsessively into the data sets, looking for patterns. One of the things they tested for, not because they expected anything but because the data were there, was age. The same pattern kept cropping up. A 1994 paper by Oswald and Andrew Clark (published in the Royal Economic Society's *Economic Journal*), on whether unemployment causes unhappiness (answer: yes, and powerfully), contained the sentence: "There is a U shape in mental wellbeing with respect to age." In a 1996 paper (in the *Journal of Occupational and Organizational Psychology*), Oswald, Clark, and a psychologist named Peter Warr found that job satisfaction is "U-shaped in age."

At that point, the result seemed an intriguing oddity. There was no particularly good theory to explain it and not much by way of confirmation, and so the researchers did not pay much attention to it. "We did what people do, which is just proceed," Oswald told me. "You're in the fog of research. That's how I think about it. You're just out there." But the age-happiness relationship persisted, and not just in their own work. Carol Graham, for example, used quite different countries and data sets, but found similar patterns. In 2004, Blanchflower and Oswald had enough data and confidence to pronounce that age, all by itself, plays a role as a determinant of happiness. In "Wellbeing over Time in Britain and the USA," which was published in the *Journal of Public Economics,* they found that marriage is very good for happiness, that unemployment is very bad, that life satisfaction had stagnated in Britain and declined in the United States (though the happiness of American blacks had risen), and that relative income matters. They also announced that age had its own, independent effect on life satisfaction: "The exact effect of age upon reported happiness is of interest. It is U-shaped."

The age effect, they said, held in both the United States and the United Kingdom, after adjusting for key variables like marital status, education, and employment. It was true of both men and women. It did not seem to be the result of changes in social or economic conditions over time, because the same pattern turned up across generations. "Something systematic appears to be at work," they wrote. "No explanation is available even in the psychology literature."

The 2004 paper, a clarion public declaration that something was going on with age, made a serious splash. Four years later, in the journal *Social Science & Medicine*, they published a magnum opus on age and happiness, "Is Wellbeing U-Shaped over the Life Cycle?" Their answer, based on large data sets spanning dozens of countries and including hundreds of thousands of people, among them more than half a million in Europe and America alone, was yes. "We show that wellbeing reaches its minimum around the middle of life," they wrote. "The regularity is intriguing. The U shape is similar for males and females, and for each side of the Atlantic Ocean (though its minimum is reached a little later among American men)." A couple of dozen or so countries did not show a U pattern, but they were mostly developing countries where the number of people sampled was small. In statistics, small samples make it difficult to find patterns amid the "noise" created by the wide variety of individuals' specific circumstances. If you imagine a sample of only three people, for example, one might be unemployed at age twenty-five, another might happily remarry at age forty-five, and the third might get cancer at age sixty-five—effects which, in that tiny sample, would completely swamp any effect of age in and of itself.

By 2008, Blanchflower and Oswald were able to cite almost two dozen other papers finding the U. For more evidence, they decided to look at mental health. If life satisfaction was low in middle age, that might imply that depression would be higher, so they obtained a database of about a million Britons between the ages of sixteen and seventy. Sure enough, they found an inverse U—a hill, as it were—with the probability of depression peaking in the mid-forties. In 2012, deepening their case, they looked at data counting prescriptions for antidepressants in twenty-seven European countries. Same result: a hill with the probability of using antidepressants peaking in the mid-forties. The following year, they came up with data on the use of mental-health drugs in two American states, New Hampshire and New Mexico: "Here the highest probability of consuming medication occurs in the age bracket 45–49. Again, a midlife peak is visible in the data."

In 2010, *The Economist,* the British newsmagazine, published an article titled "The U-Bend of Life," which made the phenomenon more widely known. Besides drawing upon the work of Blanchflower and Oswald, the article displayed a graph from a then-new paper by an American psychologist named Arthur A. Stone, of the University of Southern California, and three other authors (Joseph E. Schwartz, Joan E. Broderick, and Angus Deaton). Titled "A Snapshot of the Age Distribution of Psychological Wellbeing in the United States," the paper drew on a Gallup survey of more than three hundred thousand Americans and found the U shape, bottoming in the late forties and early fifties. Even without statistical adjustments, the pattern was visible to the naked eye.

We'll come later to what might be going on here. Suffice to say, for now, that the researchers were finding that *something* is going on—something which earlier research about midlife had missed. Life satisfaction tends to decline gradually after early adulthood, bottom out in middle age, then gradually rebound after. Andrew Oswald, for his part, is not shy about the potential significance of the data. More or less the first thing he said to me during our first conversation was: "I view this as a first-order discovery about human beings that will outlive us by hundreds of years."

Not everyone was convinced. There was a problem, potentially, with the U story, one worth recounting because it pushed the research in such an unexpected direction. Remember, the U is a big-data phenomenon. Blanchflower, Graham, Oswald, and the others find it by analyzing data sets spanning tens of thousands or preferably hundreds of thousands, and some-times millions, of people: oceans of people so large that researchers can use powerful statistical techniques to fish out patterns. The kind of data they are looking at, huge international surveys of happiness, did not exist in the 1960s, when Elliott Jaques floated his midlife-crisis hypothesis. And data aren't people, which is the reason psychologists weren't convinced by it. If you want to know how people live their lives, how their satisfaction dips and rises, you need to use much smaller samples, you need to differ-entiate between individuals, and you usually need to look in detail at their lives. You can't do big data on personal experience. Or so it seemed.

The U faced another challenge. If in 1975 you had asked a million Americans of different ages how satisfied they were with their lives, you might have retrieved an impressively large data set—but it would have been a snapshot, a statistical photo of how people felt *in 1975*. Knowing that, say, thirty-year-olds and sixty-year-olds were happier than forty-five-year-olds in 1975 might merely tell you that the three generations had ex-perienced different conditions in their lives. Maybe the forty-five-year-olds, having all grown up during the Great Depression, were scarred by hard economic times, making them generally less positive about life. The ex-ample is not hypothetical: the Depression made my father pessimistic and insecure about money, with a proclivity for hoarding. To know that the U curve is really a result of age rather than reflecting what statisticians call a *cohort effect,* you ideally need to compare people who were born in many different years but who had the same generational experience. Which, of course, is impossible. Or you need to follow individuals throughout the course of their lives—but tracking people through the course of their lives, of necessity, takes a lifetime, and many of the subjects will drop out or disappear, and keeping up with the rest costs a fortune. Even tracking people for a year is pretty hard. Partly as a result, when a few researchers had found and looked at lifetime data, the U didn't reliably turn up.

In 2002, a young graduate student at the University of Warwick

approached Oswald about taking him on as a PhD student. Nick Powdthavee was a Thai immigrant to Britain and had an idea about studying
"Buddhist economics." Instead, Oswald steered him to a data set on the
wellbeing of South Africans. Sure enough, he found the U. By the time I
met Powdthavee, he was in his late thirties and had published dozens of
articles, plus a book on happiness economics. "I've always found it," he told
me, when I had coffee with him in a basement café at the London School
of Economics and Political Science, where he was then a professor (he subsequently returned to Warwick). "In almost every data set I've looked at,
there's this U."

But, again, the South Africa data offered only a snapshot. Powdthavee
wanted a motion picture. So he, Oswald, and a third scholar (Terence
Cheng) tackled the problem head-on. They managed to find four data sets
in three countries (Australia, Britain, and Germany) that tracked people
over time, and to each they then applied a statistical technique that al-
lowed them to look at what they called "within-person changes" in life
satisfaction. In all four data sets, they found the U, bottoming at various
points in the forties. Here was evidence that the U-shaped pattern
is something actually experienced by individuals as they aged. Not all
individuals, of course, but enough to validate the pattern. "It exists,"
Powdthavee told me, adding, "It's fundamentally important."

But how fundamental? Is this a biological thing? Or a cultural thing?
A result of outside pressures or of inner design? With those questions in
mind, and acting on nothing more than a hunch, Oswald emailed a man
named Alexander Weiss.

Whole careers and important discoveries sometimes turn on quirks. Alex
Weiss has poor night vision. An American, he is a comparative psychologist at the University of Edinburgh, in Scotland. In plainer English, he
tries to learn more about human psychology by studying the psychology of

animals. He did a master's degree on sea anemones and leopard sharks, and then set out to do a PhD on the psychology of moths, but his night blindness scotched that idea. While he was looking for an alternative, a supervisor asked him to join in some work on chimpanzees.

If you are human, your personality and your general level of happiness are heavily influenced by five basic personality traits, which are, in turn, strongly influenced by your genes. The big five, as they are often called, are neuroticism, extroversion, openness to experience, agreeableness, and conscientiousness. The upbeat, positive traits among the big five often cluster together and reinforce each other to create upbeat, positive personalities, a phenomenon which Weiss and various of his colleagues call *covitality*. To a large extent, we get our personality structure and basic happiness level from our parents: in humans, subjective wellbeing (happiness, broadly defined) and personality structure not only track closely with each other, but are both quite significantly heritable (to the tune of roughly 50 percent). But how important is the biological component? One place to seek insight is in humans' closest relatives.

Along with two collaborators, R. Mark Enns and James E. King, Weiss decided to look at chimps in zoos. Lo and behold, when he looked at dominance—a major factor in both chimp personality and wellbeing, and a trait in chimps that maps fairly well to extroversion and low neuroticism in humans—Weiss found that it was both strongly heritable and strongly tied to wellbeing. That result and others like it mirrored the patterns in humans, suggesting a strong biological role in happiness, and in the personality traits that give rise to happiness. "That inspired me," Weiss said, when we spoke about his primate research. "We can learn a lot about human personality and wellbeing from studying chimpanzees and other apes."

In the course of his work on primate psychology and personality, Weiss had accomplished two useful things. First, he and James King had developed an assessment of chimp and orangutan happiness. Of course, apes can't tell us how happy they are, but they express a lot of emotion, of which keepers, who tend to know their charges very well, are quite reliable reporters. Asked, for instance, to assess the apes' positive or negative mood, how much pleasure they get from social interactions, and how successful they are at achieving their goals, multiple raters gave consistent answers, and their answers matched up with objective indicators measuring traits like physical health. Weiss thus found himself in possession of a lot of information about how apes feel.

Second, Weiss had also learned that, for chimps' personalities, age matters, and in much the same way that it matters for humans. "Human personality development is characterized by individuals' becoming more introverted, less competitive, and less emotional, and having greater behavioral controls," he and James King wrote. "This pattern is largely preserved in chimpanzees." The finding that age shapes personality in chimps is revealing, because it suggests that some of our personality *development*—as well as our personality structure—is wired into higher-primate biology. "Chimpanzees aren't out there getting jobs," Weiss told me. "You have this very different situation, yet this same basic trajectory is going on. If you adjust for the fact that chimpanzees and orangs are living fifty to fifty-five years, you find the magnitude of these age differences is super, super similar to what we see in humans." It might not be so surprising, then, to find other similarities between humans' and apes' emotional development.

One day, out of the blue, an email arrived from Andrew Oswald, an economist Weiss had never heard of. "He's like, 'I see you've done this work on wellbeing in chimpanzees and orangutans. My work has found this U shape underlying age and wellbeing, and I'm wondering if you've thought to look at this in your apes.'" He hadn't. The two agreed to meet to talk it over, and soon afterward Weiss began plowing through data on 336 chimpanzees and 172 orangutans, mostly in the United States and Japan but also in Australia, Canada, and Singapore. (The apes lived in zoos, research centers, and a sanctuary.) The results were clear. "Sure enough," Weiss told me, "there's good evidence for this U shape in our apes." The apes hit bottom at an age whose equivalent in humans is between forty-five and fifty.

The resulting paper, "Evidence for a Midlife Crisis in Great Apes Consistent with the U-Shape in Human Wellbeing," was published in *Proceedings of the National Academy of Sciences* in 2012. "Our results," wrote Oswald, Weiss, and a handful of other collaborators (including some primatologists), "imply that human wellbeing's curved shape is not uniquely human and that although it may be partly explained by aspects of human life and society, its origins may lie partly in the biology we share with closely related great apes."

The paper created a sensation. Midlife crisis in monkeys! "It was a bit overwhelming at times," Weiss told me. No one was more surprised than Andrew Oswald, who had not expected his wild hunch to pan out. He wasn't convinced until the third set of data came in, a moment still fresh in his mind when we met several years later. "I always remember the desk I was sitting at three or four times in my life when I thought, *This is going to outlive me. It's either wrong or it's absolutely fundamental to humans.*"

Good empiricist that he is, Oswald said he will breathe a sigh of relief when someone replicates the apes result. Still, when I asked how he thinks matters stand, he replied: "My betting is this is a completely universal human phenomenon." By "universal" he meant the *tendency* is universal, not that everyone will have a painful time in middle age. "I think the underlying process is the same in all humans. I could turn out to be wrong and I'm keeping an open mind, but that's what the evidence suggests."

It was the ape study that finally riveted my attention to the happiness curve. Everything suggested that my chronic fortysomething discontent was not about my circumstances, or even, in a sense, about "me," my conscious, reasoning self. And the apes seemed to seal the deal. I hadn't necessarily made bad decisions or let myself down or curdled as a human being. I didn't even need to fully understand why I felt as I did, any more than apes do. In fact, if evolution has for some reason wired into us a tendency to experience discontent in midlife, we might *expect* not to understand why. When nature sets us up with built-in physiological and psychological processes, she rarely provides built-in insight into how they work. All of which would help explain my compulsive but nonsensical daydreams about walking out on a very good writing job.

"I'm pretty sure I've gone through the U, by the way," Oswald remarked to me at one point, as if in an afterthought. His marriage split up when he was in his forties. ("I wouldn't wish that on my worst enemy.") At that point, the work on happiness did not seem likely to be particularly significant. "I was conscious that the second half of life didn't look very good. I thought there'd be a general deterioration."

Blanchflower had his own midlife difficulties. "What did I want out of life? I wanted to be famous. And I got to be a full professor at an Ivy League school, and we wrote *The Wage Curve* [his and Oswald's influential book on labor markets], and I was only forty. And we both went: *Oh! That's a bit earlier than I thought!* I think that was a midlife crisis. That was like: *Do something else.*" I asked if he had felt trapped at that time, and Blanchflower chuckled that he hadn't, but his wife had felt trapped with him. He responded to the stress by buying a snowmobile and a boat and by doubling down on work. "A lot of it was that we just worked all the time. I would work and I would spend time with my kids. I certainly didn't spend time with my marriage." His marriage, like Oswald's, broke up traumatically, and he got hit with a cancer diagnosis. The result was a period which he said can be summed up with a single word: *pain*.

About the time Andrew Oswald turned fifty, he entered a relationship with his current wife, who turned out to be as right for him as the previous match had been wrong. His perspective on life has changed, and his outlook has improved. "You're more forgiving of yourself," he told me. "It's possible to concentrate on the bits of what you've done that work well. You don't have to obsess about all the bad stuff."

Blanchflower experienced a similar turnaround. In his early fifties, he told me, "life got better." His divorce finally came through, after seven excruciating years, and his cancer went into remission. He remarried, happily; regained his health; acquired a column in a prominent newspaper; became a member of the Bank of England's board of governors. And he became a more relaxed person. "I'm less and less inclined to be a boring academic. I have nothing to prove whatsoever." He fishes, a hobby he talks about with an economist's rigor. "I go down about seven thirty at night as the sun goes down. Fishing is better if it's calm, but if it's calm, the bugs come, so you have a trade-off."

Did Danny's and Andrew's remarriages improve their mind-sets? Did their mind-sets improve their marriages? Reflecting later on my conversations with the two of them, it occurred to me that neither I nor they would ever understand how the changing slope of the happiness curve and the changing contours of their lives and choices had interacted. No data set can solve that mystery. I do know that I encountered two happy men whose lives had rounded a bend. The first time I spoke to Andrew Oswald, I mentioned that I was in my early fifties and that my contentment seemed to be on the rise. He exclaimed, "Just wait until you're sixty!"

4

....

THE SHAPE OF THE RIVER

Time, happiness, and the curve of the U

Not everyone, of course, will be unhappy at forty-five, or happy after that. In this chapter, I'll explore the meaning and magnitude of the happiness curve; but the best way to introduce the curve is by emphasizing first of all what it is not. It is not an inevitability; it's a tendency.

There is a world of difference between the two—a difference which explains why the happiness curve's real-world effects can be subtle, unpredictable, and strange. The river in the Voyage of Life has regular currents and well-charted turns; yet, paradoxically, no two voyagers experience the same journey.

Psychologists say that the notion of a universal midlife crisis is a myth. "People can certainly be unhappy in their middle adult years, and they can certainly go out and buy sports cars (or fantasize about buying them)," writes Susan Krauss Whitbourne, in *Psychology Today*. "However, whether they do so because of, or in direct relation to, their age is doubtful. Change is possible at any age, whether in crisis form or not, as we all try to achieve fulfillment." Her statement is certainly right. For everyone I encountered who had experienced the U-shaped happiness curve, I encountered someone else whose life satisfaction had taken a very different shape.

As I have mentioned, I gave almost three hundred people of middle age and above a questionnaire asking them to both rate and describe their satisfaction in each decade of life so far.* Aside from the U, the life-satisfaction trajectory I encountered most commonly—and very commonly, at that—was a rising line. People who experience this upward-slope pattern typically have unhappy or turbulent early adulthoods, a start in life they're happy to put behind them.

Take Joe, for example. When we spoke, he was fifty-seven, and his life-satisfaction ratings had risen with each decade of life: four in his twenties, five in his thirties, six in his forties, and seven in his fifties. He was born in the South and had never left. Not college-educated, he went to work after high school, first as a truck driver, then a welder. He made mistakes, including a bad marriage that began when he was twenty-three and ended before he turned thirty. He drank too much and did drugs. His divorce forced him to start over and landed him with a pile of unpaid bills, and he had to move back in with his parents, a setback he found humiliating. At thirty, though, he met the right person, and they married and had a son. Meanwhile, he took a job running cranes at a steel mill, where after more than twenty years he still works. He likes what he does and knows that stable, decently paid blue-collar employment is becoming rare. The real anchor of his values, though, is his family: "A lot of kids in my day wanted to be a fireman or policeman or astronaut. I just wanted to be a dad."

In middle age, Joe realized he needed to walk closer to the Lord. He had always been a churchgoer, he said, "but I wasn't living the life or being the example that I should." Fatherhood convinced him he needed to do

---

*Using the Cantril Ladder's venerable question, I asked respondents to rate their life satisfaction on a zero-to-ten scale. I also asked them for three words or phrases describing each decade of life. Some respondents were people I knew, some of them were random strangers, and some were adult-education students in an Osher Lifelong Learning Institute program at Bradley University, in Peoria, Illinois. I'm grateful to Bradley University professor Marjorie Getz for facilitating this research. Because its purpose was journalistic, my survey did not seek or achieve scientific validity, but the results were consistent with the academic research.

better. At fifty-seven, he felt his relationship with God was good and improving. "My wife and I were out the other day and a young man asked us what's the secret of a good marriage. We both said, 'God.' I'm a firm believer that if you don't have God in your life, it's tough." When I asked how the future looks, he said he expects to hit an eight in his sixties. "I'll have my wife and hopefully some grandchildren by then. Hopefully a place on the beach or on the lake. Life just seems to get better as you get older. I learn something each day, and it adds up."

Another common life-satisfaction pattern is the V-shaped curve. It is rarer than either the U or the upward-sloping line—mercifully so, because it's the pattern characterized by a disruptive breakdown or an acute crisis rather than a chronic malaise. An example is someone I know well, Tony. When we met in the early 1990s, he was twenty-two, a sweet-natured, baby-faced gay man who had only recently moved from a city in the South to Washington, D.C. He had an easygoing, positive personality, and bushels of talent, so he was never someone I worried about. And then, when he was forty-six, he disappeared. I asked around, but all that anyone had heard was a rumor that he had quit his job and moved to Florida. For a time, I wondered if I would ever hear from him again. When he resurfaced, it was with a story of midlife collapse.

Tony had risen fast. From waiting tables and sharing an apartment, he became an arts reporter in his twenties. By thirty, he was movie editor for a major media outlet, where he managed writers more experienced than he. Then he followed a boyfriend to Asia, wrote freelance, began a successful blog, won an award. "My thirties were fucking great," he told me, when I finally reconnected with him. "I'm feeling really successful. I'm starting to hit my stride." But he was fighting impostor complex, an incessant din of inner critics telling him his success was unearned and precarious. A move to the suburbs felt deadening and his sex life at home went flat. Tony couldn't stay faithful; his partner broke up with him. Meanwhile, he began to feel his work lacked meaning. "I was having something of an existential crisis, asking myself if even this nice job I had, this job that seems to impress other people, was producing anything of value. I escaped into booze and sex."

That turned out to be a catastrophic mistake. As his drinking became heavier, he had trouble at work. He left with a nice severance package, which only made matters worse. "That made it possible for me to sit at home quietly and drink. I did that for almost exactly six months and made myself actually ill. I got to the point where I had to get out of town. Even through the bourbon haze it was clear I would probably not make it through the winter if I didn't do something." Fortunately, he managed to pull himself together enough to call a relative in Florida, get on a plane, and checked into a hospital for medical detox. Later came weeks of intensive rehabilitation.

When I finally heard his story, after having been out of contact with him for a year, it came as a shock. Nervously, I asked my old friend if he thought he was out of the woods. He replied that his finances were precarious but he was sober. He was unsure what lay ahead but was willing to venture optimism: "I think I can keep the ship more or less aright."

When Tony's slide began, it looked very much like the onset of a typical midlife malaise, the kind that causes chronic dissatisfaction, but not an acute crisis. In fact, if Tony had not mishandled his restlessness and discontent, he might well have plodded through more or less uneventfully, as most people do. When a U curve goes bad, it can turn into a V, causing pain to ourselves and the people around us, and sometimes leading to mistakes from which our life satisfaction never fully recovers.

An example is Alan. Unlike Tony, he was a stranger when I interviewed him. A tall, slender, dignified man of sixty-five, he was the first in his South Carolina family to go to college, where he earned an accounting degree. After serving in the Vietnam, he worked in a series of white-collar government jobs, building professional momentum which lasted into his thirties. Alan was someone who enjoyed being busy and having responsibility, and he ascended into management. Around the time he turned forty, however, he fell in with shady people. One of them asked him to intermediate in a drug deal. Alan agreed and took a cut. A few months later, the seller returned for a second deal. Alan realized he was in over his head. He considered turning informant, even contacted police, but got cold feet when he reflected that he could wind up "sleeping with the fishes." Instead, he took a rap for attempted distribution of cocaine, which landed him in prison for a year.

Characteristically, he made the best of his confinement, working in the prison's law library and as a clerk on an antidrug program. On release, he managed to find a data-entry job, worked at it for several years, but then was laid off. "So I'm back out of work," he recalled of that time. "But now I have a record. It's hard to get to the level where I was, because at some point you're going to have to bring this up."

After that, Alan found a position working as a corporate mail clerk. It was a long way from management, but it proved stable. Still, when we spoke he was sixty-five and could not afford to retire. He worked alongside millennials who, he said, couldn't care less about doing the job right. He felt angry at himself for losing his way in his forties. He especially felt regret. He had never managed to rejoin the white-collar, upwardly mobile society of his youth; and he never would. "There's always something to remind you. You're riding high, and—*Wham! Boom!* After that, you feel it's hard to be around those people you knew before. It's hard to go back."

I interviewed dozens of people for this book, trying to understand in an intimate, textured way how they experience life satisfaction over time. I have learned what we all already know. There is no single, standard trajectory for human happiness. The only rule is differentness. My own path (so far) has followed a U that might have been lifted right out of one of Carol Graham's graphs, but Tony's and Alan's V and Joe's upward-sloping line are also commonplace.

Yet the U-shaped happiness curve, while not necessarily dispositive for any of us, may nonetheless influence all of us—even if what we experience in life is more like a rising line or a V. How can that be? The answer requires looking more closely at the shape of the river.

As I was working on this chapter, Danny Blanchflower sent me an email. "Take a look here," said the subject line, above a message that said: "This is the latest stuff from the U.K." Britain maintains one of the world's most thoroughgoing efforts to measure subjective wellbeing, of which its Office for National Statistics conducts annual surveys. The latest statistics, for 2014 to 2015, were in. Over three hundred thousand people of different ages had been asked, "Overall, how satisfied are you with your life nowadays?" Here is how the results look, by age group, when you graph the percentage of people saying their life satisfaction was *high* or *very high* (as opposed to *low* or *medium*).

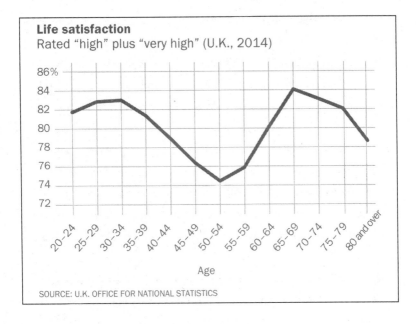

Life satisfaction
Rated "high" plus "very high" (U.K., 2014)

Age

SOURCE: U.K. OFFICE FOR NATIONAL STATISTICS

As is immediately apparent, satisfaction declines from youth through middle age, bottoms out in the early fifties, and then rises to a peak at age seventy before roughly leveling off (with a mild decline) until advanced old age (eighty and beyond). People were also asked how happy and anxious they felt yesterday, measures of affect rather than satisfaction with life, and those indicators followed the same general pattern, with anxiety and unhappiness peaking in the early fifties and then falling through the sixties. You don't need a PhD to interpret the graph; in fact, this is the kind of data which leads Blanchflower to roll his eyes and say, "How hard is that to see?" when psychologists say they can't find a U.

The pattern is telling us something interesting about the happiness of people of different ages. In Britain, in 2014, the average middle-aged person was less happy about his or her life than was the average young person or older person. But what is it telling us about age itself? That is a different question.

Over lunch one day, Andrew Oswald illustrated the distinction by using one of his obsessions: fruits and vegetables. (As it happened, we were sharing a vegetable plate.) A few years ago, rummaging around in large data sets, he had discovered, in Britain, a "remarkable relationship" between eating fruits and vegetables and being satisfied with life. That became grist for a paper he coauthored with Blanchflower and Sarah Stewart-Brown. You might have thought there would be a lot of research on connections between diet and happiness, given how much everybody cares about both subjects, but in fact their study, Oswald said, is among only a few to have looked for a relationship. What they found was this: "Happiness and mental health rise in an approximately dose-response way with the number of daily portions of fruit and vegetables"—all the way up to seven daily portions, which is about as much fruit and vegetable matter as anyone can ingest.

But wait: People who eat a lot of vegetables are likely to be different in many ways from people who do not. They may have higher incomes (poor people have less access to fresh fruit and vegetables) and healthier lifestyles (smoking less, exercising more); they may be younger and better educated; they may just be happier to start out with. There are all kinds of reasons why what looks like a connection between diet and happiness might be the result of some third factor influencing both. What you really want to know, then, is not whether people who eat a lot of vegetables are happier on average, but whether eating vegetables is in and of itself associated with happiness and mental health. The more interesting finding of the fruit and vegetable study is that the answer is yes.

Oswald and his coauthors adjusted their analysis for all kinds of factors which might influence happiness, including, for instance, age, income, marriage, employment, sex, race, exercise, smoking, religion, body mass, and even consumption of other foods like fish, meat, and alcohol. In effect, they used statistical techniques to compare like with like across a variety of dimensions, which large data sets allow them to do. If adjusting for income or education or fish consumption had made the effect of eating fruits and vegetables go away, then that would suggest that income or education or fish consumption is what really matters. In fact, however, "the pattern [they write] is robust to adjustment for a large number of other demographic, social, and economic variables." They find what they call a fruit-and-vegetable gradient, and its effect on happiness and mental health appears quite significant.

Their result does not prove that eating more fruits and vegetables will, by itself, make you happier. I wouldn't be surprised if that were the case, but in the social sciences establishing causality is difficult. What the fruit-and-veggie gradient *does* reveal is a genuine association: some sort of independent relationship between the two variables, and thus something which cries out to be explained.

Age, of course, is different from diet inasmuch as we can't control it. If someone develops a way to escape midlife blahs by becoming younger, no doubt many people will avail themselves of it, but that day seems far off.

Still, the question which most intrigued Oswald and Blanchflower and me, once I got my head around it, is whether *age itself* has an apparent effect on how happy we are.

The answer, again, is yes. In fact, the happiness curve shows up more clearly and consistently after filtering out people's life circumstances than before. Here is an example, from an analysis by Carol Graham and her colleague Milena Nikolova of the biggest data set out there, the Gallup World Poll, whose survey set of 160 or more countries covers about 99 percent of the world's population. If you just look at people's assessments of their own lives compared to the best possible life they can imagine for themselves (one of the most widely used gauges of overall satisfaction with life), the results turn out like this:

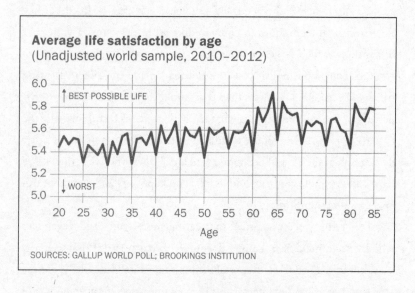

Average life satisfaction by age
(Unadjusted world sample, 2010–2012)

SOURCES: GALLUP WORLD POLL; BROOKINGS INSTITUTION

If there is a visible trend, it is that people get happier over time, with an upward bump around retirement age. But once Graham and Nikolova adjust for income, gender, education, employment, marriage, health, and so on—in other words, filtering out other factors influencing life satisfaction—here is how the relationship between age and life satisfaction looks:

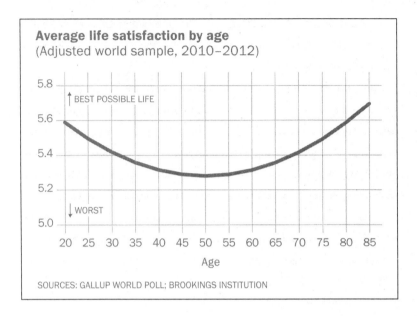

Average life satisfaction by age
(Adjusted world sample, 2010–2012)

SOURCES: GALLUP WORLD POLL; BROOKINGS INSTITUTION

There's the U. Once Graham and Nikolova factor out the other things that are going on, your age, in and of itself, has a clear relationship with how happy you are.

The smoothness of the curve is something of a tip-off. Real-world responses from actual people are jiggly. The U curve, by contrast, is a statistical projection, or prediction, of how satisfied people *would* be if they were the same in all measurable respects except for age—not, obviously, a real-world condition. When I first encountered this finding, one reaction I had was: *so what?* We are each a huge bundle of variables, and what we care about is how they all add up—how happy we actually *feel*—and not how happy we might feel if only one thing in our lives were important. If I want to know, at age twenty, how happy or unhappy I may be at age forty, I'll need to know whether I'm in a good marriage, whether I have enough food to eat, how my health is, and all the rest. Knowing the independent effect of age on happiness tells us no more about our actual lives than knowing the independent effect of pitching on baseball tells us about who actually wins the game.

The answer lies in understanding what the happiness curve is really saying, which is this: it is perfectly possible to be very satisfied with your life in middle age, *but it is harder.*

Returning to Thomas Cole's metaphor of the river, I might say: the happiness curve is like an undertow that pulls against you in middle age. That doesn't mean you can't row against it. Or perhaps your load has become lighter, or your rowing skill has improved, or your muscles are stronger, or you have managed to improve your boat. Or perhaps, like Joe, you have come through a worse stretch upstream, when you were younger, so the middle portion of the river seems comparatively tame. If one or more of those things pertains, you may not even notice the more challenging current in middle age. You may think: *why would anyone believe this portion of the river is difficult?*

Or you may not.

I was someone who, after going to war with myself over my sexuality in my teens and early twenties, had had a blessed life. I enjoyed good health, did well in my career, had lots of friends. I felt excited and energized in my twenties and early thirties as I came into my own as a journalist and came out of the closet as a gay man. I certainly pulled hard on my oars. I pushed myself and took some serious risks, such as when I quit a good job to attempt a wildly ambitious book, which failed twice before it finally got published. But I was someone who had never experienced an unfavorable current. Events and circumstances had flowed in my favor. In my late thirties, therefore, when the U sloped down and the background current changed, I felt the change keenly. Rowing against the undercurrent was noticeably harder; the river ahead seemed longer; my destination, farther away. The circumstances of my own life had sensitized me to an unfavorable shift in the undertow.

I think this kind of sensitization may be common for people who reach middle age without having experienced major difficulties in earlier adulthood. Joe rated his happiness in his forties at six, which is relatively low. But he experienced his forties as a relief after his unhappy, unsettled twenties and his better but still difficult thirties. On the other hand, Tony's trajectory is more like mine. He made a fast start and went from strength to strength as a young man, but was then all the more sensitive to the ennui which caught up with him in his late thirties. I doubt the happiness curve, by itself, caused his collapse in his mid-forties; that had more to do with bad decisions he made, notably drinking too much, moping too much, and failing to reach out for help before he lost control. I do think, though, that the curve's downslope contributed to his malaise, which set him up for the trouble he ran into.

Of course, the undertow would not matter if it were faint. Then it would be a statistical curiosity, something real but not usually noticeable, or at least noticeable only in situations like mine, where everything else is going well in life and no unexpected jolts come along. You may have noticed that, in the chart above showing the happiness curve for the entire world, the difference between the most and least happy portions of the curve is not even a full point on a scale of one to ten.

Actually, however, less than one point still turns out to be quite a bit. Most people restrict themselves to a narrow band in the upper-middle portion of the scale. Eighty percent of people rank themselves between seven and nine, and anything below six is rare enough to indicate serious misery. (Tens almost never appear. People like to leave room for improvement.) Because the rest of the world is not generally as happy as the United States, the average global response is in the five-to-six range, a tick or two lower than in America. Either way, a decline of a point or even half a point is significant.

How significant? The same statistical manipulations which allow economists to tease out the effects of particular variables on happiness also allow them to estimate how large those effects are. In their landmark 2008 paper (which I discussed in the previous chapter), Blanchflower and Oswald find that going from age twenty to age forty-five decreases life satisfaction by about a third as much as becoming unemployed—and unemployment is

one of the worst things that commonly happen to people. "That is sugges-
tive of a large effect on wellbeing," they write. In another paper, which looks
at more than two dozen European countries, they find that being middle-
aged nearly doubles a person's risk of using antidepressants, after controlling
for other variables. Most recently, in their longitudinal study (also discussed
in the previous chapter) of how individuals experience the effects of age on
happiness over time, Oswald, Nick Powdthavee, and Terence Cheng find
that the effect of going from about age twenty to about age forty-five is
comparable "to a substantial percentage of the effect on wellbeing of major
events such as divorce or unemployment." That kind of magnitude is no
guarantee that you or any particular person will feel the undertow, or will
have trouble with it if you do feel it. But it does explain why the undertow,
while too weak to heave me into a full-tilt depression, was strong enough to
bother me day in and day out for a decade or more.

In a way, I had it easy. Having enjoyed an enviable launch in early adulthood and then been spared major setbacks or trauma, I experienced the U's
downturn as an unwonted, unwarranted sourness. But if you're already in a
depressed or dissatisfied emotional state, or if you're struggling with difficult conditions, then the negative undertow can amplify your other problems. One of the more painful interviews I did for this book was with a
woman named Nancy, a stranger who emailed me thanking me for an article I wrote about the happiness curve. "It made me feel better about the
unaccountable—and very deep—funk I find myself in at age forty-two,"
she wrote. Later, in an interview, she told me she was someone who had
always struggled with depression. It ran in the family. Her great-grandmother
had been institutionalized, her grandmother had been hospitalized, her
mother, she said, was a "nutty buddy." Her twenties, like so many people's,
were fun and exciting. She took an office job in an exciting city, then went
back to school, and enjoyed a life of carefree discovery. But, she said, "There
was always the background of depression." Antidepressants, which she
finally began in her late twenties, were life-changing, but they did not elim-

inate the depression, only reduced it. In her early thirties, she became a mother, but she experienced parenthood as a source of stress and anxiety. By the time she turned forty, chronic depression had become a fact of life.

"Even with all that, when I turned forty, something got worse," she told me. "A couple of years ago—I don't know—I wake up either sad or angry. It's worse, and it's not life-related." I asked if she could think of a reason for her downturn. No, she replied. Nothing had changed or gone wrong in her life. "I still have the same problems. I'm in a job that's pretty perfect for me, other than low money." Her kids were older and at an easier age, which should have reduced the emotional pressure. Her marriage was okay. "I think I'm just sadder," she said—now fighting back tears, a catch in her voice. "If the depression is the same, and if my life is the same, *why am I sadder?*" As was also true of me, she not only felt bad, she felt bad about feeling bad; but, unlike me, she was depressed to begin with. If other things are more or less equal, entering the trough of the curve can make an already bad situation worse.

Where does that leave us, in terms of thinking about happiness and age? In his book *Authentic Happiness: Using the New Positive Psychology to Realize Your Potential for Lasting Fulfillment*, Martin E. P. Seligman, one of America's most prominent psychologists, posits a formula for happiness:

$H = S + C + V$ where H is your enduring level of happiness, S is your set range, C is the circumstances of your life, and V represents factors under your voluntary control.

His formula is elegant and seems intuitively right, and it offers some guidance for thinking about how to become happier. We can't do much about our happiness set point, which is mostly a function of our genes and personality. We can work to change our life's circumstances and our own behavioral and emotional patterns in ways that help us be happier. All well and good. But the happiness curve suggests that the formula is missing a term and should look like this:

$$H = S + C + V + T$$

where T stands for time, or perhaps more specifically, aging. T—whether you are at age twenty-five, forty-five, or sixty-five—matters, but it is not the *only* thing that matters.

You can see right away that H, happiness, can get complicated. If C and V, your circumstances and voluntary choices, are changing in ways that make you feel dramatically better about life as you move into middle age, then time may not matter to you. For example, Perry, seventy-two and semiretired, was aware of nagging midlife discontent, but it was swamped by improvements in his circumstances. In young adulthood, he was wounded twice in Vietnam, got married to the wrong person and painfully divorced, and then watched his career as a police officer go up in smoke after he cited the commissioner for drunken driving. ("I made the right decision. You took an oath to enforce the oath, and nowhere in that oath did it say, 'With exceptions.'") As sharply as circumstances had zigged south for him in his twenties and early thirties, they zigged north in his mid-thirties when he met a "wonderful woman" and began a new career as a safety officer for a shipping company. "Life turned around," said Perry. The result was that his satisfaction rating jumped from only three in his early thirties to seven in his forties—and then, once time started working in his favor, to eight in his sixties and nine in his seventies. By contrast, in Nancy's case, her circumstances and voluntary choices remained mostly steady over time, but in her forties the negative pull of T (middle age) compounded the depressive effects of S (her low emotional set point). Result: misery. And what if different elements are moving in different directions? Well, then it all depends. That is why individual cases vary so widely, even though the U-shaped undertow is quite strong.

In my amended version of the equation, two of the four terms (our emotional set point and our age) are beyond our personal control. One term (our voluntary choices about our lives and attitudes) is entirely under our control. The fourth term (our circumstances) is partly under our control and partly not; one of our challenges in life is to control and improve our circumstances. So the message here is not as simple as fatalism ("You can't do anything about your happiness, it's wired into your personality") or stoicism ("Control your emotions and attitudes, because the rest is not really up to you"); nor does it support the idea that we can be as happy as we choose simply by thinking positively. It clearly does not support a crude story about the inevitability of an emotional crisis or meltdown in middle age.

What it does say is something which I believe is important, even fundamental, and insufficiently or incorrectly appreciated by science and society—a point which I'll spend most of the rest of this book trying to unpack. *Time matters.* We cannot reverse its flow or alter our age, but we can comprehend time's effects and adjust to them, both individually and socially, in ways that make us happier. We can become smarter about that central feature of Cole's *Voyage of Life,* the hourglass. In the first three paintings, the hourglass remains squarely in the Voyager's field of view; yet he pays no attention to it. The baby is too young to be aware of time; the youth gazes at the castle in the sky; the middle-aged man looks heavenward. In the final, fourth painting, the hourglass is gone, knocked away by the travails that have battered the boat; the voyage has reached its end and earthly time is no longer important. The Voyager has overlooked what was right in front of his face all along. Perhaps he should have paid more attention to time, and perhaps we should, too.

The passage of time is inevitable and inexorable; the clock ticks at the same rate for all of us. To understand the happiness curve, however, a distinction is important. Unless we happen to be traveling at nearly the speed of light, *time* is an absolute concept. *Aging* is a more subtle, more relative phenomenon. For one thing, people age at visibly different rates. Anyone who has attended a high school or college reunion will have played the mental game of comparing his or her own aging process with others'. Some people look a good ten years older or younger. Some people, at age fifty, are more physically active and fit than in their days of beer and pizza. Others struggle with painful backs and aching knees and have been forced to relinquish their vigorous self-images.

Moreover, how old we think of ourselves as being depends not just on our bodies, but also on how long we expect to live, and how long-lived and vital the people around us are at any given age. A fifty-year-old person in a poor developing country, where health care is rudimentary and nutrition is sketchy and life is physically taxing and the average age is quite young, will seem very old compared to a fifty-year-old person in today's America, where it's said, with much justification, that fifty is the new forty. In China, average life expectancy has risen from the low forties in 1960 to the mid-seventies today, an increase of more than thirty years in just two generations: one of the most staggeringly impressive accomplishments in all of human (or probably galactic) history. True, much of that gain has come from reduced infant and child mortality; the average Chinese person in 1960 did not drop dead at age forty-three. Nonetheless, being forty-three years old in China means something very different today than it did in 1960. Aging, unlike chronological time, is a *social* concept.

When I use the shorthand "time matters" or the letter T in the happiness equation, then, I am really mashing together two different things. Which is it that shapes the U? *Aging,* a relative concept that changes across eras and cultures? Or *time,* which is absolute? The answer has to be: both.

The discovery of a relationship between age and happiness among our closest primate relatives implies that time itself—chronological age rather than social age—matters. After all, chimps age physically, but they don't know how old they are or celebrate birthdays and retirements. Among species, only we humans tally our years since birth and use incendiary devices and unhealthy comestibles to demarcate the increments. Only humans carry in our heads a statistical forecast of how long we expect to live, and use it to count down our remaining years. Only humans are obsessively aware of where we stand in the aging process relative to others around us. That's why a fifty-year-old feels, and effectively *is,* so much older in a society where the average life expectancy is only sixty than where it is eighty.

We might expect, then, where you live would inflect the way your age and happiness interact—if you're human. The chimps and orangutans we met in the last chapter live in three countries and two hemispheres, some in zoos and some in sanctuaries, but their U curves look almost identical. That stands to reason: assuming they are housed and treated more or less comparably, apes have no reason to care which country they are in. It would be surprising if apes in Japan had midlife problems, but apes in Australia did not. The same is not true of humans. Consider this chart, based, again, on Carol Graham's and Milena Nikolova's analysis of Gallup World Poll data:

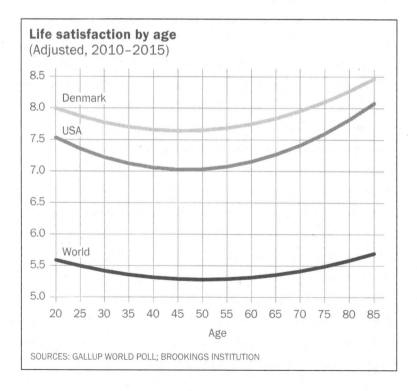

Life satisfaction by age
(Adjusted, 2010–2015)

Denmark

USA

World

Age

SOURCES: GALLUP WORLD POLL; BROOKINGS INSTITUTION

The lowest line is the same worldwide happiness U curve we already saw above. Here, however, it is compared with the age-happiness curves of two countries, namely the United States and Denmark. The general patterns are the same; but at every stage of the curve, Americans are happier than the world as a whole. Age may tend to push their satisfaction downward in midlife, but you would still rather be an average American at age forty-five than an average person in the world at age twenty or seventy. That is not too surprising: America is a stable, wealthy, and generally desirable place to live, which is why so many people want to live there. On the other hand, Denmark, the uppermost line, is happier still. In general, Scandinavia is a very happy place to be. According to the 2016 *World Happiness Report,* six of the world's eight happiest countries were in that part of the world (for the record: Denmark, Finland, Iceland, the Netherlands, Norway, and Sweden).

It thus turns out that different countries and regions show different age-curve patterns. Countries' happiness curves bottom out at different average ages, and they can show very different relationships between early and later stages of life. Below, for example, are curves for six places, again from Graham's and Nikolova's analysis of Gallup World Poll data.

On each curve, the star indicates the bottom of the curve, where life satisfaction touches its nadir and begins to improve; the dot indicates the average life span in that country or region. In this data set, the United States and the United Kingdom look similar, which is not surprising given their fairly similar cultures and economies. The pattern is the same in Latin American and Caribbean countries, but the overall level of life satisfaction is a notch lower there, perhaps because life is not as easy. In all three places, the turnaround begins in the forties. In China, satisfaction is yet another notch lower, but the upturn later in life is significantly steeper. So China is a relatively unhappy place overall, but it is a place where age brings striking improvement. Germany, on the other hand, is a fairly happy country— sixteenth in the world, according to the 2016 *World Happiness Report*—but

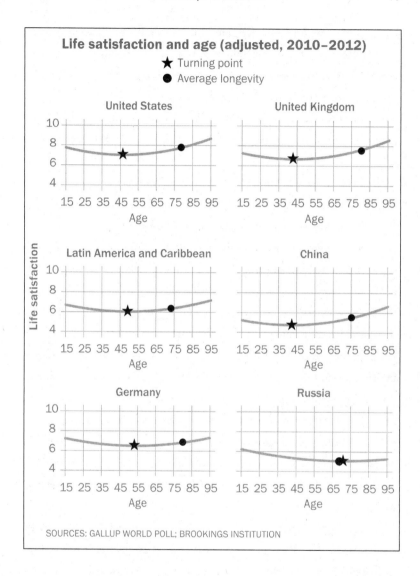

Life satisfaction and age (adjusted, 2010–2012)

★ Turning point
● Average longevity

United States

United Kingdom

Latin America and Caribbean

China

Germany

Russia

Life satisfaction

Age

SOURCES: GALLUP WORLD POLL; BROOKINGS INSTITUTION

the clock seems to be set somewhat differently there, because happiness does not bottom out until the mid-fifties. On average, Germans live through more years of downswing than upswing. We don't necessarily need to shed tears for them, because their relatively unfavorable *trajectory* of happiness is offset by their relatively high *level* of happiness. Would you rather live in a place with a higher happiness level overall, or a place with more years of increasing happiness? Take your pick. But try not to pick Russia. In the 2016 *World Happiness Report* it was the world's fifty-sixth happiest country, and, according to Graham and Nikolova, the curve there does not turn until the average person is dead. That combination of a low *level* of happiness and a late-turning *trajectory* of happiness is the perfect mix for misery.

It turns out that these things—happiness level and happiness trajectory—may be connected. Not long ago, when Carol Graham and Julia Ruiz Pozuelo looked at forty-six countries where the Gallup World Poll had surveyed an especially large number of people from 2005 to 2014 (the extra data density produces more statistically reliable results), they found U curves in all but two of them. Going further, they divided the countries into three groups: the most happy set, the least happy set, and a group in the middle. Finally, they looked at the turning point in each group of countries: that is, the age at which people start feeling better, so that the river's undertow begins to work in their favor instead of against them. They found that the turning point was earliest (age forty-seven) in the happiest countries and latest (age sixty-two) in the least happy ones. In other words, they found a kind of rich-get-richer phenomenon: people in happier countries not only enjoy higher levels of life satisfaction, they also enjoy more years of *rising* satisfaction, because they get past their midlife dip earlier. The chart below shows how that relationship works.

The same pattern holds for individuals, as well as countries. When Graham and Ruiz Pozuelo looked at the world sample, they found that the happier people are, the earlier their upswing—and, therefore, the more years they spend (other things being equal) enjoying rising satisfaction with their lives. The reason is unknown, but the result, as with so much about happiness, seems neither particularly logical nor particularly fair: the undertow helps soonest those people and countries who need its help the least.

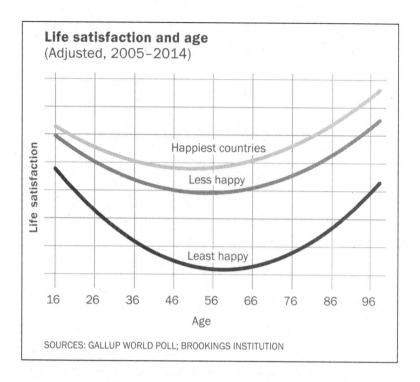

Life satisfaction and age
(Adjusted, 2005–2014)

Happiest countries

Less happy

Least happy

Life satisfaction

16   26   36   46   56   66   76   86   96

Age

SOURCES: GALLUP WORLD POLL; BROOKINGS INSTITUTION

The fact that the relationship between happiness and age is different in different places tells us something important, aside from "Don't be Russian." Whatever is going on is partly biological and genetic. The happiness curve would not show up in as many data sets and places as it does, including among apes, if it were not to some extent hardwired. But it is not *entirely* biological or genetic, because genes don't vary much between countries, but the pattern does. The happiness curve, then, must be about both time *and* aging.

So now to the really hard question. Something complex is going on. What is it?

5

· · · · · · · · · · · ·

THE EXPECTATIONS TRAP

Midlife malaise is often about nothing

At age forty-six, Anthony believes he has peaked. His best personal growth and most exciting days are behind him, or so he thinks.

He is very likely mistaken. I would lay a bet that his best years are ahead of him. He, however, is incapable of seeing that. The happiness curve manufactures discontent from what seems to be thin air, and then, having done so, entices us to give up on doing better just as things are about to turn around. It's an insidious trick, one whose mischief Anthony is experiencing.

He is a professional whom I had met at a few social functions. When he filled out my life-satisfaction questionnaire, I noticed a downward-sloping curve, declining from his twenties. Nothing unusual there. But when I saw that he used the word *peaked* to describe his forties, I decided to ask him about it.

His twenties, he told me, were a time of reveling in newfound independence and rapid intellectual growth. He thrived in school, had an exceptional mentor, met and became engaged to his future wife. His thirties brought the typical dose of reality. The job market in his field was tough, he and his wife endured two disruptive moves, and in the midst of one of those moves, both of their fathers died. They were devastated. "For a year after that," Anthony said, "I went through life like a robot." A year's journey through grief brought Anthony back to normality, but it was a new normal. "It had a permanent effect on me. I describe it as the last death of childhood."

Professionally, things went better. In their mid-thirties, Anthony and his wife both landed dream jobs. But then, in his early forties, he began to feel stagnant. "Reality bites, and it's pretty clear I had peaked. I had reached my limits, given my IQ and creativity. It was going to be hard to grow more. Let me put it this way: it became clear that I'd done as well externally as I possibly could. So I had a period of depression during that time, maybe a year, a year and a half."

When I interviewed Anthony, his depressed period was several years behind him. Using my zero-to-ten scale, he rated his life satisfaction an eight, the same as in his thirties. He said he feels fortunate. Still, what I heard, listening to him, was a man adjusting to the idea that the best is behind him. He accepts that he will never be one of the top people in his field, and he is coming to terms with physical decline. He's on a cholesterol medication. His body doesn't recover as quickly. The other day, after reading in the paper about someone his age who dropped dead on the Stair-Master, he thought: *something like that could happen to me.*

So he feels he has *peaked*? "Definitely. I am over the halfway point in terms of age. Physically for sure. And mentally the decline has clearly begun."

I wondered if he could imagine recapturing the satisfaction and spirit he had enjoyed in his twenties. He replied firmly: "No. That was a very high-growth period. I don't see that happening. There's just not enough time."

Anthony is not an unhappy person, but he finds himself working to accommodate what he assumes are diminishing prospects. He feels that his capacity for both outward achievement and inner satisfaction is waning. It isn't that things are bad. It's that things are unlikely to get better. What is missing in his voice is not happiness. It's optimism.

Here is what I would have been able to explain to Anthony had I spoken to him only a few days later, after I interviewed a young German economist named Hannes Schwandt. Precisely *because* Anthony's optimism has ebbed and he feels he has peaked, chances are his pessimism is misplaced and his emotional peak is yet to come. If Schwandt is right, Anthony is a leading candidate for a pleasant surprise.

It's hard, actually, to remember journalistic etiquette and call Hannes—I mean, Schwandt—by his last name, because he may be the least formal person I've ever interviewed. When I went to meet him at Princeton University one spring day, he bounded downstairs to meet my husband and me in the lobby of the social sciences building and gave us an exuberant welcome before sweeping us off on a campus tour, showing us dinosaurs and chemistry labs while frequently checking his cell phone and talking so fast (in English—not his native tongue) that it was hard to keep up. When we finally alit in the little office he shared with another researcher, students kept coming by to ask where to pick up some T-shirts. Six feet, balding, and trim, with prominent features and beefy hands, Schwandt was in his early thirties and still on the threshold of his first professorial appointment (in Zurich), but he was already enjoying the kind of success which most postdoctoral researchers can only dream of.

Originally from Hamburg, Germany, and schooled in Munich, Schwandt began his graduate work in business economics but quickly got bored. He liked math, but he was more interested in improving society than maximizing profits, and he was frustrated with the tyranny of mathematical modeling. "You spend a lot of time with a lot of fancy models, and you learn very little about anything in real life. We had this class on macroeconomics and unemployment, but I didn't learn anything about unemployment. I went to the professor and said maybe we should do something on the history of unemployment, and he said he couldn't even really think without a model." (Shades, there, of Andrew Oswald, an earlier generation's rebel against dry mathematical economics.)

He thought about quitting economics altogether, a fate averted when he read a lecture by Richard Layard, a pioneering happiness economist whose approach made sense to Schwandt (and whose work I've mentioned in chapter 2). After reading Layard, Schwandt found it bizarre that the economics profession had left to others the study of wellbeing—of what it is that gives people satisfaction. After all, the idea that people always make rational choices, much less choices that reliably improve their wellbeing, is demonstrably wrong. "It could well be that we're making choices that aren't optimal for us," Schwandt said. "And revealed preferences will never tell you this."

It would be one thing if people were just randomly guessing wrong about their utility, but that, too, is demonstrably untrue. Experiments show a whole assortment of ways in which people's irrationality is not random but systematically biased. To name just one example (from a famous 1990 experiment by the Nobel Prize–winning psychologist Daniel Kahneman and colleagues Jack Knetsch and Richard Thaler), people who would be willing to pay, say, only $3 for a mug will then, if given that mug, demand more like $7 to part with it a few minutes later, as if their simply coming into possession of the mug had increased its value. People seem averse to losing what they have, even when they would be better off getting something new. If people exhibit this "endowment bias" consistently, then they will also consistently forgo opportunities to better their lot by trading upward—at least by traditional economists' definition of *upward*. Humans, it turns out, are shot through with biases of this kind.

In 2007, Schwandt, still a first-year PhD student, began wondering if people's expectations were rational about something quite central to their wellbeing: their own satisfaction with life. "I was open to the idea that rational expectations are wrong, and I thought it would be a good test just to check."

At the suggestion of a mentor, Schwandt dived into data from a German study which had followed the same group of individuals for almost fifteen years, from 1991 to 2004. Not only had the study stayed with its subjects for more than a decade, it included both western and eastern Germany, thereby allowing for comparison across two very different political and cultural contexts. Most unusual of all, the study asked people, not only about their satisfaction with their lives, but also how satisfied they *expected* to feel five years down the road. By comparing expectations with subsequent reality, Schwandt could look at how right or wrong people had been about their future happiness.

The result astonished him, not just because the pattern was there, but because it was there for both men and women, and it was there for both eastern and western Germans (people whose prior experiences of life, in the Cold War years, had been very different), and it was there within individual people as well as groups of people. It didn't go away when Schwandt checked for major events like recessions which might have disrupted people's lives. It persisted when he performed statistical adjustments for things like income and demographics. As he would later write: "This pattern is stable over time, observed within cohorts, within individuals, and across different socio-economic groups." The pattern was so strong—in fact, plainly visible to the naked eye, without any statistical manipulations—that at first Schwandt thought he might have miscoded the data. He hadn't. "I thought: this *must* matter."

At first, he wasn't sure precisely why it might matter, though he had a general idea. He was aware of the happiness curve, and was intrigued by the lack of an explanation for it. For a while, though, he went back to his more mainstream work on the economics of health and wellbeing. He had not, after all, received much by way of encouragement. "This was my first project in my PhD. I remember presenting this in front of a group of macroeconomists, and they were literally laughing at me. I still remember: They found it really ridiculous that I would do this. They asked me literally why anyone would care about expected life satisfaction."

One economist who did not think his findings were ridiculous was Andrew Oswald. When they connected at a conference, what was supposed to have been a brief breakfast turned into a two-hour conversation. "He said, 'Wow, this is so important,'" Schwandt recalled. And so, returning to his work comparing expectations with reality, Schwandt developed an article which was published in 2016 in the *Journal of Economic Behavior and Organization,* under the title, "Unmet Aspirations as an Explanation for the Age U-Shape in Wellbeing."

Here is what Oswald saw in Schwandt's paper that so excited him:

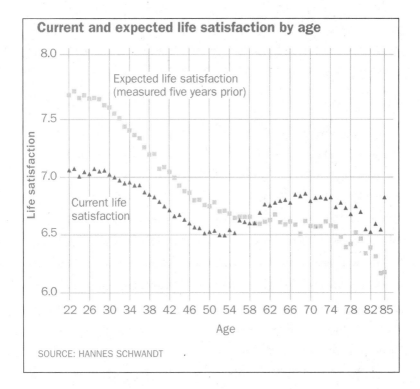

Current and expected life satisfaction by age

SOURCE: HANNES SCHWANDT

And what does the graph show? Germans in the database, whose ages range from seventeen to ninety, were asked to rate their current and future life satisfaction on a standard scale of 0 ("completely dissatisfied") to 10 ("completely satisfied"). The triangles show how satisfied people actually are at every age. The squares show how satisfied they had expected to be five years prior. The curves are lined up to compare prior expectations with subsequent reality. For example, twenty-five-year-olds expect their satisfaction to rate about 7.5 when they reach the age of thirty; but when they actually are thirty, their satisfaction is only 7. In other words, they are not as happy with their lives as they expected to be. In yet other words, they're *disappointed*. When the line of triangles is below the line of squares, people are disappointed with their state of contentment. When the line of triangles is above the line of squares, they're pleasantly surprised.

A couple of things are immediately apparent from the graph. The line of triangles—current life satisfaction—shows the U pattern (until old age, when survey subjects get sick and die off and the data gets thin and messy). The bottom is just where one might expect, at around age fifty. No surprises there!

Second, however, is this: young people consistently overestimate their future life satisfaction. They make a whopping forecasting error, as non-random as it could be—as if you lived in Seattle and expected sunshine every day. "These errors are large," Schwandt comments, in his article. Young adults in their twenties overestimate their future life satisfaction by about 10 percent, on average. Over time, however, excessive optimism diminishes. Perhaps because they have been disappointed so regularly in the past, and perhaps because they feel that most of life's adventurous, healthy years are behind them, their expectations fall. Not to 0: a drop from 7.5 to 6.5, though big, is not catastrophic. People are not becoming deeply depressed. They are becoming, well, *realistic*.

Look what happens in the fifties. The U curve begins swinging upward.

Meanwhile, expectations have almost completed their downward drift. The expectations gap closes—and then reverses. Life satisfaction in late middle age and beyond, contrary to prior expectation, is growing, not shrinking. But expectations have plateaued at a low level. For a good twenty years, every year brings, not another dose of regret and disappointment, but another pleasant surprise. So there is the undertow, and its reversal. The forecasting errors that bring so much grief in the earlier part of life switch sign in the latter portion. The current shifts.

All of that—the expectations gap and its reversal—is fairly readily apparent at a glance. Hannes Schwandt, however, being an economist, did some math to seek relationships which may not be so obvious. The expectations-versus-reality gap turns out to have a peculiar self-referential characteristic, which helps explain why so many people, I among them, have felt, in middle age, that obnoxious sensation of being both puzzled and trapped.

Recall that people are not being asked here to rate expectations for their future *situations* in life. The question is not, say, "How much income do you expect in five years? How much health? How good a job?" Those would be questions about objective circumstances. Instead, people are being asked about something subjective: how satisfied they expect to *feel* in five years, and then, later, how they actually do feel. And feelings can operate on themselves. Disappointment and regret can make us dissatisfied. Dissatisfaction can add to our disappointment and regret.

The result turns out to be something which is quite easy to model mathematically—Schwandt wrote an equation for it—and which quite elegantly matches up with observed results. He calls it a *feedback effect*, and it helps explain why sometimes people with little to be dissatisfied about nonetheless feel so dissatisfied, and then feel dissatisfied about feeling dissatisfied. After showing me some equations, Schwandt explained it this way:

"Let's say you're at this stage where you feel midlife discontent. And let's say things are really bad, that there are a lot of challenges in your life or things have turned really sour. Then you're depressed, but at least you're like, 'Wow, there are good *reasons* to be depressed.' It's clear to you why you feel bad and that's kind of the end of the story. You probably also share your problems more with other people, or other people acknowledge why you're dissatisfied.

"But say you're on a track where everything looks nice. Then you feel discontented. Instead of just saying, 'I'm discontented because of this and that thing,' and that's it, you say, 'I'm discontented and I don't know why,' and this makes you more miserable, and this makes the forecasting error even larger. So you keep the circumstances constant, but you *feel* bad about them. Since you feel bad about them you're disappointed, your life satisfaction decreases and you feel even worse about that. You're in a downward spiral. If your objective life circumstances are actually really good, this feedback effect might just be stronger—because you're more disappointed about being disappointed."

In his paper, Schwandt writes: "The mathematical model shows that this mechanism has explanatory power even in a world in which the utility derived from life circumstances is constant over age." In other words, the math demonstrates that downward spirals can happen quite independently of one's actual circumstances in life. The feedback effect can and often does afflict people who do not experience any severe crisis or shock, people who, on the contrary, are doing fine. Schwandt writes: "The feeling of regret about unmet expectations further increases the gap between expected and realized life satisfaction, leading to yet greater disappointment and a further lowering of life satisfaction." That is a pretty good description of how I felt in my mid-forties. It was a frustrating and mystifying place to be.

Schwandt's model helps explain why the happiness curve keeps appearing *after* economists factor out life circumstances: that is, why age itself, independent of other things that may be going on, keeps showing up as associated with lower satisfaction in midlife. Sometimes the people who are, relatively speaking, least affected by objective circumstances will be most trapped in feedback loops.

One can dismiss such objectless disappointment as a yuppie problem or first-world problem (though in fact the happiness curve turns up in many developing countries). One can dismiss it as whining. Which was exactly what I did when I experienced it. Whining was something I felt I had no right to do, given my privilege and good fortune. My dissatisfaction reduced my self-esteem. It made me dislike myself. It made me embarrassed to tell people I was in a rut.

Ironically, such embarrassment, although perfectly justifiable from a moral or objective point of view (everyone loathes a whiner, especially when the whiner is oneself), is a cause of yet more dissatisfaction and disappointment. All the things we have learned since childhood about the shame of ingratitude can turn against us by accelerating Schwandt's weird spiral of disappointment. Counting my blessings, as I did on the threshold of forty, was a worthy exercise morally; I'm glad I did it. But, in light of Schwandt's equation, I am no longer surprised that it didn't help. Unknowingly, by trying to explain to myself why I ought to be more satisfied, I was giving myself more reason to dwell on the gap between how satisfied I felt and how satisfied I thought I *should* feel.

You see, then, the peculiar character of the feedback effect. Like the 1990s television comedy show *Seinfeld,* midlife slump can be *about nothing.* That very fact can itself be profoundly troubling. I think of my friend Simon. In his mid-forties, he has had his share of ups and downs, and his pattern is a familiar one: exciting twenties, progress toward goals in his thirties, turbulence in his forties, including some hard knocks. At last he had achieved success and prominence in his chosen field, becoming a media figure in a major market. "I've done everything I want to do, for the most part." So did he feel content? "No. Exhausted. I feel at times like an amazing fuck-up who has gotten away with stuff, who has been lucky. I've thought of running away to Brazil. Changing my name and becoming a hotel clerk." His dissatisfaction mystified and troubled him at a deep level that seemed not just emotional but spiritual. "I think it must be something internal," he told me. "I see life as a challenge to overcome rather than an adventure to be enjoyed. If I did a deep psychological dive, I might say that nothing will ever make me content. Maybe there's something deeply psychologically wrong with me."

There's something wrong with me. That is the feedback trap talking.

Now look at what happens as people move through their early decades of adulthood: the expectations gap steadily narrows. You might think this would be a good thing: my actual feeling of disappointment shrinks as I shed my unrealistic optimism. So why the U-shaped curve, indicating steadily less satisfaction through middle age? Partly because of the feedback effect. But also, Schwandt thinks, because of what he calls a "hump-shaped regret function." As he told me, "Life satisfaction depends on circumstances right now minus the regret that you feel about the sum of missed chances in your past life." In plainer English, his math suggests that feelings of disappointment are *cumulative*.

"When you're young," Schwandt explained, "you don't really feel so much regret, because even if things don't turn out so well at the beginning, you still think there's time. You don't really care so much." When you're twenty-five, a disappointing year is just a bump in the road. Next year will be better!

But then what if, where life satisfaction is concerned (remember, we're talking about the inner, subjective world, not about what's actually happening to you), next year brings another disappointment? Things are pretty good, but you're not as content as you expected to be. Then the same thing happens the next year. And the next. And the next and the next and the next. After a while, it dawns on you that disappointment seems to be a permanent feature of life. This has a couple of effects. On the one hand, your expectations for future satisfaction fall—pretty quickly, as the graph shows. So the hard work of realigning your happiness expectations is being done. But meanwhile, until the realignment happens, you're being hit from two directions at once. "On the one hand," Schwandt told me, "you feel all this disappointment about your past. And then also your expectations evaporate about the future. So in midlife you're feeling miserable about the past and the future at the same time."

This would go a long way toward explaining why, for example, Anthony, at age forty-six, though not depressed, is certain he has peaked. He has found that getting most of what he wanted does not make him as happy as he expected, a fact to which he is resigned—and which implies even less satisfaction in the future, as his physical and intellectual faculties decline. He is looking at his future *circumstances* and drawing what seems a logical conclusion about his future *satisfaction*: the best is behind him. He can't intuit that when Schwandt's lines cross, when reality begins to outperform expectations, the spiral changes direction. Positive feedback replaces negative as disappointments become pleasant surprises, and as growing satisfaction and gratitude reinforce each other.

So the story of expectations realigning with reality has a happy ending. But the only way *out* (to paraphrase Robert Frost) is *through*. The passage through is not generally traumatic; remember, we're dealing with larger and smaller amounts of satisfaction, and with disappointment relative to high expectations. But it is a grind.

"Resigned," Jasper said, when I asked how he feels about his life. We met at the neighborhood gym. He had seen an article I wrote about the happiness curve, and we struck up a conversation because, having recently turned forty, he felt himself inching toward the trough of the happiness curve. He had risen rapidly as a young lawyer in his twenties, a period he describes as "fun, future-oriented"; but in his thirties came the realization that the practice of law was a "soul-sucking grind," that he was not the husband he wanted to be, and that he and his wife could not have kids. He had responded, readjusted: left the rat race, gone back to school, adjusted to childlessness. Now, in his early forties, he was managing a family dental practice, but only, he hoped, temporarily. He had set his sights on a new career teaching and writing about the things he cares most about.

With so much to look ahead to, I wondered, why was he *resigned*?

"I suppose by the time we hit forty," he said, "most of us have run up against a reality that can look pretty different from the future we anticipated for ourselves at age twenty-five. There's a definite spiritual maturity, a deepening self-awareness and introspection that result from embracing the truth about ourselves and our frailties and failures as well as our successes. So I wouldn't say I'm not grateful for the wisdom that comes with experience. But there are times when I miss having a more simple and naïvely optimistic outlook on life—even if I know now that such an outlook required almost willful disregard of life's realities."

Jasper was in the process of bidding farewell to what Hannes Schwandt describes as a forecasting error, and what Thomas Cole depicts as a castle in the sky. Jasper missed the high expectations of the past, even though he knew they had misled him. Objectively, he was in the process of bringing his life into closer alignment with his values. But subjectively his optimism about his future life satisfaction had waned, and its decline was itself a source of regret.

The natural question for me, pondering Hannes Schwandt's expectations gap, was: Why? Why the big forecasting error? It turns out there are answers to that question, but they move us from economics and big data, Schwandt's world, to psychology: the construction and organization of our minds.

Tali Sharot, Israeli by birth, is a cognitive neuroscientist at University College London, where her duties include directing the Affective Brain Lab, a center which studies how emotions affect cognition and behavior. She is particularly well known for her work on what she calls *optimism bias* (in fact, she has written a book by that name). Positive forecasting errors, she has found, are no biological mistake. They appear to be wired in. For all that they mislead and sometimes immiserate us, we may need them to survive and thrive. "It's hard for us to get out of bed unless we can say, 'Oh, it will be a great day, I'm going to succeed in what I'm doing,'" she told me. In a 2011 article in *Current Biology,* she described optimism bias this way:

> [Students] expect higher starting salaries and more job offers than they end up getting. People tend to underestimate how long a project will take to complete and how much it will cost. Most of us predict deriving greater pleasure from a vacation than we subsequently do, and we anticipate encountering more positive events in an upcoming month (such as receiving a gift or enjoying a movie) than we end up experiencing. Across many different methods and domains, studies consistently report that a large majority of the population (about 80 percent, according to most estimates) display an optimism bias. Optimistic errors seem to be an integral part of human nature, observed across gender, race, nationality, and age.

People expect to have above-average longevity and health, underestimate their likelihood of divorce, overestimate their job success, and so on. They expect positive events in the future, "even when," as Sharot and several coauthors reported in the journal *Nature,* in 2007, "there is no evidence to support such expectations."

What happens if you give people accurate information? Will they correct their biased beliefs? In experiments, Sharot and various colleagues ask people about the likelihood that various bad things (a robbery or a cancer diagnosis, for instance) will happen to them over, say, the next five years. Once their answers are recorded, the subjects are informed of the actual odds, and then asked again whether the events will happen to them. It turns out they are better at assimilating positive than negative information. Sharot calls this the "good news/bad news effect." If you put people in a brain scanner and perform the same kind of exercise, positive information and negative information appear to be coded by different regions of the brain— so the bad is not simply the inverse of the good. Moreover, Sharot and her colleagues found they could make the optimism bias disappear by aiming bursts of magnetic energy at a specific region of the brain. The implication is that we are wired to accentuate the positive and screen out the negative, not just in our emotional outlook, but in our basic cognitive functioning.

Well, most of us, most of the time. There is an exception. Mildly depressed people predict the future accurately. It turns out that they are just as good as nondepressed people at taking in positive information, but they are more responsive to negative information, and thus more realistic. "They see the world as it is," writes Sharot in a 2012 ebook, *The Science of Optimism: Why We're Hard-Wired for Hope*. "In other words, in the absence of a neural mechanism that generates unrealistic optimism, it is possible all humans would be mildly depressed." In fact, humans aren't the only ones who seem wired for optimism. Ingenious experiments find that birds are, too. And mice. And other species.

Why would nature bias us to be optimistic, and therefore subject to continual disappointment? Perhaps because realism is bad for you. "Hope keeps our minds at ease, lowers stress, and improves physical health," Sharot writes in *The Science of Optimism*. "This is probably the most surprising benefit of optimism. All else being equal, optimists are healthier and live longer." In fact, "optimism is not only related to success, it leads to success." Optimism inspires entrepreneurs to launch start-ups, despite dismal odds. I know: I tried a start-up. I was confident it would succeed. It failed. But I'm still glad I was unrealistic enough to try.

Optimism bias as a general idea is well established. Less firmly known, but tantalizing, is the idea, which researchers are now getting hints of, that optimism bias is not age-neutral. Rather, it seems to reach low ebb in middle age. Sharot writes, in *The Science of Optimism*:

> How easily people learned from good news was relatively stable across age groups; they were pretty good at age nine, and they were still pretty good at ages forty-five and seventy-five. However, how well people learned from bad news followed an inverse U shape. From the time we are children, we slowly acquire the ability to alter our beliefs accordingly when we receive bad news (like learning that things we love, such as candy, may be bad for us). This ability seems to peak around age forty, and then it slowly deteriorates as people grow older.

In other words, people in middle age may be more likely than others to suffer from what has been called *depressive realism,* a heightened receptivity to lessons from the school of hard knocks.

"Why," I asked Sharot, "might depressive realism be more common in middle age?"

"Unclear," she replied. Maybe because the brain changes as it ages. Or maybe because stress is often high during midlife, and stress and anxiety reduce optimism bias. To mention the obvious, people might simply be learning from experience. Of course, the explanation could include all of the above, and more. For the young to sally forth optimistically into the world, taking risks and pushing limits, might serve the species' interest; a subsequent recalibration in maturity might also be useful.

The research does not imply that middle-aged people are depressed. They still have an optimism bias. It is just smaller, noticeably so. They have received a dose of depressive realism. Jasper might be inclined to agree.

As my diary writing and blessing counting attest, when I was Jasper's age I, too, had begun to feel, and feel disturbed by, declining optimism. My passage through my thirties had been smooth. I was fine with not having kids (a different internal conversation if you're gay than if you're straight). I didn't need or want a change of career. No health trouble or financial problems. Having experienced no setbacks, I assumed I was in a temporary funk, a phase which would pass pretty soon (after all, there was no reason for it!). What finally got my attention, convincing me that something peculiar was going on, was an event that happened when I was forty-five. A positive event. *Spectacularly* positive. I had come to accept that my low-key style of journalism lacked the sort of sizzle that appeals to competition judges, and so when I won a National Magazine Award, the magazine industry's equivalent of the Pulitzer Prize, it came as a complete surprise. It filled me with pride and gratitude and a sense of earned success. For about a week. Maybe two.

Then, creepily, with a mind of its own, the dissatisfaction oozed back. Soon it was as if the award had never happened. As ever, I found myself awakening most mornings to an unbidden, unwanted internal monologue badgering me about my underachievement. That was when I began reckoning with the reality that my nagging sense of disappointment had taken on a life of its own. It had become, apparently, a feature of my personality, always hunting for something to be dissatisfied about, and inventing spurious dissatisfactions if no real ones were on hand. Faced with the irrational persistence of my disappointment, I started to doubt my capacity to feel gratitude and satisfaction. That, I think, was when Schwandt's feedback loop really kicked in. *How*, I wondered, *could even the most tangible of achievements fail to turn me around?* What I didn't know was that the problem wasn't me; it was my elephant.

Jonathan Haidt started his career on a disgusting note. Today, as a psychology professor at New York University, he is one of the world's most innovative thinkers about the ways in which intuition, the sum of our involuntary sentiments, shapes human reason and cognition. Born in 1963, he suffered what he calls an existential depression during his senior year in high school, deciding that without God life must be meaningless. He turned to philosophy for answers, but discovered that psychology was more fun. After college, he spent a couple of years writing computer programs for the Bureau of Labor Statistics in Washington. Somehow, in the Mixmaster between his ears, his interests came together to propel him toward the empirical study of moral intuition. For his dissertation, he chose an intuition which had received little formal study: disgust. His doctoral dissertation was called *Moral Judgment, Affect, and Culture, or, Is It Wrong to Eat Your Dog?*

In a career's worth of subsequent experiments, Haidt has found that gut feelings like disgust influence our reason much more than the other way around. He likes to compare reason to a press secretary, pushed forward by our rationalizing minds to justify choices we make at a gut level. "The central insight that I had in moral psychology," he told me, "was: keep your eye on the intuitions, the gut feelings, and the reasoning follows."

Memorably, and now famously, Haidt likens the reasoning mind to a rider perched atop an elephant. Historically, he notes, a common metaphor for thinking about emotion and reason is that of a horse and rider. But riders direct horses, absent a snake or stampede. That metaphor clashed with Haidt's findings, including those in a natural experiment that he had conducted upon himself. "At the time I was single and I was dating," he recalled. "I would make some big mistake in my dating life, and I would *see* myself making a mistake, and I saw that I was going to go ahead and make it, even though I knew it was the wrong thing to do. I knew what the right thing was and I knew all the psychology about the wrong thing, but I couldn't stop myself."

Apparently, if he and his experimental subjects were riding something, it was no obedient horse. "Elephants are really smart, and they're really, really big, and I felt like a small boy perched atop a giant elephant. If the elephant didn't have any plans of its own, the boy can kind of prick it and turn it this way and that." But if the elephant has its own ideas, it goes whichever way it pleases. The rider is left to rationalize the elephant's direction or look on in frustration, or both.

The elephant, for Haidt, is the mind's many automatic, involuntary processes; the rider is the mind's controlled, voluntary processes. Unlike Freud's subconscious, the involuntary, nonconscious form of mental processing is not some swirling cesspool of guilt and taboo and childhood trauma. It is more like a system of cognitive shortcuts allowing us to function in everyday life, because we don't have nearly enough time or capacity to think through every decision from scratch. Disgust says *Ick!* sparing us the trouble of deciding whether to touch or eat something unfamiliar and potentially hazardous. The automatic processes, unlike the ones under conscious control, happen unbidden; they tend not to slow down when you're tired; they do not require willpower or concentration. You are not aware of the process, just the output—for example, realizing someone is attractive. "It's just *bang*," Haidt said. "You're aware of the attraction, though a huge amount of neural computation went into that attraction."

When, at forty-five, I won that journalism prize, I—the rider—was very pleased. So I gave the elephant a pep talk: *This is great! This is a lifetime achievement, a validation of my whole career! Yay! Quit sulking! Be pleased! And stay pleased!* So . . . why didn't the elephant stay pleased? When I asked that question of Haidt, he replied by asking me if I had seen the movie *2001: A Space Odyssey.*

"Sure," I said.

"And who's running the spaceship in that movie?"

"HAL, the onboard computer."

"And what is HAL's goal?"

"To complete the mission."

"And does HAL care if the crew is happy?"

"Well . . . no."

The elephant's mission, said Haidt, is not to make us feel satisfied with what we accomplish or do. "The elephant's mission is to make us successful in producing offspring: in doing the things that will lead to the successful completion of the mission of life on earth. The elephant is especially concerned that you get prestige. The elephant was created by evolution to complete the mission. And happiness is not the goal of the mission."

The elephant, as we have seen, is biased toward optimism. It is also biased toward disappointment. In his fine 2006 book, *The Happiness Hypothesis: Finding Modern Truth in Ancient Wisdom,* Haidt enumerates various ways in which the elephant undermines the rider's efforts to savor success. One is the *progress principle*. We set many goals in life: status, friendship, finding a good mate, accumulating resources, rearing children so that they will give us grandchildren and great-grandchildren. But the mental reward for success, a shot of encouraging dopamine, comes mainly not when we meet some big life goal that we've set for ourselves intellectually, but when we take some short-term positive step. "Here's the trick with reinforcement: it works best when it comes seconds—not minutes or hours—after the behavior," writes Haidt. The elephant "feels pleasure whenever it takes a step in the right direction." In other words, "when it comes to goal pursuit, it really is the journey that counts, not the destination. Set for yourself any goal you want. Most of the pleasure will be had along the way, with every step that takes you closer. The final moment of success is often no more thrilling than the relief of taking off a heavy backpack at the end of a long hike." That is the progress principle: "Pleasure comes more from making progress toward goals than from achieving them." For me (or for my dopamine system), winning that prize was not like taking off a heavy backpack, but it was of startlingly short duration. Just another step on a path.

Toward what? Having only just arrived, my elephant was already craving more dopamine, demanding progress toward some new goal—even though I had none in mind. That is the *adaptation principle*. "We don't just habituate, we recalibrate," writes Haidt. "We create for ourselves a world of targets, and each time we hit one we replace it with another. After a string of successes we aim higher; after a massive setback, such as a broken neck, we aim lower." Unfortunately, the rider is not in on the secret. "Whatever happens, you're likely to adapt to it, but you don't realize up front that you will. We are bad at 'affective forecasting'—that is, predicting how we'll feel in the future. We grossly overestimate the intensity and the duration of our emotional reactions. Within a year, lottery winners and paraplegics have both (on average) returned most of the way to their baseline levels of happiness."

From the elephant's point of view, this kind of constant recalibration may be adaptive, keeping us abreast of changes in our environment. From the point of view of the rider trying to appreciate what he or she has accomplished or accumulated in life, it is not so good. "When we combine the adaptation principle with the discovery that people's average level of happiness is highly heritable," writes Haidt, "we come to a startling possibility: In the long run, it doesn't much matter what happens to you. If this idea is correct, then we are all stuck on what has been called the 'hedonic treadmill.' . . . We continue to strive, all the while doing things that help us win at the game of life. Always wanting more than we have, we run and run and run, like hamsters on a wheel."

To all of which, add the phenomenon we encountered in chapter 2: the social-competition treadmill. Haidt describes it:

> The elephant was shaped by natural selection to win at the game of life, and part of its strategy is to impress others, gain their admiration, and rise in relative rank. *The elephant cares about prestige, not happiness,* and it looks eternally to others to figure out what is prestigious. The elephant will pursue its evolutionary goals even when greater happiness can be found elsewhere. If everyone

is chasing the same limited amount of prestige, then all are stuck in a zero-sum game, an eternal arms race, a world in which rising wealth does not bring rising happiness.

I confess that, after I won my big award, I got some joy from the improvement in my prestige; and, I won't lie to you, I still do. But my elephant kept gazing up the social ladder, not down; it quickly took on board my success, recalibrating; it demanded more achievement. Recalling my plight, I suggested to Haidt that the elephant's priorities seemed designed to make us unhappy. He demurred. "They're not designed to make us miserable. They're designed to motivate us to be *successful*. A life of contentment is not motivating for success. Contentment means you can stop."

This is not to say we are always dissatisfied or disappointed. As Haidt emphasizes, the trick is to depend less on trying to talk the elephant into being satisfied, as I was doing in my forties, and instead to give it an environment where the things it wants and the things the rider wants are in closer alignment. That would be an environment rich in the ingredients of sustainable satisfaction: ingredients like a high-trust social environment, adequate health and income, a goodly amount of control over our lives, and, above all, strong and supportive social bonds. When I asked Haidt if the elephant metaphor had affected the way he leads his own life, he replied: "Absolutely! I see my own life and my own mind much less as a machine, much less as a project or city to be built, and much more as giving myself the right kinds of experience and exposure and letting time do the work. Life is about training and educating the elephant and the rider, and getting them to work together in harmony."

A life in memory, like a great painting, changes with the light it is seen in. In my mind's eye, I am almost twenty again, beholding for the first time

Thomas Cole's quadriptych in the National Gallery of Art. To the younger me, the swaddled innocence of Cole's *Childhood* certainly rings true. So do the (literally) sky-high aspirations of *Youth*. Standing on the foothills of maturity, I want to make a mark on the world, though I have no settled ambitions.

I had no way to know what the light of hindsight and recent scientific learning would show. I would do well professionally. I would find love and commitment, albeit not oriented as I expected. I would have everything to be grateful for. But the castle in the sky? Perhaps that glittering elusive palace is not the objective situation we expect to attain—our material and social ambition—but the happiness we expect to reach: our *subjective* ambition. After all, one of the most striking facts about *The Voyage of Life* is that the Voyager is alone. There are no other people, no cities, no society. One interpretation is that Cole was naïve about the importance of social connections in life. Another is that he was portraying not life's circumstances but its psychology: the inner world, where we are all, finally, alone. Perhaps what he is telling us is that our inner river will bend away from satisfaction, and that the rapids and crags are within ourselves.

Cole was a visionary whose time was far removed from our own, so I can't say exactly what he meant. What I can say—or, more precisely, see—is what the twenty-year-old version of me got wrong. I was certain in youth that I would be better off objectively by middle age. That forecast was accurate. My conditions improved. But I also made another youthful forecast: that my satisfaction would keep pace with my accomplishments. That forecast was off. Yes, I was appreciative, but nowhere near as appreciative as I had believed I would or should be. The closing of the optimism gap, plus upward social comparison, plus the hedonic treadmill and my elephant's other tricks to keep contentment out of reach: all of those things, as the years ticked by, conspired to create a sense of disappointment which I couldn't shake by force of will. And *that* was disappointing. In my forties, caught in the feedback loop, I was stumped and stuck.

If Cole were painting his Voyage of Life today, he would need to add a fifth painting, one between *Manhood* and *Old Age*—but I'll come back to that. First, I linger for a moment on what is, to me, the most interesting (if also the least pleasant) place on the happiness curve: that in-between region of middle age where Schwandt's lines are in the process of converging and crossing. Here, the expectations gap is closing, but has not yet closed. Disappointment will soon end, but still seems endless. Realism has arrived, but not yet settled in. Here is the bottom of the U, a treacherous zone.

It is important to see what this time of unfinished transition is not: a *crisis*. At least, not usually. The whole point of Schwandt's research—and Sharot's, and for that matter Andrew Oswald's and David Blanchflower's and Carol Graham's—is that the curve implies no disruption or discontinuity in our emotional wellbeing. Change is gradual and cumulative, a buildup of increments of disappointment as youthful optimism bias is squeezed away. In fact, as Schwandt's math shows, negative feedback implies that we can still feel a cumulating sense of disappointment even without any objective disruption or emotional trigger at all. The idea of midlife "crisis" thus misses the point. Instead, to understand what's going on in this transitional phase, and why people's experiences of it vary widely, consider the stories of three people I interviewed: Randy, Mary Ann, and Margaret.

Randy, at forty-four, is an example of someone who feels the undercurrent of disappointment all the more keenly for having had smooth sailing. His emotional set point is healthy, his external conditions comfortable, and his personal choices wise, but his sensible steadiness has given full rein to the effects of time. He achieved his career goals and has a happy marriage and a thriving son, but, for the reasons we've seen, arrival didn't bring satisfaction. Going by the statistics, he has been on the downslope of the curve for a few years and might not hit the upturn for a few years more, and so he is in that particularly difficult period near the bottom when disappointment seems eternal. When I asked him to characterize his forties, he replied: *tired, fatalistic*. Why *fatalistic*? "I've been in the same job more than ten years. In the field that I'm in, which is downsizing and changing rapidly, I'm feeling that things are now less up to me to change and they're more predecided. In my twenties, I felt I had the power to do what I want to do and try new things and experiment. Now I feel like if I want to stay in the kind of lifestyle that I have, which is a nice house, supporting a child, saving for college, going on vacation with my family, here's what I'll need to do: I'll need to stay in a job that's well paying, even if I don't always enjoy it. That's what I mean by fatalistic. There's less room for experimentation."

Does he ever have escape fantasies? "Of course." On a vacation in Mexico, kayaking on a beautiful lagoon, he admired the sunset. "I thought, I want to do *this*: pull up stakes and live in Mexico and look at the stars at night." Sometimes he fantasizes about retiring early. "Can I really do this for another twenty years? Am I going to get up at six a.m. every day and keep doing what I'm doing? I just have to shake my head. No. I don't want to. So I am trying to imagine what else I can do."

I asked: "Are you having a midlife crisis?"

"I'm at midlife. But a crisis seems to me something that's sudden and then suddenly resolved. There's probably a better word for something that's long-lasting." He said he imagines an uptick in his life satisfaction a few years hence: from six to maybe seven. But in the next breath he acknowledged that his optimism is, to some extent, forced. "I try to stay optimistic because, if I didn't, there wouldn't be much point in going on. By whatever means, I've been able to develop a pretty strong core to deal with things." To me, this sounded less like optimism than like sol-diering on.

Talking to Randy, I thought of what Hannes Schwandt said: *On the one hand, you feel all this disappointment about your past. And then also your expectations evaporate about the future. So in midlife you're feeling miserable about the past and the future at the same time.*

Randy isn't miserable. When I see him interact with his affectionate wife and his exuberant eleven-year-old son, I know he isn't clinically de-pressed. I believe him when he says he realizes he's lucky. But he is at that wearisome juncture where the past feels like a stream of accumulating dis-appointments and the future is still around the bend.

Randy's case contrasts tellingly with that of Mary Ann. Like him, she is a forty-four-year-old professional. Unlike him, in midlife she encoun-tered the kinds of catastrophes we all dread. The result, though, is that she seems to have shifted her disappointment curve—thereby advancing the realism and acceptance which people with fewer problems rely on time to bring.

Unlike most people I interviewed, Mary Ann is someone who embraces the term *midlife crisis,* and it is easy to see why. In rapid succession, her mother received a cancer diagnosis; then Mary Ann herself received a can-cer diagnosis, which was a false alarm; then she received another cancer diagnosis, which was *not* a false alarm. Meanwhile, her husband ran into an exotic and hard-to-treat health problem, and her father-in-law died.

"I've hit my midlife crisis," she told me. "All the sorts of things that are supposed to precipitate midlife crisis hit—*poof*—in my forties. You come smack-dab slamming into the concept of your own mortality. It makes you feel really old, really fast. You're facing mortality, you're feeling old, you're thinking there are more achievements behind you than ahead. These are the hallmarks. I'm textbook in some ways."

Mary Ann's feelings are complicated, though. Describing her forties, she used the words: *anxious, reflective, appreciative.* Why, amid all the jolts, *appreciative*? She and her husband are healthy now, and her expectations have been reset by their ordeal. "Once you come through, you think: *my god, I do have a great life.* I'll just sit outside sometimes when the weather is nice and think: *yes!*" On the Cantril Ladder scale, she rates her current life at seven: down from the eight she gave her twenties and thirties, but not bad. She sees the future as unlikely to bring the kinds of adventures she once had, but she seems to be making her peace with that. "I don't feel so old that I don't feel surprises are possible," she said. "I don't rule out the possibility of big shifts. I just don't expect them." And is that okay? Again, a mixed answer. "No one's happy about coasting or sliding. But I'm not flipping out about it. I'm too old to sweat the small stuff."

Mary Ann actually is not old at all, but she uses the phrase *too old* to refer, not to her objective age, but to her subjective position on the happiness curve. Schwandt suggests that the presence of objective difficulties in midlife—things like health crises—can mitigate emotional difficulties by helping people understand and accept their disappointment, thereby protecting them from a negative feedback cycle. I would not for a moment say there was anything desirable about Mary Ann's bruising trials, but her encounters with mortality and suffering may have boiled off unrealistic optimism which otherwise would have taken longer to leach away. Her family's crises seem to have taken her on a shortcut to the mature realism of the latter portion of the expectations curve. Her chronological age is the same as Randy's, but her life-satisfaction age seems, perhaps, ten years ahead of his.

If the transition to realism sounds dreary and gloomy, take heart. The draining away of unrealistic optimism, although a grind when underway, can cast a freshening light on life. Take Margaret. An Australian in her early fifties, she has rounded the bend that probably lies a few years ahead for Randy. Her forties brought uncertainty, unsettledness, a series of jobs that didn't feel right, but her fifties? *Industrious, settled,* are the terms she uses. When I probed, I learned that by "settled" she means that she has settled *down,* but also that she has settled *for.* Her job still isn't quite the right fit, but it is pretty good and she can settle for it. "It's good enough. I've come to terms with the fact that I've accepted an area of work that's not my ideal, but it's still very satisfying." Meanwhile, she finds satisfaction in pursuits which might have seemed less worthwhile to her younger, more ambitious self. A piece of jewelry broke, so she took a jewelry-making course. She learned to knit. She took sewing lessons. "I come out of it feeling so refreshed and relaxed, like I've had a big rest. It's using a different part of the brain. I feel like there's more of a balance." She describes herself as happier than she has ever been. I can tell that Margaret is surprised by the pleasure she is getting from what she calls her "little courses." She uses the word *awakened* to describe her life.

On Hannes Schwandt's map, Margaret has passed the crossing and reached the place where expectations are realistically low and satisfaction surprisingly high. On Thomas Cole's map, she is out of the rapids.

Talking to Jasper and Randy and Margaret, and to many others, it dawned on me that we don't have a good vocabulary for the rich and ambivalent mixture of emotions they are encountering in midlife. Clinical words like *depression* and *anxiety* don't fit; dramatic words like *crisis* don't fit, either, at least not reliably. *Malaise* is pretty good, but it is one-dimensional and needs fleshing out. I hear *fatalism* and *resignation* from Randy, something like *acceptance* from Mary Ann, and something closer to *satisfaction* from Margaret. I hear, in Randy, a note of mourning for optimism lost, but in Margaret, a note of relief at letting go of the ambition that is optimism's burden (Jonathan Haidt's "heavy backpack"). From Mary Ann I hear notes of sadness, but also notes of lightness. And so on. The feelings my midlife interviewees describe are too complex and rich to fit easily into any standard emotional box.

The unscientific but, I think, revealing survey research I did for this book drives home the emotional ambivalence and richness that characterize the midlife passage. When asked to rate and describe their state of satisfaction in each decade of life, my respondents send clear signals about their twenties (*fun, exciting, hopeful, busy, uncertain, adventure, ambitious, free*) and their sixties and seventies (*happy, satisfied, content*). But in describing their middle decades, respondents proffer a messy mixture of positive and negative and neutral. At the bottom of the happiness curve, it seems, you can't tell a simple story about the textures of life, because expectations and reality and personality and choices and age are all hurling themselves at you and interacting with each other.

Amid all the complexities, though, one finding turned up invariably: *no one sees around the bend in the river.*

Remember, the optimism which diminishes through the middle decades of life is optimism about our future life satisfaction. The long downturn of the happiness curve conditions us to expect disappointment, and so naturally a turnaround is the last thing we foresee.

There is a famous scene toward the end of the film *The African Queen* in which the protagonists, their boat trapped in a swamp and their view blocked by tall reeds, give up on ever reaching open water, not realizing that it is only a few yards away. The happiness curve plays its own version of that wicked trick. In a manner of speaking, the bend in the river hides itself, lurking out of view just when we would most benefit from a glimpse of it.

Cole, in *Manhood,* seems to make the same point. From our point of view, the calm of the ocean, not far away, is visible through a gap in the crags; but the worried Voyager, looking heavenward and surrounded by high rocks, does not perceive it.

And what of *The Voyage of Life*'s missing fifth painting?

In 1840, Cole, looking past *Manhood*'s rapids, saw the still waters of impending death. In *Old Age* the boat is becalmed, progress has subsided, and the future lies not in this world but the next. Cole had every reason to see the period after midlife that way. In his day, the average American twenty-year-old could expect to live to the age of only about sixty; and, of course, high childhood mortality meant that large numbers of people never even made it to adulthood. Cole himself died at the age of forty-seven. From where he sat, not much lay beyond *Manhood* except death. He could not have foreseen a world of much longer, healthier lives: a world in which the Voyager enjoys a decade or two (or three) of vitality and improving happiness before death finds him—the scene Cole didn't paint.

Today, of course, we live in that world, at least if we are fortunate enough to be denizens of an advanced country with good health care and high incomes. Today's average twenty-year-old American can expect to live to about the age of eighty. In theory, we should be able to see what Cole could not. Oddly, however, we don't. Those who feel trapped and squeezed between the pincers of Schwandt's narrowing expectations gap make a forecasting error that perversely mirror-images the forecasting error of youth. Where the twenty-year-old was too optimistic, the fifty-year-old is too pessimistic. That is part of what can make the middle years such a slog: the hard knocks of repeated disappointment lead us to make the biggest forecasting error of all.

Fortunately, the depressive realism of middle age turns out to be . . . well, unrealistic. Life gets better. Much better.

THE PARADOX OF AGING

Why getting old makes you happier

At the beginning of her twenties, the same age when I was contemplating Thomas Cole at the National Gallery, Laura Carstensen was in an orthopedic ward, contemplating twenty-one broken bones. Her past had been injudicious, and her future seemed unpromising. She was not someone you would have guessed would ever wind up as the world's leading expert on aging and happiness. But the Voyage of Life takes quirky twists, as Carstensen was about to discover. Four months in the hospital would put her on a path to a scientific career and, ultimately, the likely solution to the happiness curve's most counterintuitive riddle: why getting old makes us happier.

Carstensen has straight brown hair, cut to shoulder length, with a touch of honey and a gray streak above the right temple. On the day we met she wore black pants, a red leather jacket, hoop earrings, and a necklace composed of concentric gold circles. Her face is broad and friendly, and, despite her eminence, she is naturally disarming to talk to and irrepressibly curious about others. Interviewing her at Stanford University, where she directs the university's Center on Longevity, I had trouble imagining her as the teenage rebel she once was.

Born in 1953, in Philadelphia, she was one of five children. Though her parents were highbrow—her father a professor, her mother an artist—she hated high school and wasn't interested in learning. "It was an era when everyone was rebelling," she said. "The Vietnam War was going on. We were protesting anything we could protest." At seventeen, she got married. The decision, itself a form of protest, was not what you might call well thought through. "I knew that the only way that I could move out of the house," she said, "was to go to college or get married, and I didn't want to go to college."

Aimlessly, after getting married, she worked as a waitress, then a telephone operator. At nineteen, her marriage went sour, and she had a son, hoping a child might repair the relationship. It didn't work. She demanded a divorce, was refused, left her husband, and moved back into her parents' house with her toddler. If all that was not enough turmoil, a week later she rode back from a concert with a friend who steered the car off an embankment. She was fortunate to survive, but her body was shattered. "I ended up in the hospital for four months, most of it in an orthopedic ward," she said. "I had punctured lungs, I couldn't see. It was a horrible accident."

Trapped in the ward with three elderly women, she was bored, deeply bored. So the most important man in her life made a suggestion: Why not audit a college course? Choose a lecturer, he told her, and I'll attend class for you, with a tape recorder. That way she could listen in bed at the hospital whenever she wanted. For no special reason beyond being interested in people, she chose psychology.

As the course unfolded, it touched on social psychology, which ponders people's interactions with others. Carstensen, her curiosity aroused, began to observe how differently she was treated than the ward's elderly residents. It occurred to her to wonder: how much of aging is really a reflection not of biology but of how society views and treats us?

And so, healed and now hooked, she entered and finished college, then graduate school, then launched an academic career—always guided by her father, Edwin, the man who had traipsed back and forth to the orthopedic ward with tapes of psychology lectures. A biophysicist whose credits included topics like "finite amplitude ultrasound in tissues" and "cavitation in lithotripsy," he was, she told me, the most intelligent and curious person she has ever known. "He accepts nothing at face value," she said, "and he likes to say there is nothing more important in science than finding out that you're wrong." As her career launched, she quickly had occasion to remind herself of her father's skeptical dictum: her first major piece of research made no sense.

Carstensen set out to study the social interactions of old people in nursing homes, expecting to find that residents who had the fewest social interactions would be the least happy. Social connections, after all, are central to emotional wellbeing. But she was wrong. "What I found was that the people who interacted the *least* were the people who were doing the best, psychologically."

There was another surprise: "I began the study of aging absolutely expecting, as basically everybody did at the time, that the study of aging was the study of decline and decay, how people fell apart. And I was reading in textbooks that depression rates soar in old age, and if you live long enough you'd eventually get depressed. Just old age itself was a form of psychopathology. I never questioned that. I took it as the premise for the work I was doing." But depression kept not turning up, at least not at unusual rates, except in depressing environments. What did keep turning up was, in fact, the opposite. Emotionally speaking, older people were doing well.

Although she had no way then to know it, what seemed like a wrong result would eventually lead her to understand why the ostensibly improbable is true: aging changes who we are, and what we perceive, in ways that make us happier—even when our bodies betray us.

My father used to say that growing old isn't for sissies. He often expressed fear of aging, and especially of being "frail elderly." He and others of his generation, having watched their own parents fade into what seemed like lonely decrepitude, or having seen them languish in the corridors of smelly nursing homes, perceived little to look forward to in the latter decades of life. Middle age had brought my father the disruption and stress of divorce, single parenthood, and a solo law practice; he was, in those years, prone to rages and obsessive worry. So no one, I suspect, was more surprised than he when, as he aged past an unfortunate (and brief) second marriage and into his late fifties, his tightly wound personality uncoiled and his outlook on life lightened. He lived twenty years after retiring at age sixty, and those years (apart from a hard medical landing at the very end) were his happiest. Even before he retired, his rages became infrequent and then disappeared, a gift to himself and our family. When he was in his mid-fifties, I asked him where his anger had gone. He thought for a moment and then said: "I just stopped having five-dollar reactions to nickel provocations."

In my own surveys, where I ask people to rate and describe the decades of their lives, I have heard variations of my father's tale—the sense of unexpected satisfaction in one's sixties and seventies—so often that I just about stopped keeping track. As I mentioned in the previous chapter, the vocabulary of middle age is dense with conflicting, high-stakes words, but descriptions of the sixties and seventies are dominated by variants of the words *happy* and *satisfied* and *content*. The other side of that coin is that words like *challenge* and *ambitious* fade—and along with them *stress*. Asked to rate their life satisfaction with a number, respondents score their sixties and seventies highest, with only a slight decline in the eighties. My survey methods are inexact, but I do not need a microscope to see that the modal story for people in their sixties and seventies is of being very satisfied with life.

One snowy morning, I visited my ninety-four-year-old neighbor Nora, a casual acquaintance until I sat down with her that day and asked about her satisfaction with life. She was someone who had always had a cheerful emotional thermostat, but she had seen her share of hardship: a poor childhood without electricity or running water; her husband's death at the age of only fifty-two; a difficult adjustment to retirement; the loss of a grown grandchild; the challenge of caring at home for an older sister with dementia. Nora was hobbled by a broken kneecap and was a recent cancer survivor, and she noticed her mental acuity diminishing when she played bridge; just a few weeks prior, she told me, she had caught herself making mistakes she had never made before. Of course, at ninety-four, she had lost many friends, including two entire bridge tables. She wasn't housebound, but she couldn't go about much, and after an hour of activity she needed to sit and rest.

Those are the sorts of struggles and losses which made my father expect the worst from aging, but Nora's judgment was unequivocal: "one hundred percent satisfied with everything." She scored her life satisfaction a perfect ten. The key to her longevity, she said, is good genes. And the key to satisfaction? "I would say enjoy every day as it comes. Take what the day brings. Accept it. I think it's acceptance as much as anything. Acceptance, and not worrying." It's not that hardship and loss don't exist. It's that, as she told me, "You don't mind it as much."

I should say, here, that Nora's acceptance did not strike me as passivity or resignation. It was more a kind of *savoring*: of the moment, of the day. Her life might be objectively slower and emptier than in earlier times, but it was subjectively rich and satisfying. As I interviewed her, I wondered whether I will achieve as much equanimity if I reach Nora's age. Fortunately, a lot of science suggests that my chances are good.

I am not promising bliss in your eighties. As always, the motto of this book is: Your mileage may vary. Just as there is no guarantee of having a midlife slump, there is no guarantee of having a late-life upswing. We are talking about tendencies. The river has regular undercurrents, but no two voyages are alike.

Still, the undercurrent in latter decades turns out to be quite strong;

and the evidence for it is also strong. I have discussed, in earlier chapters, the difference in perspective between economists, who look at big data sets and find the happiness curve turning up incessantly, and psychologists, who look at individual lives and find little evidence of midlife crisis. I have also argued that the two viewpoints are reconcilable, if we remember that the psychologists are looking at particular voyagers while the economists are looking at the undertow. All of that is true of middle age. But when we reach the later decades of life, economics and psychology come into alignment, with the result that both kinds of evidence, from big data and from individual people, show the same pattern. As I explored the research literature, I found studies looking from every angle and coming back with the same basic finding, which is that my father's view of aging—as a process of emotional as well as physical decline—is wrong. Just a taste of the research:

Stress declines after about age fifty. A lot of people have found this result, including me. When I ask people for words or phrases to describe each decade of life, *stress* figures noticeably for the twenties, rises high in the thirties and still higher in the forties, and then drops to below-twenties levels in the fifties—and keeps dropping from there. The words *busy* and *work* follow a similar pattern, which implies that withdrawal from the workplace is part of the picture. But not all of it. Stress begins falling, and falling steeply, a decade and more before retirement age.

That point came home to me forcefully in a conversation with Arthur Stone, the University of Southern California psychologist whose work on the happiness curve I mentioned in chapter 3. He is trained as a clinical psychologist and for years has looked at how people's bodies and minds are affected by stress and pain and fatigue and other everyday challenges. Gallup, he said, had asked an immense sample of Americans—1.5 million—whether they experienced a lot of stress in their life yesterday, and the pattern was "incredibly strong." Between the ages of eighteen and fifty, half or more said yes (they had had a lot of stress the day before). "Then what happens from age fifty to age seventy is it drops to about twenty percent, and it drops in a linear way. That's going from half to one in five, and that's in the face of chronic health problems. The effect size is huge. The steepness and the regularity of the drop are extraordinary, too. It's just rare in science that you see patterns like this."

So he and two USC colleagues, Stefan Schneider and Joan Broderick, looked at two other gold-standard data sets. Same result: "noisier," Stone told me, "but it's exactly the same kind of drop from age fifty to seventy." Then, trying to explain what caused stress to decline so sharply, they adjusted for about twenty variables, pretty much everything you can think of that might explain stress's diminution (health status, kids, marriage, and so on). The pattern didn't change. In fact, it grew stronger, as if age itself were reducing stress. Or perhaps some as yet unknown variable reduced stress. Either way, Stone's own straw polls were consistent with his finding. He said he had taken to asking people if they would like to be twenty again. "I was amazed that, except for one person, everyone in their fifties and sixties said, 'Nope, I would want to be the age I am today.'"

Emotional regulation improves. "Young people are miserable at regulating their emotions," Laura Carstensen said, summarizing research by herself and others. We all remember the high emotional highs of our young years, and the low emotional lows. Extreme emotions are exciting, but, as Arthur Stone's straw poll implies, many of us who have aged past the high-drama years would rather not relive them.

Thomas Cole's depiction of youth places the Voyager in Edenic surroundings: the river is placid, the landscape lush, the sky blue. What Cole could not have captured in a single painting is that the emotional weather of youth is changeable; only a moment or two later, the Voyager might be drenched in a thunderstorm or whipped by high winds. Part of the reason emotional weather tends to settle down with age may be the accumulation of life experience. "On average," the Cornell University psychologist

Elaine Wethington told me, "people do seem aware that they learn some- thing as they age, and it seems to calm down their emotions. 'I don't let that stuff bother me anymore.'" Other reasons, which I'll come to soon, may have more to do with aging itself, and even biology. Whatever the reasons, the relief which emotional smoothing brought to my father is common. With age, we give fewer five-dollar reactions to nickel provocations.

Older people feel less regret. The cranky codger figures prominently in the standard caricature of age, and no one would deny that older people, like younger people, complain. But the stereotype about bitterness is, if anything, the opposite of the truth.

A few years ago, a group of German psychologists decided to look at how people at the two ends of adult life process regret. Led by Stefanie Brassen of the University Medical Center Hamburg-Eppendorf, they gath- ered three groups of experimental subjects: emotionally healthy young men whose average age was twenty-five, emotionally healthy older men whose average age was sixty-six, and depressed older men, also averaging sixty-six years old. All were given a task much like the games which con- testants play on the TV program *Let's Make a Deal*: They were shown an array of eight mysterious squares ("boxes") and told to "open" them sequen- tially. When selected, seven squares would reveal a nugget of gold, which the players could collect, but behind one square was a devil, randomly as- signed. Subjects who picked the devil lost all their prior winnings. Thus, in each round, the subjects had to decide whether to stop playing and pocket their haul or keep playing and risk getting zonked (the *Let's Make a Deal* term for betting and losing everything).

As every gambler or game-show junkie knows, getting zonked is a frus- trating experience. Unlike *Let's Make a Deal* contestants, however, these people got zonked while experimenters watched their brains in fMRI ma- chines. The experimenters also measured subjects' physical reactions. In a 2012 *Science* magazine article—evocatively titled "Don't Look Back in Anger! Responsiveness to Missed Chances in Successful and Nonsuccessful

Aging"—Brassen and her colleagues reported that the emotionally healthy older group showed less regret when getting zonked than did the emotionally healthy young group. By contrast, the *depressed* older group was just as regret-prone as the young people were. What to make of the finding? The experimenters theorize that healthy aging helps people accept what they can't control, a positive change which depression negates.

Older people are not depression-prone. As for depression itself, here, too, the stereotype is wrong. In 2002, surveying the literature, the psychiatrist Dan G. Blazer remarked that depression is "less frequent (or no more frequent) in late life than in midlife." Its prevalence is quite low: 1 percent to 4 percent of the elderly are affected by depression in any given year. (Depression does become more common among the oldest old, reaching 13 percent.) Recall, too, the finding by Oswald and Blanchflower that antidepressant prescriptions in Europe (and two U.S. states) peak in the forties.

Age also often brings better skill at coping with depression and adversity when they crop up. "In midlife there is this confluence of stresses," the prominent happiness economist John Helliwell told me, "and there's some evidence that a rise [in subjective wellbeing] comes as life stresses diminish. But there's also this skill that rises with age of being able to put bad things in context and being able to cherish the good ones."

Less stress, less dwelling on life's downsides, better emotional regulation, better coping: looking back, I believe I saw those changes in my father. True, he did remain congenitally pessimistic, someone who seemed to relish finding the dark lining in every silver cloud. But in that respect he turns out to have been somewhat unusual. Most people experience the positivity effect.

You recall, from the previous chapter, how the squeezing out of unrealistic optimism can bring seemingly relentless discontent in middle age, but sets the stage for years of pleasant surprises later on. The kind of evidence I have just adduced about emotional regulation helps explain the turnaround: some combination of experience and neurological development rather unexpectedly improves our resilience and reduces our tendency to experience stress and regret, even in the face of stressful and regrettable situations. But there is more going on. Lots of evidence confirms a *cognitive* factor. That is what Carstensen and other researchers have termed the *positivity effect*. Older people register a higher ratio of positive to negative information, which feeds back to support positive emotions.

Tali Sharot, the cognitive neuroscientist whom we met in the last chapter, has studied the effect. "In comparison to their younger counterparts," she and four other scholars wrote in a 2014 paper titled "Optimistic Update Bias Increases in Older Age," "older adults remember faces displaying positive emotions more than those displaying negative emotions, have less rich autobiographical memory for negative events, and experience less negative arousal when anticipating monetary loss." As we saw in the previous chapter, older people dwell less on negative information than do younger people. Surveying voluminous evidence in a 2012 article titled "The Theory Behind the Age-Related Positivity Effect," Carstensen and her Stanford colleague Andrew E. Reed, writing in *Frontiers in Psychology,* note that the positivity effect turns up in working memory, short-term memory, autobiographical memory, "and even false memories." Older adults tend to lean toward the positive when confronted with all sorts of inputs: word lists, emotional faces, upsetting or heartwarming pictures, and health-related messages. Older adults remember their own choices in life more positively, too: the flip side, perhaps, of experiencing less regret.

People grow more positive about each other, too. In one study in the mid-1990s, Carstensen, along with the psychologists Robert Levenson and John Gottman, brought in married couples—some married happily, some less so—and recorded them with hidden video cameras as they discussed their conflicts. The scientists' observations and the subjects' own reports agreed: older couples, compared with their middle-aged counterparts, expressed less anger, disgust, belligerence, and whining. That was still true after the scholars controlled for overall marital satisfaction, so that they were comparing marriages of equivalent quality. The older couples were also more likely to express affection than were younger couples, even when tensions were comparably high.

As that kind of evidence piles up, experts are increasingly willing to draw a conclusion which is striking in its sweep and implications. As the University of North Carolina sociologist Yang Claire Yang has put it, "With age comes happiness."

Now, the positivity effect is not enough to make every day joyful; but it is large enough to be a big factor in life. One team of scholars (Angelina R. Sutin and five colleagues, writing in *Psychological Science* in 2013) finds the age upswing to be roughly similar in magnitude to the effect of having a college diploma rather than only a high school diploma, and education is among the things that matter most to wellbeing. "Older adults maintain and may even improve their emotional wellbeing despite the inevitable physical and social losses that occur with aging," they find. In France, a 2013 study (by Kamel Gana and four colleagues) followed almost nine hundred individuals as they aged through their seventies. After controlling for variables like education, gender, and health, the authors found a "linear increase" in average life satisfaction with age. Carstensen and seven colleagues, writing in 2011, made the same point a different way. "The peak of emotional life may not occur until well into the seventh decade."

The *seventh* decade! I was astonished when I first read that statement. Apparently I am not alone. "Despite empirical evidence to the contrary," Carstensen and her colleagues write in their 2011 article, "old age is persistently viewed as a time of sadness and loss by younger people. Older people share these pessimistic views about the 'typical' older person."

It's the "I'm okay, you're not okay" syndrome. Even older people who are very satisfied with their own lives often think that most *other* people their age are unhappy. In a 2006 study directly on point, Heather P. Lacey, Dylan M. Smith, and Peter A. Ubel asked two groups of people, one young (average age: thirty-one) and the other older (average age: sixty-eight) to estimate both their own and an average person's happiness at the ages of thirty and seventy. Sure enough, older people were happier than younger people. But everyone, old and young alike, believed that happiness *declines* with age. Everyone also overestimated the happiness of young people, and underestimated the happiness of old people.

If you hear, in these upside-down assumptions, an echo of Hannes Schwandt's findings that people's expectations about life satisfaction are way off target, you're right. Even after decades of being surprisingly happy, many older people believe they are only temporarily defying emotional gravity. One eighty-four-year-old woman I interviewed, who still played tennis and worked with passion and enjoyment, saw only gloom when she looked ahead five years. "My god, I'll be so aged," she told me. "I can only imagine it will be horrible then."

The writer Eleanor Cooney once said, "There's no such thing as a lucky old age, because old age by definition means precisely that your luck has run out. Some people's luck runs out more egregiously than others, to be sure, but everyone's luck runs out if they live long enough." That has to be right. Doesn't it? The body wears out, we lose capacity, we acquire chronic illnesses, and we drop dead. No fun. Yet the interplay of age, health, and happiness is not as simple as we assume.

When he was seventy-seven, my father developed what doctors said was a harmless tremor. He also became depressed. The tremor got worse, and not long after he turned seventy-nine, he got a new diagnosis: Parkinson's disease. Ah! Frightening as that diagnosis was, it was consistent: depression is a common symptom of Parkinson's. Fortunately, the doctors said, Parkinson's progresses slowly, and so he would have many active years. And there were medications for it. But the medications failed, and the disease progressed, quickly and aggressively, not at all as the doctors had predicted. (Much later, we learned why, when a neurologist diagnosed my father's condition as multiple system atrophy, a faster, crueler, and deadlier affliction than Parkinson's.)

Yet even as my father declined physically, his depression lifted. He often complained that he hated being ill, yet somehow, even at the very end, his everyday spirits remained surprisingly good. Only a week before he died, withered and unable to walk more than a few steps, he said brightly one morning, "Where are we going today?" and organized a trip to the art museum.

Human resilience is an amazing thing, but there is more to the story than just hanging on in desperate circumstances. Some years ago, Dilip Jeste, a University of California (San Diego) geriatric psychiatrist whom we'll get to know in the next chapter, discovered that schizophrenic patients he was studying tended to get better as they got older. As they aged, instead of declining, they were more compliant with their medications, had fewer psychotic relapses, and had less need for psychiatric intervention. That was surprising, because it cut against conventional wisdom about the course of the disease. It occurred to Jeste to wonder if the findings were unique to people with schizophrenia, so he and a group of colleagues conducted a telephone survey of about two hundred nonschizophrenic people over the age of sixty, asking them to rate on a scale of one to ten how successfully they were aging. "Successful aging" isn't a precise term, but it maps reasonably well onto life satisfaction, and people's self-ratings turn out to be good predictors of their mortality and morbidity in old age; so apparently people know successful aging when they see it. "It was really a big surprise," Jeste told me. "We found that a large majority of people had physical impairments of various degrees. Based on objective ratings of physical health, I would have assumed ratings of three to five." But the mean score was above eight, and most people were in the seven-to-ten range—and self-rated successful aging *increased* with age.

Amazed, Jeste repeated the experiment, this time on a larger scale and randomizing the participants to avoid the possibly of a biased sample. With ten colleagues, Jeste interviewed 1,300 people to assess their general health, their levels of depression and anxiety, their memory and cognitive functioning, their physical and mental health, and so forth. Same result. People in the study ranged in age from fifty to ninety-nine, and the average was seventy-seven. In a study published in 2013 in *The American Journal of Psychiatry,* the researchers found that older age was associated with physical and cognitive decline, but also that, "contrary to our hypothesis, older age was associated with a higher score for self-rated successful rating." People in their fifties rated themselves in the mid-sevens; people in their sixties in the low eights, and the numbers just kept rising—even into the nineties! Physical ailments and disabilities didn't seem to matter, except at the extremes, and even there the researchers found contrary examples. (One person with metastatic cancer gave himself a nine.) Statistical tests of whether the real culprits might be other factors, such as education and finances and ethnicity, came up negative. The tendency of successful agers to live longer was part of the story, but not all of it. Even as people became more afflicted with disability, their self-rated successful aging increased. Old age, even very old age, apparently is *not* necessarily when our luck runs out.

I do not mean to imply that getting frail or infirm makes you happy, in old age or at any other time of life. The point is that most people remain surprisingly happy *despite* getting frail and infirm. One of the most interesting bits of research I ran across is a German study of health, aging, and happiness, conducted by Ute Kunzmann, Todd D. Little, and Jacqui Smith and published in *Psychology and Aging* in 2000. Looking at people aged 70 to 103, they find that declining health reduces positive feelings. That stands to reason. But after they adjust for health, thereby gauging the underlying effect of aging per se, they find age is associated with *more* positivity (and less negativity). "Surprisingly," the authors write, "not only did poor functional health suppress the effects of age, age also suppressed the effects of poor functional health." To put that remarkable statement a bit more plainly, age seems to protect people from some or all of the emotional toll of poor health. If so, then contrary to what my father assumed would happen, age was helping him cope.

Now, a logical question to ask, in the face of a quite counterintuitive result, is whether the positivity effect is really a senescence effect. Could the protective effect of aging be an artifact of older people's weakening grip on reality? It wasn't true in my father's case: amid the ravages of his neurological meltdown, his mental acuity remained intact. In fact, Carstensen and colleagues find that the positivity effect is *stronger* in older people with sharper minds; impairment of cognition impairs positivity, too. In a 2012 paper titled "The Emotion Paradox in the Aging Brain," the University of California (San Diego) psychologist Mara Mather notes that, although it's true that the brain shows many changes with age, and that most such changes tend to reduce brainpower, emotional processing is an area in which mental decline is *not* in evidence. Moreover, although older people are more distractible, one thing they are *less* distracted by is negative emotional stimuli. Older people are just as good as younger people at *perceiving* negative stimuli, Mather writes; the difference comes next, at the processing stage, when elders' cognitive systems put more attention and emphasis on the positive. With age, apparently, we lose not our emotional sharpness, but our tendency to have our day ruined by annoyances and setbacks.

Perhaps, then, positivity comes about because older people lose their emotional edge. Are they becoming emotionally numb, so that they are not feeling either depression or joy? Wrong again. Carstensen and her various colleagues find that old people feel both negative and positive emotions as intensely as young people do. What seems to change with age, rather, is that older people experience negative emotions with less frequency, and for shorter spells. The storms are still strong, but they come less often and don't linger as long. Also, when storms do boil up, older people have better control over their feelings.

So perplexing is the positive effect of age on life satisfaction in the later years that psychologists have dubbed it *the paradox of aging*. "We tend to think we know what makes people happy," Carstensen told me. "It's having a long, bright future. It's being in charge of things. It's having people focus on you and think you're the handsomest or prettiest person in the room. But all these things that we think make people happy decline with age. And the paradox is, we get *happier*."

We have seen, in earlier chapters, any number of paradoxes about happiness: happy peasants and frustrated achievers, the hedonic treadmill, and so forth. The paradox of aging may be the most important of all, because it suggests that our standard assumptions about life's emotional trajectory are backward. As we age, physical and emotional health do not track in tandem. They move in counterpoint. Why?

"It hit me," said Carstensen. We were in her office at Stanford University, and she was recalling the early 1990s. Her research was not going according to prediction: the elderly subjects of her study seemed uninterested in making new friends, and their social circles were shrinking, yet they were happy. She feared she was on a wild-goose chase. "I'm running study after study trying to find out if I can identify the pathology in older people's pathetic social lives. None of my studies were working. I thought I would never get tenure."

She didn't find the answer; it found her. "I was just talking to the people in my studies," she recalled. "I remember talking to two sisters one day. They lived in a senior residence, an apartment building for older people. They were saying friends have died; we don't have a lot of people anymore. And I said, 'But there are a lot of people here. There are people you could get to know.' And they turned to me and said, 'We don't have time for those people.'

"It occurred to me—so many people had been telling me this over the years, as I was asking these questions. *Why don't you want to make new friends? Why don't you want to explore? Why don't you want to expand your horizons?* And they were talking about *time*.

"It hit me: they weren't talking about time in the day, because they seemed to have plenty of that. They were talking about time in a different way. They were talking about *life*time.

"And all of a sudden, just this realization. You can't make a new *old* friend when you're eighty. It isn't going to happen. The numbers don't work."

What if the social lives of these seniors were not withering but being pruned? What if age brought a shift in emotional priorities? "What people were saying," Carstensen told me, "is they're very interested in the people they care about and the ones they really love. But they're not interested in just any person whom one could sit down in front of them, or they were much less interested than when they were younger. And that was the selectivity theory. Emotions stay intact, but people make increasingly careful decisions about what they invest in and in whom they invest."

In other words, perhaps our basic goals and choices in life are not time-neutral, but change with our time horizon, altering not just what we do from day to day, but how we feel, and even what we perceive. In a series of experiments in the 1990s and beyond, Carstensen and other researchers set out to test the theory. They gathered people of different ages and asked them to imagine whom they would want to meet if they had thirty minutes free: the author of a book they like; a family member or close friend; or a recent acquaintance with whom they had much in common. "What we find is that older people overwhelmingly choose a member of their family or a close friend. Younger people's choices are distributed pretty randomly across the three choices."

Then the researchers asked the same people whom they would choose to see during the same half hour if they were about to move across the country and had only thirty minutes left before leaving. Suddenly, the younger people answered like the older ones: they showed a strong preference for close friends and family. Flipping the scenario, the researchers asked what people would do if they learned they would have twenty additional years of life. Now older people answered like young people, choosing strangers and book authors as often as close friends and family.

Carstensen and her colleagues also looked at Hong Kong during the time when it was being handed over to Communist China, a time of uncertainty and anxiety. News headlines blared "the end of Hong Kong." During that window, young people in Hong Kong showed the same preference for friends and family as did older people—a preference that disappeared after about six months, once the situation had stabilized and residents had calmed down. "When the fragility of time, or of the future, is primed, that's when we see these effects," Carstensen told me. "And it takes about six months for life to return to what it was before. I've had friends who have had heart attacks, and they say, 'I am so done with this rat race. I am going to focus on what's important. That's my family.' And within six months they're back in the rat race."

Carstensen found some of the same effects in the immediate aftermath of the terrorist attacks of September 11, 2001: young people temporarily put more emphasis on the present and on the really important relationships, instead of longer-term goals. She also looked at gay men with and without HIV. Uninfected men's priorities were like those of other young people, but those who had the virus and were symptomatic had priorities more like those of older people—and those with the virus, but without symptoms, were in between. (Recall, in this connection, Mary Ann, whose health crisis seemed to have accelerated her passage through the trough of the U.)

In 1999, Carstensen, along with Derek M. Isaacowitz and Susan T. Charles, published a seminal article in *American Psychologist*. It was titled "Taking Time Seriously: A Theory of Socioemotional Selectivity," and it laid out what has become the reigning explanation of the paradox of aging. The monitoring of time, the authors argue, is basic to humans. Young people are primed to seek out new information and new people, hoarding knowledge and acquaintances as a hedge against the uncertain future. "When time is limited, however, short-term goals, such as social connectedness, social support, and emotional regulation, assume highest priority. Under these conditions, focus shifts from the future to the present. Individuals seek out social partners with whom they experience close ties, and emotional experience is characterized by greater complexity."

I saw just such a change in my father. Starting in junior high school, he and a group of friends had gathered several times a year to share selections from books and articles and poems. "Reading Out Loud," they called their meetings. The group managed to stay connected for seven decades; in fact, it assumed growing importance for my father and everyone else. It became my father's extended family; even as illness sapped his strength and travel became perilous, he made his way to meetings. What had been a source of pleasure became a source of meaning as he and his oldest friends drew closer and cherished each other more.

Far from dwelling on the past as the stereotype would have it, older people focus more than other age groups on the here and now. "Older people are mostly present-oriented, less concerned than the young with the far distant future," write Carstensen and her colleagues, in "Taking Time Seriously." When time becomes short, "social interactions are navigated carefully in order to ensure that their emotional quality is high." An elderly couple, for instance, will be more likely to appreciate what is good in their relationship and overlook what is troubling.

Living in the present. Taking each day as it comes. Savoring the positive. Dwelling less on the negative. Accepting. Not overreacting. Setting realistic goals. Prioritizing the really important people and relationships in life. Those attitudes read like a list of what both modern psychology and ancient wisdom have told us for years about how to find satisfaction in life. You would not necessarily want young or middle-aged people to be so present-oriented, because young people need ambition and society needs entrepreneurs. But it is easy to understand how socioemotional selectivity theory helps explain the surprising upturn in late-life satisfaction. Carstensen's theory implies that *age changes our values.*

I asked Carstensen if people usually realize their values readjust with age. "Yes," she said. "If you ask people if their priorities are changing, they absolutely know that." But there is an unconscious dimension, too, one which alters not just how we set our goals, but also how we experience everyday life. "Goals direct cognitive processing," Carstensen said. "That's as close to a law as anything we have in cognitive psychology. If goals are changing systematically with age, we should see differences in the types of information people attend to and remember." That would help explain experiments finding that older people are more likely than young people to focus their attention on happy faces than on negative or sad ones; that they are more attentive to positive memories; that older adults' brains, when observed in MRI machines, show comparatively less neural responsiveness to negative stimuli and less encoding of negative material. "It's a big effect, a whopping effect," Carstensen told me.

That helps explain the virtuous cycle of the late-life upslope of the happiness curve. Our increasing emphasis on emotionally meaningful goals focuses our *conscious* goals and priorities on the things that matter most for satisfaction, reducing the urge to obsess about regrets and disappointments. At the same time, the change in goals also directs our *unconscious* attention toward the positive. We like more of what we see, and we see more of what we like. Changes in our priorities and in our perceptions reinforce each other.

And thus we arrive at a possible solution to the paradox of aging. How can it be that we become more satisfied with life even as our bodies betray us? Carstensen, in her 2009 book *A Long Bright Future: Happiness, Health, and Financial Security in an Age of Increased Longevity,* puts the answer this way: old age "has its share of hardships and disappointments. It's just that by the time people get there, they're more attuned to the sweetness of life than to its bitterness." I would put it a slightly different way: *our values change faster than our bodies.*

In my own interviews with older people who were encountering physical limits and frailty, I looked for insight into the satisfaction of the later years. I found a lot of satisfaction, but not as much insight. As was true with people in the trough of the happiness curve, most people on the curve's upslope were better at describing their subjective situation than at explaining it. James, for example, is a lawyer by training, now mostly retired. At eighty-three, he has had to shed commitments. He can't do all the meetings. He makes mistakes. "I just can't do the work. I don't trust myself." Travel, photography, and pro bono projects fill some of the gap, and he enjoys a group of friends—the "Same Boaters," as they call themselves—who meet every week and organize programs. Still, he is someone who looks to his professional work for fulfillment, even as an octogenarian. "I don't like not having a lot of phone calls every day," he said. "I don't like the idea of people offering me seats on the subway. I don't like falling apart physically. I don't have as much professional connection with people as I would like."

Yet when James took my Cantril Ladder quiz, he scored his satisfaction at nine, almost the top of the scale. Despite the losses, he told me, he feels that his life is not *worse* so much as *different*. When I asked why, he said, "I intellectualize more than feel the disabilities of age." Meaning what? "I don't like the *idea* of being old. I think about being old as having certain disabilities, and intellectually I know that. But I haven't emotionally absorbed them in any way. I don't feel these disabilities present big emotional issues for me. They're sort of sand traps on the course that you have to walk around, but they're not handicaps that make life miserable."

My friend Robert, seventy-nine, has had to give up skiing ("You age, but the mountain doesn't") and he may soon have to give up sailing, his passion. "I have to spend a remarkable amount of time looking after my body," he told me. Yet he rates his satisfaction at nine, higher than ever before. After the striving and turbulence of midlife, he works part-time and sets his own schedule. He has learned to relax. He no longer feels he has a list of things to accomplish. When I asked if he is surprised to feel so good emotionally, he replied in the affirmative: "I never frankly expected to live this long." To him, every day is a pleasant surprise.

No guarantees, your mileage may vary, and all that. I am not suggesting that every ninety-four-year-old will be, like Nora, "one hundred percent satisfied with everything," or that ill health has no emotional consequences, or that frailty is fun. I am suggesting that Laura Carstensen is right when she says, of aging: "Society gets this wrong and individuals get it wrong."

Growing old in modern, prosperous countries like the United States is not like growing old in the past or in disadvantaged places. In the United States, just since I was born in 1960, the average life span at birth has increased by almost ten years, from less than seventy to almost eighty: a fantastic improvement. Worldwide, the increase in longevity has been even more spectacular: almost two decades, from the low fifties to the low seventies. For many of us, it's as if someone sliced open our life spans at age sixty and added fifteen healthy, positive years.

Yet our workplaces, retirement plans, and physical environments are still tailored as if we were healthy and happy only through our early sixties. Retirement begins in the sixties, even though, today, most people can look forward to many productive years ahead; public pensions kick in a decade and more before the decrepitude for which they were designed. Popular culture, meanwhile, tells us that youth is vibrant and happy, the best time of life, and middle age will bring "crisis," and then old age will bring functional and emotional decline—when the reality is that youth tends to be a time of challenging emotional extremes, middle age a time of grinding but productive adjustment, and the gray years are generally the happiest of all.

Carstensen likes to imagine a different world, one in which expectations about aging align with the reality of aging. "Right now, as people grow older, I think they get a message from society that says: 'Go away, make room for younger people,'" she said. "'You're incompetent. We'll take care of you. We won't take *good* care of you, because we don't have enough money, so don't gobble up all the resources. But go away.'" If we understood the trajectory of happiness and age as it really is, she believes, we would perceive late adulthood not as a burden but as a gift: an unprecedented, unconditional grant of more time to realize our goals, to be with our loved ones, to pursue our dreams.

So how might the cultural story change, I asked Carstensen, if today's upside-down stereotypes were turned right side up? At the social level, she replied, we would do much more to include older people and exploit their talents, turning them into fiscal assets rather than liabilities and bringing them back to the center of social life. At the individual level, we would tell young people a different story about their trajectories. "The older you get, you'll have more physical problems, but you'll have a lot of knowledge. You're also going to come to find yourself with the freedom to care about what matters most to you, and pursue *those* goals, and not pursue the goals that other people say should matter to you."

Carstensen revels in that prospect. "I mean," she told me, "I think that could make people maybe want to get old!"

Here, then, is what I think we know. Time and aging fight happiness in midlife, then switch sides. They redirect our priorities and reshape our values—without, at any stage, informing us of their perverse plan or preparing us for it.

Why might they do that? I'll have more to say about that in the next chapter. Here, suffice to say that they seem to be playing a deep game. For it appears that humans are not alone in changing our priorities with advancing years. In a 2016 study of a population of Barbary macaques, Julia Fischer, of the German Primate Center, and Alexandra M. Freund, a University of Zurich psychologist, along with three of Fischer's colleagues, found that the monkeys maintain full interest in social interactions in old age (and younger monkeys continue to seek out the elders' company), but they focus their interactions on fewer partners. In other words, the macaques become choosier about their friends and seem to invest more in anchor relationships: the same sort of social selectivity that older humans demonstrate.

Though that research is too preliminary to depend on, it echoes the finding that great apes experience a U-shaped happiness curve; and it hints that hardwired biology alters our values as we age. But distinctively human psychology and self-awareness are at work, too, as Carstensen showed when she induced older people to prioritize like younger people, and vice versa, by manipulating their time horizons. As with the happiness curve itself, so with the paradox of aging: biology and psychology, human nature and human culture, absolute time and relative aging—all interact. Just what kind of intricate dance they perform together, and which partner leads, remain to be discovered. Be that as it may, time is not merely the neutral background against which action occurs in our life, a blank slate upon which events scratch their marks. Aging is not merely a chronological series of birthdays, a downward course of physical decline, or a more or less predictable progression of situations and environments which we march through. Together, performing their dance, time and aging are independent actors, with a trajectory of their own, weaving patterns through and around our lives and psyches, patterns which are not necessarily transparent or even comprehensible to us as we experience them.

In her twenties, Laura Carstensen was a divorced single mother in graduate school. Could she pass the next test? Find a job? After graduate school she landed at Indiana University, and then, only three years later, at Stanford: a promising trajectory, but as she pushed toward tenure in her thirties, she was told that her research wasn't relevant to psychology. She did get tenure, of course; yet success brought not relief but even more anxiety. "My forties were for me the worst," she recalled. "I've blocked out that time in my life. It just felt like everything could collapse. I knew I was good by that time. I was publishing; I was getting grants. I was being recognized in various ways in my profession. But it might not be good enough. It felt like the bar was extremely high and the possible loss was large. I felt under pressure constantly to prove something. I felt that people constantly look at you and decide whether you're good enough."

She was in her fifties when her satisfaction curve turned upward. "I think you're coming out of the fog in your fifties," she said. At age sixty-three, when we spoke, she was happier than ever before.

I asked her: "Don't you still get evaluated, bid for grants, cope with judgmental critics and competitive colleagues? Don't you still have all those stresses?" Carstensen's six-word response: "I don't care. I. Don't. Care." Meaning not that she ignores other people's opinions and needs—far from it—but that she no longer sees every day as another harsh referendum on her accomplishments. "At this point in my life," she said, "I take criticism to heart intellectually, but it doesn't hurt me emotionally like it did in my youth." She added, "I feel so privileged. I *feel* it now. I didn't feel it in the early years."

"So," I asked, "have you peaked?"

"I'm pretty much here," she replied. "I do not worry about aging. I worry about *physical* aging, yes. Not a lot, though."

"You don't expect your life to get better emotionally?"

"I don't think my life *could* get better emotionally."

Perhaps she is wrong about that.

CROSSING TOWARD WISDOM

The happiness curve has a purpose, and it's social

In early 2015, the world's best and most successful blogger shut down his website and walked away. He was fifty-one.

Andrew Sullivan was thirty-seven when he began *The Daily Dish,* as he called his blog. The form, then, was still new. People were already creating self-published journals online, mixing opinion with news items and links and occasionally the odd bit of reporting (and often it *was* odd). Some prominent journalists had taken up the form. But Sullivan took it to the next level. He had graduated from Oxford University, earned a PhD from Harvard, launched a career in journalism, and become editor of *The New Republic,* one of Washington's most influential publications—all before the age of thirty. Even by the standards of Washington wunderkinds, he was a star. Blogging, though, tantalized him with an opportunity to reinvent himself and his profession. Writing in his own voice, without intermediation, he could connect directly to readers, building not just an audience but a community, thereby both exploiting and advancing an infant medium whose potential seemed boundless.

He succeeded. The *Dish* became a must-read for people in the United States and around the world. It pioneered a business model, managing to operate in the black at a time when traditional journalism was plunging deep into the red. It built a fiercely loyal following. And then Sullivan stopped.

A few months later, I asked him why he had walked away. He cited the mental and physical strain of running a business, of nonstop writing and editing and emailing and keeping up: "The sheer number of people you have to be in contact with. The sheer amount of data you're processing." He cited factors in his personal life. He cited, in other words, the stresses that can and do lead successful people to experience burnout in midlife.

But Sullivan wasn't just tired. The river had turned. His values had changed, and his blogging work no longer aligned with them. "I was so absorbed in virtual reality," he told me, "that I had neglected actual reality, the friends I cared about, the family I love."

I asked about the influence and attention he was abandoning. After all, as he himself reminded me, walking away at the peak of success is "just not something one does in America." He replied in terms that would not have surprised Laura Carstensen. "In my forties, I felt the attenuation of my ambition." Meaning what? "It means that the worldly ambitions that I might have had, I increasingly see as distractions from the life I really want to live."

I pressed him. What if people say, *What ever happened to Andrew Sullivan?* "It doesn't bother me. I'm hardly free of ambition, vanity, or ego. But compared to my mid-twenties, it's drastically reduced."

I asked what he might do next. "I don't know where I'll be," he said, "but I'm pretty sure I won't be chasing after glittering prizes. And that, I think, will make me happy."

I first met Sullivan when he was twenty-eight years old. By the time he closed the *Dish,* we had known each other for more than two decades. It was true: I had never seen him so happy.

Elliott Jaques, introducing the concept of midlife crisis in 1965, regarded it as a time of danger, but also of opportunity. "It is essentially a period of purgatory—of anguish and depression," he wrote. But it can also bring commensurate rewards. "The sense of life's continuity may be strengthened. The gain is in the deepening of awareness, understanding, and self-realization. Genuine values can be cultivated—of wisdom, fortitude and courage, deeper capacity for love and affection and human insight, and hopefulness and enjoyment." He described midlife crisis as a "process of transition [that] runs on for some years." Although, in researching this book, I have come to believe that Jaques got some important things wrong (beginning with the use of the word *crisis* for something that is usually gradual and undramatic), I think his idea of midlife as a transition is right.

As I interviewed people about their midlife transitions, and their lives afterward, I heard reflections like Andrew Sullivan's again and again, always suggesting a reorientation of personal values away from ambition and toward connection. I came to believe that the feelings and themes I heard add up to more than just a hard-knocks lesson in realism or a random suite of changes in the brain. The transition has a direction: something you could even call a purpose. As we saw in the previous chapter, the upslope of the happiness curve has an *emotional* direction, which is toward positivity. But it also has a *relational* direction, which is toward community. In other words, this a social story, although we rarely experience it that way.

Perhaps the most dramatic example I encountered was Paul. He was fifty, a professor I met not long ago when speaking at a college in New England. I had hardly expected to make an intimate connection with him, because I was there on business and he seemed like an ordinary guy, one of those pleasant people you shake hands with and forget. My ears pricked up, though, when he mentioned that for years he had been a dedicated, even compulsive rock climber—and that he had shattered both legs in separate climbing accidents. I had not met many people whose response to shattering one leg would be to go right on and shatter the other, so I began asking some questions about his life. He decided to trust me with his story, which turned out to be a case study of how the turn in the happiness curve can change the way we see others.

The first couple of decades tell a familiar tale. In his twenties, Paul moved fast. He described his twenties with the words *intense, ambitious, immortal.* "I got married when I was twenty-four years old to my high school sweetheart. There was this sense that life was this big adventure. I got very invested in outdoor sports. When I started climbing, it wasn't recreational; it was go big or go home." In his thirties, after floundering for a while and working odd jobs, he began the professional climb that would lead to his professorship. "It was just a very intense time. I was just kind of running around all the time, putting everything I could into everything I was doing." He adopted the same take-no-prisoners attitude toward rock climbing. He would set his sights on a semi-impossible route and not rest until he had conquered it, only to start all over again when the next season began. Paul strived to be the perfect climber, the perfect professor, the perfect husband, the perfect father, the perfect soccer coach. Everyone saw him as successful, a winner. But even as he conquered society's crags, he knew, in his early forties, that something was wrong.

"I started having these weird symptoms. I started being obsessive-compulsive about what other people were saying about me. I started to question my moral center, the foundations of my identity. I didn't know what was happening to me. I had just gotten tenure. I had a beautiful wife, beautiful children. And yet I was living in this very dark place."

Unsettled, uncertain, he took a semester off, entered counseling, yet spiraled down. "When you don't know what's happening, it takes on a life of its own. I was so worried about other people judging me. I was judging myself. I would sit around the dinner table with my family, hoping to go back to work, but I couldn't function. I couldn't be in the room with them without nearly collapsing, mentally. I had to go up to my room, and it literally felt like the walls were caving in on me.

"It was a terrible time. My oldest might have been in sixth or seventh grade. Watching me struggle had a massive impact on his life. He thought his father had his act together. As did all my friends. When they found out I needed to take time off and collect myself, they couldn't believe it. I remember this profound sense of loneliness that was existentially frightening. I felt I was at the brink of this abyss."

Was anxiety the problem? Depression? Some of both, Paul replied. Yet the psychiatric jargon didn't really explain anything. "I think the reason it happened was that I didn't like myself. I didn't trust myself. I didn't think of myself as a good person. I'm very driven, but I ended up measuring myself through how others perceive me." A single poor evaluation by a student, he had felt, was an indictment, a failure.

With psychiatric help, Paul battled his way back. He resumed his life, now trying to be more forgiving of himself. Normalcy returned. But, under the surface, the crisis had primed him for a larger change—a change in values. "There's a great egocentrism that drove my past," he said. "What really has changed me is a move from being goal-driven about Paul."

One of Paul's fields of study is Native American literature. A former student suggested to Paul that he visit a reservation in South Dakota to explore service-related learning opportunities for his students. He went, for a week. "From the first moment I was there to the moment I left, I felt that every single thing I was doing had more purpose and meaning than anything I'd ever done in my life. It sounds corny; it sounds cliché. But I'm putting a rivet in a socket in the house I'm fixing, and I feel like this rivet has *purpose*."

When he returned from South Dakota, he brought home a question: Could he maintain a sense of purpose? Could he weave it into his everyday life? He knew he tends to overdo things, so he had to be careful. "I had to step back and say, *Am I romanticizing this? Will I flame out from the intensity?* I felt very ashamed of where I'd been for the past forty-seven years. Yes, I was a compassionate and kind teacher; I did as much as I could for my family, though I neglected my family for climbing. But it really triggered in me this sense of obligation to help people who didn't have what I had. I knew it intellectually the whole time, but to get on the ground, to meet people, and to see other people in nonprofits, incredibly bright and talented people who have given their lives—that, for me, has transformed my life. I began to think about how to make my whole life more purposeful in terms of helping people, particularly *these* people."

Today, he spends six weeks a year on reservations in the United States and Central America. He has developed educational programs and an oral history project for Native American communities he works with, and he is on the board of a nonprofit that works with Native Americans. Yes, he still rock climbs, but only a few times a year. Leg-shattering routes no longer tempt him. "Those things are not at the top of my list anymore."

Listening to his tale, I suspected that the visit to the Sioux reservation, though transformative, was almost incidental. The trigger for his values change might just as easily have been a visit to an orphanage in Vietnam, or a week teaching low-income kids. The real change, of course, was in Paul. So I asked him: "What do you feel happened to you?"

Two things, he said. First, he became better able, finally, to forgive and trust himself, and with that came a sense of mastery, of competence. "You *can* be forgiving of yourself. I'd be lying if I said I didn't have moments of stress, when I have to sit on the stoop with my wife and say I need to sit back and take a breather. I think what's increased my life satisfaction is the ability to handle those things, to put those things in perspective. To understand that it's all going to be okay. Even if things get hairy, I think I have a tool belt now."

Second, and seemingly even more important: Although Paul will always be intensely goal-oriented, his goals shifted outward, away from what psychologists call egocentricity and toward other-directedness. "In the past, I worked to help people," Paul said, "but at the end of the day I did that because it was a goal I set for myself. On the reservation, I feel humbled. Yes, you need an ego to work there, to think you might make a dent. But you have to be humble, to listen to people, to try to understand." In describing how he had changed, he used a phrase which stayed with me because it seemed so apt: he feels "a deeper sense of recognizing other selves."

Paul's life satisfaction is high. He rates it at nine on my Cantril Ladder test, higher than the seven of his twenties or the six of his thirties or the five of much of his forties. He finds himself, at fifty, in a world with a narrower time horizon, but a broader people horizon. He finds himself feeling less ambitious, in the conventional sense of ticking off life goals, but more competent. "I'm optimistic about my fifties. If things are good now, with a gathered wisdom of sorts, in the next thirty years or the next one year or however long I have left, I could leave the earth and each of my kids would say, 'My dad was all right, not because he *accomplished* X and Y and Z, but because he *cared* about X and Y and Z.'"

Paul's story, with its chaotic meltdown, fragile recovery, and transformational change, is dramatic: the tale of a sudden, wrenching change in values. Usually, the change is much more gradual and subtle.

More typical, for example, is David, age fifty-four, an entrepreneur whose start-up business finally took off after ten years of painful, sometimes desperate struggle. In his twenties, he had drifted, flailing, clueless; in his thirties, he got a good job and made a name for himself; then, at forty, when he was at the top of his game, he risked everything to pursue his dream of a start-up—only to flounder financially and emotionally. Every day brought struggle, threw up some fresh problem. Professionally, he felt at sea. Meanwhile, his marriage broke up. Therapy helped, but he did not talk to friends. "If you're too despondent, others get despondent, so I had to keep up appearances."

By the time he was fifty, the business had stabilized. By his mid-fifties, when we spoke, it was firmly established, and David was happily remarried. But he also found himself changing. "I think my impostor syndrome is dead. Finally. My sense of mastery is higher." For the first time in his adulthood, his life satisfaction was high—though he said his affect had not fully kept pace. (Remember, life evaluation is not the same as one's day-to-day emotional state.)

I asked: "Have your values changed?" Definitely! "I get a huge amount of pleasure in trying to help people succeed in things." David was teaching. He did a lot of mentoring. "I like to try to help cool things come into existence, regardless of whether my name is associated with them." He noticed himself worrying less about that checklist of accomplishments with which his younger self was so preoccupied. When he and I spoke, he was just back from a trip to California. Somewhat to his own surprise, he had canceled all his Silicon Valley business appointments and instead spent the time reconnecting with a friend from junior high school. That just seemed more important.

And so, in his forties, David had passed through not only a professional transition, but a personal one, too—yet without the kind of drama that Paul experienced. Most transitions seem to be of the quieter sort, but are just as developmentally profound. Another example is that of Christine, who experienced a series of challenges at midlife. Her mother's death shook her, and a series of jobs caved in beneath her, forcing her to start over, not once but several times. At one point, she found herself on the brink of losing her family's medical insurance and running out of savings. The scramble from job to job had denied her, in her fifties, the sense of professional arrival which many people achieve in their thirties and forties, yet with two kids and a husband to support, she didn't have room in her life to do anything but keep going. Despite the stress, though, at fifty-three she reported her highest life satisfaction ever. When I asked what had changed to improve her sense of wellbeing, she replied by talking about what had changed in herself. She felt a sense of mastery. "I can *do* life. I have a sense of what my limitations are, what my strengths are, and I can now organize my life so I can play to my strengths." And, she said, "I no longer feel an obligation to save the world."

When I probed, I found that she no longer felt a need to save the *whole* world. Earlier in life, Christine had imagined holding big, important roles that make a dent in the world's problems. In her twenties, she joined the peace movement and planned to end nuclear war. Had her ideals collapsed? Not exactly. "I can't save the world," she said. "I can save my little corner of it." She had acquired a new passion, volunteering at a wild-bird rehabilitation center. "If I can rehabilitate a raptor, that's focused, concrete, makes a difference." The ambition and idealism were still there, but she had scoped them to fit her ambit of control. She was less invested in the abstract and general, more in the concrete and specific.

And so, although some people, like Paul, experience an existential crisis and an internal drama at the bottom of the happiness curve, many of us make the turn gradually and mundanely and inconspicuously; often we are only indistinctly aware of it ourselves. Yet the critical and gradual paths both lead us in the same direction: toward others, and toward wisdom.

When I interviewed Andrew Oswald about the happiness curve, he was eager to talk about the data and its many implications. Empiricist that he is, he was more reluctant to talk about explanations. Instead, he suggested I call someone whose work he found intriguing: an unorthodox psychiatrist named Dilip Jeste.

Jeste was sixty-nine when I first encountered him in 2014. He spoke in a lilting Marathi accent, a legacy of his upbringing in India, and cut a modest figure. He was on the short side and slight of build. When we met, in San Diego during the summer, he was wearing a baggy blue blazer and a sweater, because, as he told me, he is always cold. His clothing and build made him look his age, but he moved and walked like a much younger man; when we left his office to visit his lab across campus, I had trouble keeping up with him. His mind is equally quick. It needs to be, because it occupies parallel worlds.

Born in 1944, the son of a lawyer, he was one of five children and grew up in a small town near Mumbai. In seventh grade, to learn English, he moved to the city of Pune, where he discovered the library in the U.S. consulate and began voraciously consuming books. One of them was Sigmund Freud's *The Interpretation of Dreams*. "It was like an Agatha Christie mystery," he recalled. "Instead of starting with a murder, you start with a dream."

Solving the mind's riddles, the young Jeste thought, should be his life's work. Deciding on psychiatry, he began medical training in India and then continued in the United States, at a series of gold-plated institutions: Cornell, the National Institutes of Health, George Washington University. Finally, in the mid-1980s, he landed at the University of California at San Diego. At this writing, he is still there—now with a very long string of titles (Director of the Sam and Rose Stein Institute for Research on Aging; Distinguished Professor of Psychiatry and Neurosciences; several more). His office wall is covered with plaques, certificates, and awards. As they imply, Jeste became what one might fairly describe as a pillar of the American psychiatric establishment. In 2012, as president of the American Psychiatric Association (he was the first Asian American to attain that position), he supervised the first major revision of psychiatry's diagnostic manual since the mid-1990s. His field, primarily, is geriatric psychiatry and the study of successful aging. In the previous chapter, I mentioned his finding that people report higher subjective wellbeing as they move through the late decades of life, even while they grow more infirm. He is also a brain researcher, someone who spends a lot of time (and money) putting experimental subjects inside deafening magnetic-resonance imaging machines to observe their mental circuits firing. The day I visited him, he was conducting an experiment to learn more about how older brains process compassion.

I dwell on Jeste's scientific credentials because he has another side which is quite different, one which challenges mainstream psychiatry in fundamental ways. For one thing, he is an evangelist for something he calls *positive psychiatry,* an extension into medicine of positive psychology. This is a new idea. Psychiatrists, being physicians, concern themselves with treating mental disorders. If they ameliorate your depression or anxiety, their job is done. As Jeste puts it, if they take you from minus five to zero, they're finished. He thinks psychiatry can and should do more: it should apply itself to making well people happier and more resilient, taking them from zero to plus five, thereby enhancing wellbeing and preventing psychiatric problems.

Positive psychiatry has yet to catch on in the psychiatric world, partly because improving happiness, rather than treating illness, is not in the medical curriculum. Jeste, however, studied a different curriculum. He grew up in India, immersed in one of the world's great wisdom traditions: specifically, in the teachings of *The Bhagavad Gita.* "It's cultural, growing up in India," Jeste told me. "We read the *Gita.* The whole thing is about wisdom."

Jeste was struck early in his career by a puzzle. *Why would life satisfaction rise as people move into old age, even in the face of physical decline?* The trend was too strong to be happenstance. "I started wondering whether the life satisfaction we were seeing in older people was related to their becoming wiser with age, in spite of physical disability. So then the question is: *What is wisdom?"*

Jeste imagined he might be able to conjoin two divergent traditions by developing a neuroscience of wisdom. The first step might be to define wisdom in a scientifically rigorous way. The second might be to measure it. The third might be to understand which parts of the brain are most involved with it, and thereby to explore whether wisdom has a physiological basis. A fourth, one hopes, might eventually be to learn how to cultivate and enhance wisdom.

Medical traditionalists were skeptical (and still are). Jeste recalled being told by colleagues: "Do anything, but don't utter the word *wisdom*. No one will take you seriously. It's not a real concept. It's a philosophical concept rather than a neuroscience concept." He took their skepticism as a challenge.

When he set out, he couldn't find any articles on wisdom and neuro-biology (apart from ones mentioning people named "Wisdom"). By 2010, he was cranking them out himself. Top journals were publishing his papers, which were packed with sentences like this one: "Two brain regions were identified as being common to different domains of wisdom—the pre-frontal cortex (especially dorsolateral, ventromedial, and anterior cingulate) and the limbic striatum." Damage to those domains, he found, can lead people to behave in ways that most of us would agree is unwise, yet without affecting intelligence.

But what are the "domains of wisdom"? Alone and with colleagues, Jeste combed through wisdom about wisdom: ancient and modern texts, Eastern and Western texts, traditional and scientific texts. When I asked what he had gleaned, he replied: "The concept of wisdom has stayed surprisingly similar across centuries and across geographic regions." Again and again, modern scholarly definitions mention certain traits: compassion and pro-social attitudes that reflect concern for the common good; pragmatic knowledge of life; the use of one's pragmatic knowledge to resolve personal and social problems; an ability to cope with ambiguity and uncertainty, and to see multiple points of view; emotional stability and mastery of one's own feelings; a capacity for reflection and for dispassionate self-understanding. By comparison with modern Western sources, the *Gita* places more emphasis on controlling one's desires and mastering materi-alistic cravings. But, write Jeste and Ipsit V. Vahia in a 2008 article in the journal *Psychiatry,* "A comparison of the conceptualization of wisdom in the *Gita* with modern scientific literature shows several similarities, such as rich knowledge about life, emotional regulation, contributing to common good (compassion/sacrifice), and insight (with a focus on humility)."

Jeste told me, "All across the world we have an implicit notion of what a wise person is." Of course, culture imposes many variations on the theme. Yet there is more than enough consistency across eras and societies to suggest that wisdom is not just a random label meaning different things to different people in different places. Rather, wisdom is its own recognizable quality. Its ubiquity, Jeste believes, suggests it is something important for *Homo sapiens*—and something hardwired, at least in part. "The concept of wisdom is universal," he told me. "And so it has to be biologically based. I think there are brain changes that are conducive to feeling better and improving some aspects of old age." No one supposes there is a "wisdom organ" somewhere in the brain. But much might be learned, Jeste believes, by understanding how wisdom works, and how it may be embedded in our circuitry.

If wisdom has a biological basis, then it presumably also has an evolutionary basis. Presumably it evolved because it helps people do better in life. But why might it persist, and often increase, among the elderly, including older women, who are past their fertile years? In biology, the so-called grandmother hypothesis posits that postmenopausal women improve their lineage's prospects by investing in the wellbeing of their children and grandchildren. A grandmother effect likely helps explain why human females undergo comparatively early menopause and then long outlive their fertility, a phenomenon seen in only two other species, short-finned pilot whales and orcas. In studies of orcas, marine biologists find that having postmenopausal mothers and grandmothers in the group greatly improves the survival prospects of younger males, even (in fact, especially) when they are well into adulthood and are siring offspring of their own. Something analogous may be true of humans.

"Wisdom is useful at any age," Jeste said. "But in older age it becomes especially important. From an evolutionary point of view, younger people are fertile, so even if they're not wise, they're okay. But older people need to find some other way to contribute to the survival of the species, and that is through the grandmother effect of wisdom."

Perhaps. The biology and neuroscience of wisdom are chapters yet to be written. As of now, the work which Jeste and others like him have embarked upon proffers more questions than answers. But a science of wisdom is being born.

Until I met Dilip Jeste, it had never occurred to me that the concept of wisdom might have scientific meaning, much less that wisdom might be quantifiable. But that turned out to be the case, as Monika Ardelt was able to demonstrate.

I called on Ardelt at the University of Florida, where she was a sociology professor. In her office, Post-its, cartoons, photographs, and children's drawings adorned every vertical surface. Every inch of shelf space was crammed with books. But her conversational demeanor was orderly and precise. She was born in 1960 in the German city of Wiesbaden and grew up in a smaller town near there. She was only a child when she first felt the pull of wisdom. "I had this one uncle who fascinated me," she said. "He didn't say a lot. He had this completely white hair and sat there while others were gossiping and would smile. There was this very positive aura around him. Just being with him made me calm. You felt good sitting with him there. That was fascinating to me, because the rest of my family wasn't like that. He was modeling acceptance, equanimity."

In her late twenties, she came to the United States for her graduate studies. Hunting for a dissertation topic, she hit upon adult development and successful aging. "I was always fascinated by wisdom," she told me, "but I didn't think of it as a topic of scientific study." But one day when she went to the library to look up a data set, her eye chanced upon a 1990 book edited by the Cornell University psychologist Robert Sternberg: *Wisdom:*

Its Nature, Origins, and Development. "I was like, I can't believe it! There are people who actually study wisdom!" That led her to a pioneering 1980 paper by the psychologists Vivian Clayton and James Birren, which had conceptualized wisdom as an alloy of strengths in three domains, each reinforcing the others. One is *cognitive,* the domain of knowledge and reason—of understanding and learning. Another is *affective,* the domain of emotion and empathy—of feelings about ourselves and others. The third is *reflective,* the domain of self-understanding and dispassion—qualities which allow us to get some perspective on ourselves and others.

The tripartite paradigm posits that wisdom can be analyzed as a set of measurable psychological components. This happens to map rather well onto the Buddhist conception of wisdom, a good example of the kind of convergence across eras and cultures that Jeste emphasizes. Here is how the economist Jeffrey Sachs summarized the Buddhist approach in the 2013 *World Happiness Report*:

> The Eightfold Noble Path prescribes eight "right" responses to transience and interdependence. These are grouped into three dimensions: a cognitive dimension (right view, right intention); an ethical dimension (right speech, right action, right livelihood); and a mental-concentration dimension (right effort, right mindfulness, and right concentration). The cognitive dimension is to understand the nature of reality itself: always in flux, impermanent, and interconnected. The ethical dimension is to avoid causing harm to others through the wrong kind of behavior, such as lies or livelihoods that bring harm to others. The concentration dimension is to train the mind to avoid false attachments to transient pleasures.

The Buddha, of course, did not have modern psychological testing at his disposal. Ardelt did. She wondered if she could sift the hundreds of questions in standard psychological tests and select some which reliably identify people and behaviors that most of us would recognize as *wise*. In time, she developed a thirty-nine-item questionnaire—subsequently simplified, by herself and others, to twelve questions. Sure enough, people who are identified by peers or interviewers as comparatively wise ("wisdom nominees") score higher on the Ardelt test. People's overall wisdom could thus be compared, as could their relative strengths in wisdom's three domains. Meanwhile, other wisdom tests appeared, and the various tests turned out to produce consistent results. In science, anything you can quantify is real. So it's official. Wisdom is real!

I took Ardelt's thirty-nine-question wisdom test. I tried as hard as I could to be unsparingly honest about myself, as Ardelt emphasized I must. Some questions seem obviously related to wisdom, like, "I always try to look at all sides of a problem." Other questions are more oblique: "Sometimes when people are talking to me, I find myself wishing that they would leave." (True in spades!) My results placed me toward the higher side of the "moderate" range. I think I know why I don't qualify for the top category. I score well on the reflective elements; I'm good at seeing many points of view and thinking objectively about problems. But I do less well on questions about sympathy and compassion ("I often have not comforted another when he or she needed it"). I am not someone who instinctively reaches out to help others, or who intuitively grasps how to do it. Besides being something I need to work on, my empathy shortcomings hurt my wisdom grade, because my own wisdom, fundamentally, is not about me.

What, then, is this quality which Jeste is brain-mapping and Ardelt is testing? Scholars disagree on the fine points but have arrived at a strong consensus on the big ideas.

Wisdom is a package deal. It entails a variety of traits, but its magic lies in the *integration* of those traits, so that they support and enrich each other. Someone who had a lot of brainpower or knowledge without much empathy or compassion might be clever or expert, but also manipulative and devious, and therefore unwise. Someone who had a lot of compassion without much reflection might be generous and kind, but impulsive and impractical, and therefore unwise. Someone who had a lot of reflectiveness but not much knowledge might be thoughtful but naïve, and therefore unwise. In *Star Trek,* undoubtedly the wisest of all television shows, a recurrent theme is that the most blazingly intelligent character, the Vulcan Spock, lacks the instinctive empathy of Dr. McCoy and the pragmatic decisiveness of Captain Kirk. None of the three alone is wise. Wisdom arises from the (sometimes tense) interaction of the triumvirate.

Because it depends on such interactions, wisdom is also a *dynamic* quality, not a static one. Even within individuals, it varies from situation to situation and day to day. Igor Grossmann, a young social psychologist at the University of Waterloo, in Canada, has found that there is more variation in wise reasoning *within* individuals than *between* individuals. That is one reason it is so important to surround ourselves with diverse people and multiple points of view: in any given situation, the wisest reaction may not originate with whoever is ostensibly the wisest person.

Grossmann's experiments also suggest that wise thinking can, to some extent, be learned or induced: for instance, by asking people to talk about a situation in the third person, as if it had happened to someone else, instead of in the first person, as if it were their own experience. That seems like promising news, and it makes me wonder if schools should spend more time teaching young people how to think with detachment rather than how to pass standardized tests.

Wisdom is not intelligence or expertise. You might think that people with the fastest mental processors would bring more cognitive power to bear on reflection and therefore would be wiser; but voluminous research finds that raw intelligence and wisdom simply do not map to one another, at least not reliably. In a 2013 paper, Grossmann and four colleagues found no association between intelligence and wisdom. In fact, on some dimensions, such as wise reasoning about intergroup conflicts, they found that cognitive ability and wisdom were negatively related. Many other studies have come to similar conclusions.

Similarly, expertise alone is no guarantee of wisdom. "Wisdom means that wise people *know* something," Ardelt said. "So this is knowledge. But wise people don't necessarily know the latest development in quantum physics. What wise people know about is *life*. They know particularly about the interpersonal aspects of life: how to relate to other people, how to understand other people. And the *intra*personal aspects of life: understanding yourself."

The point is not that being bright or knowing quantum physics is inimical to wisdom, or that you can grow wiser by becoming stupider. It is that if you want to become wiser, you must become *wiser,* not smarter or better informed. At some level, we all know that Ardelt and Grossmann and *Star Trek* are right to see wisdom as different from intelligence, and as more complex and precious. So why is it that, these days, the highest compliment we pay, so often, is "She's very smart"?

Wisdom is balanced. Wisdom balances strengths in multiple domains, so that none dominates and each supports the others. It entails balance in other respects, too. A wisdom characteristic that comes up consistently across eras and cultures is *emotional* balance. Wisdom does not imply always being calm and tranquil, by any means; but it does imply being good at emotional regulation, and thus being less likely to fly off the handle in a provocative situation. (No five-dollar reactions to nickel provocations, as my father put it.) If you are wise, you are better able, in the poet Rudyard Kipling's words, to "keep your head when all about you are losing theirs."

Another kind of balance also characterizes wisdom: the ability to maintain emotional and intellectual equilibrium in uncertain, ambiguous situations. That is challenging, because humans are wired to seek certainty and clarity, even if we attain certainty by overlooking important nuances.

"The urge to resolve ambiguity is deeply rooted, multifaceted, and often dangerous," writes Jamie Holmes, in his book *Nonsense: The Power of Not Knowing*. "In times of stress, psychological pressures compel us to deny or dismiss inconsistent evidence, pushing us to perceive certainty and clarity where there is neither." Jeste argues persuasively that being able to exercise good judgment amid uncertainty and ambiguity is one of wisdom's core traits.

Wisdom is reflective. As I mentioned, Ardelt and others of her school of thought regard wisdom as combining competence in three areas. One domain is cognitive (relating to knowledge and intellect), the second is affective (relating to compassion and emotion), and the third is reflective— but *reflective* means something more than mere contemplation. "The reflective dimension of wisdom is basically defined as the ability to look at phenomena and events from different perspectives," Ardelt said. "It's also the ability to look at yourself from an outside perspective. By doing this, by looking at phenomena and events from a different perspective, people get a broader understanding of the world, but also a broader understanding of themselves. That reduces ego-centeredness. It also helps develop greater sympathy and compassion for other people."

The English language lacks a precise word for the quality Ardelt describes. In colloquial usage, *reflection* and *self-understanding* and *self-awareness* imply inward-looking navel-gazing or mental self-absorption: an egocentric kind of self-exploration, which is not the right concept. Other psychologists have used the term *self-transcendence,* but that sounds like an LSD trip. *Dispassion* and *objectivity* are also in the right neighborhood, but they can imply aloofness or calculating indifference. Whatever we call the ability to get distance from one's own passions and viewpoint, it opens paths to the cognitive and compassionate elements of wisdom. "I think the reflective dimension is the most important of the three," Ardelt said. "It gets you to the other two."

Wisdom is active. Reflection, however necessary, is not sufficient.

"Behavior or action is an essential part of wisdom," Jeste, Katherine Bangen, and Thomas Meeks write. "An individual may think wisely, but unless she acts wisely, she does not truly embody wisdom."

Acting wisely is harder than reasoning wisely, even (perhaps especially) for the hyperintelligent. Recall how the psychologist Jonathan Haidt found he was incapable of following his own better judgment about dating. His "rider" saw the best path to travel, but his "elephant" had its own ideas. To extend Haidt's metaphor, when we talk about wise behavior and wise reasoning, we are not talking about either the rider's ratiocinations or the elephant's instincts. We are talking about how we think and behave when the rider and elephant jointly identify the best path and travel it in harmony.

Because wisdom requires us to act, it has the further interesting quality of acting upon us. "Wisdom is *realized* knowledge," Ardelt told me. "It transforms the individual. Intellectual knowledge does not, necessarily. You just know more." In 2004, Susan Bluck of the University of Florida and Judith Glück of the University of Vienna collected people's stories of doing, saying, or thinking something wise. Most people recalled their wise moments as teaching a valuable lesson or overcoming a problem, for example by wresting a positive outcome from a negative situation. Ordinary knowledge and intelligence won't typically have any of those life-inflecting effects.

Wisdom is good for us individually. Recent studies have shown wisdom to be associated with, among other things, better physical health, better mental health, happiness, life satisfaction, mastery, and resilience, along with less addiction and impulsivity. We cannot be completely sure which way the causality runs: flourishing may increase wisdom, as well as the other way around. But here is another clue that wisdom is, in and of itself, a good influence: the same positive relationships hold *within* individuals, not just between them. Examining time diaries (in which people recorded their emotions and reactions over the course of the day), Grossmann and several colleagues found that when people are in wise-reasoning mode they experience more intense positive emotions and less intense negative ones, and they have better emotional regulation, and they are more forgiving.

Wisdom is good for us *collectively.* Has any healthy society ever wished for *less* wisdom? Of course not, and for good reason. Wisdom confers what economists refer to as "positive social externalities." In other words, the benefits of having wise people and behavior in our midst spill over to make life better for the rest of us, wise and unwise alike. This is perhaps the single most distinctive and important trait of wisdom, one which all modern definitions agree upon and emphasize. "One of the most consistent subcomponents of wisdom, from both ancient and modern literature," write Dilip Jeste and Thomas Meeks, "is the promotion of common good and rising above self-interests."

If you think about it, wisdom's characteristic strengths have in common their utility for social problem solving. Wise reasoning helps people put themselves in others' shoes; it focuses not on abstract intellectual inquiry, but on navigating interpersonal conflicts and other social problems; it is demonstrated in action, not merely in thought. It improves our lives by improving the quality of our relationships—which, because every relationship involves at least one other person, improves others' lives, too. It expresses itself by proffering actionable advice, spreading itself around; and, when good advice is taken, wisdom is contagious. Temperamentally, it leans toward equanimity and balance, traits essential to compromise and conflict resolution. I can't count the number of times a wise friend has talked me down from some high dudgeon, whether by pointing out that the person I'm angry with might have a point, or by suggesting that I might be reading sinister motives into a mistake or a misunderstanding, or by helping me see that the smart thing to do is let the matter go. Wise counsel is sometimes most high-minded or principled, but just as often it encourages us to "rise above principle and do what's right," as the novelist Joseph Heller put it. It expresses itself, often, in counterpoint to ideology.

I believe the single most fundamental trait of wisdom is this: You cannot be truly wise on a desert island by yourself. You can be shrewd, resourceful, intelligent, skilled, and much else besides. You can exhibit various elements of wisdom: putting yourself inside the head of a rescuer, or possessing useful knowledge about survival, or making levelheaded decisions. But so long as you are a society of one, you are only *potentially* wise. Wisdom is oriented toward social harmony and the good of the people around us, not just toward ourselves.

In 1996, in his book *The Sense of Reality: Studies in Ideas and Their History,* the philosopher Isaiah Berlin penned a memorable description of wisdom in the political sphere:

> What is called wisdom in statesmen, political skill, is understanding rather than knowledge—some kind of acquaintance with relevant facts of such a kind that it enables those who have it to tell what fits with what: what can be done in given circumstances and what cannot, what means will work in what situations and how far, without necessarily being able to explain how they know this or even what they know.

Berlin aptly captured wisdom's ineffable, yet distinctive and tangible, quality of social practicality. So did a politician who confronted one of the hardest social problems America ever faced. In 1962, a thirty-nine-year-old Mississippi state tax collector traveled to Centre College, in Danville, Kentucky, to give a speech which he called "In Defense of the Practical Politician." His name was William F. Winter, and he would go on, in the early 1980s, to become one of Mississippi's most estimable governors. Still later, he led the University of Mississippi's William Winter Institute for Racial Reconciliation, where he was still active as I wrote this chapter. But in 1962 he was an obscure official trying to think his way through the country's most intractable and antagonistic conflict, namely race relations. "He was a moderate in a state in which the very word 'moderate' had been successfully transformed into a term of vilification and abuse," observes the writer and social philosopher David Blankenhorn, who, growing up in Mississippi in the 1950s and 1960s, bore witness to that fraught era. Profiling Winter in *The American Interest* magazine in 2016, Blankenhorn recalls 1962 as a time when angry Southern populists, caught up in the passions of racial politics, denounced compromise as surrender and swore to fight, fight, fight (a political tendency which has by no means vanished).

Winter spoke in a different vein. "Willingness to compromise involves great courage," he told his audience at Centre College. "Some of the most courageous public officials I have known have been the quietly dedicated men of reason who have worked under the most unrelenting pressures to gain acceptance of unpopular but necessary agreements, while bombastic orators denounced them as traitors or worse." Practical politicians, he said, do not prefer to compromise. Like anybody, they would rather have things their own way. But they know when the time has come to compromise, and then they know how to do it. Americans, he said,

> owe much to the practical politician and the adjustments he brings to the inexact science of government. If he is less than certain, it is because he knows . . . that certitude is not always the test of certainty. If he is less than an intellectual, it is because he knows that not all answers are found in books. If he is less than perfect, it is because he is dealing with less than perfect men.

Winter was describing a bundle of characteristics which we cannot manage without if we hope to share a diverse, divided country. He was describing wisdom.

Back, then, to Thomas Cole's river, the stream that runs through our story. As the sands fall in the Voyager's hourglass, the river's course and current twist. An undertow pulls toward disappointment and pessimism in the middle passage, even (or especially) if our situations seem objectively good; then it changes direction, pulling toward surprising emotional rewards in later decades. Knowing the hydrology of Cole's river, we are in a position to ask an important question. Do the river's current and its peculiar reversal have a purpose—for individuals, for society? Does the undertow of age double back on itself for a reason?

Yes. We are a social, tribal species. We evolved to coexist in groups, and we rely upon our social instincts to maximize the odds of passing our genes down to thriving children and grandchildren and beyond. It would make sense for us to be programmed to be striving and ambitious and competitive in youth, to seek altitude as fast as we can in early adulthood, to attain status and the social and material and sexual perquisites that go with status. It would also make sense for us to shift toward a different role once prime childbearing and parenting years are past: a role more oriented toward the good of society, toward the flourishing of those in our communities and groups, toward helping navigate the challenges of life in the tribe. And it would make sense for there to be a transitional passage in between: a sometimes awkward, grueling, confusing period of being neither here nor there. If wisdom increases with age, we can tell a meaningful and ultimately heartening story about the social and possibly biological logic of the happiness curve. The curve is the current we cross toward a less egocentric, more satisfying perspective on life.

If wisdom increases with age. I would like to be able to say that contemporary science proves that age increases wisdom, or even that age and wisdom consistently go together. As of now, however, research is ambiguous. Some studies find that wise reasoning rises with age. Igor Grossmann and his four colleagues reached just that finding in their 2013 study on wisdom and intelligence. But in another paper, in 2014, Grossmann and Ethan Kross found no meaningful difference in the wise reasoning of older and younger adults. In yet another study, published in *Psychological Science* in 2012, Grossmann and six colleagues studied wise reasoning about interpersonal conflicts in America and Japan. They found that wise reasoning improved with age among Americans, but not among Japanese. And so it goes, in research by Ardelt, Jeste, and others.

Looking at the evidence, I do not think we can say that aging automatically or necessarily makes anyone wiser. Here, though, is what I think we can say. Other things being equal, the aging process makes it *easier* to be wise in later life. It gives us, so to speak, better equipment.

More balance and equanimity; more contentedness and less regret; more mastery and practical experience; more comfort with inner and outer ambivalence and conflict; more emphasis on investing in social relationships and on what my interviewee Paul called "recognizing other selves": in recent research, those changes tend to be associated with both age and wisdom. To adopt Paul's metaphor, they are wisdom's tool kit. We hear them alluded to in the stories I told at the beginning of this chapter and elsewhere in this book. Andrew turns away from "glittering prizes" and toward friends, family, and religion. Paul gives up his status-conscious quest for perfection and discovers meaning in his work on Native American reservations. David turns his entrepreneurial energies toward helping others launch projects. Christine saves birds rather than the world. In all their accounts, and many others which I do not have space to include, we discern elements of growing wisdom: movement toward equanimity, toward pragmatic problem solving and reflection, toward other-directed priorities.

I've interviewed many people who expressed satisfaction in their fifties and beyond. Few have spontaneously invoked the term *wisdom*. Today the word is barely part of our everyday vocabulary. Yet anyone attuned to wisdom's wavelength will hear its signal loud and clear. I recall, for example, interviewing Chip, a military retiree and part-time limo driver who, in his mid-sixties, rated his life satisfaction at eight, an all-time high. When I asked why, he said he had developed patience which he had lacked in his youth; that he had become less judgmental of others; that material things had receded in importance. ("I'm not a millionaire," he said. "I'm not even a thousandaire. I'm not unhappy about that. A lot of money is trouble.") Perhaps most telling, he said he had learned how to avoid the conflicts that once had been endemic in his life, with the result that his fourth marriage was succeeding, after three prior failures. "When I was younger, the least little things set me off," he said. "I'm the kind of person now, before I will argue with you I will see if there's a way to settle a thing. I'll try to see if there's a way to compromise. If not, we'll put it on the shelf and try to get it done later." Wise words!

Of course, we shouldn't bemoan the world-saving, egotistical ambitions of youth. David could not advise young entrepreneurs on their start-ups without first having succeeded with his own. Both slopes of the happiness curve serve a purpose. That purpose is not to help us be happy (or unhappy) as individuals. If the undertow steers us first toward grandiosity and restlessness and volatility and status competition, and later toward realism and satisfaction and equanimity and sociability, and if there is often an unpleasant, worst-of-both-worlds transition in between—well, our individual feelings are quite incidental. If my interpretation of the evidence is correct, the happiness curve is a *social* adaptation, a slow-motion reboot of our emotional software to repurpose us for a different role in society. It came into being because it helped our tribes survive and thrive.

Thomas Cole depicts the life's voyage as an inner, solitary journey, bereft of human companionship or society. He depicts the subjective psychology of aging. That is an impressive accomplishment for someone who was working in the 1830s and 1840s, when the invention of psychology was decades in the future. Still, I can't resist pausing to savor an irony at Cole's expense. *The Voyage of Life* may be a subjective portrayal of an interior journey, but if my argument is correct, the river's winding track was laid down and its banks were carved by precisely that which is missing from Cole's paintings: our collective interactions with others, writing themselves, over the course of eons, into our culture or our genes or (most likely) some combination of the two.

In that important respect, Cole's solitary river voyage is a social journey after all. We humans share it and collectively shaped it, even though we travel it one by one.

Understanding how the happiness curve reorients us toward communitarian values helps, I think, make sense of a paradox I alluded to in chapter 5. The downslope and trough of the happiness curve represent a squeezing out of optimism: a long, slow adjustment toward what psychologists have called depressive realism. We reduce our expectations of our future happiness. Emotionally, we lower our sights and learn to settle. Settling increases our contentment.

Settling? That sounds dreary. It sounds like grudgingly accepting contentment of a diminished and impoverished sort: like resigning ourselves to the abandonment of our youthful dreams and the deflation of our youthful hopes. It sounds like, well, depressive realism.

Yet depression, deflation, and diminution are not at all what most people experience. Not even close. In my interviews with people who had navigated the transition, I rarely heard notes of disappointment or resignation. I heard that life after the reboot seemed richer, more than compensating for any losses.

Partly, that must be the result of the psychological changes we saw in the previous chapter: the positivity effect, socioemotional selection, and the rest. Partly, though, it is a function of something Aristotle understood without the benefit of fMRI scans and big data: *Wisdom enriches us.* It changes our values, not just our knowledge; and in doing so it changes who we are and how we perceive the world.

Jerry Hirsch, who was in his early seventies when we spoke (he let me use his real name), gave an evocative description of the change. He was the chairman of the Lodestar Foundation, a philanthropy in my home-town of Phoenix, Arizona. In the first portion of his career, he had made serious money, building shopping centers. He thought his life was good—until his marriage caved in when he was forty-eight. After divorce came depression, a suicide attempt, hospitalization, and a hard look at his life. "I realized my tombstone would say, 'Before there was Hirsch, there were 426 Kmarts, and now there are 693 Kmarts.' Is that what I want my legacy to be? I said no. There has to be something else." He went back to school, then studied spirituality, "always searching for what would give my life more meaning." He settled on philanthropy. "I concluded if I wind up helping someone, it would give me more meaning in my life. Coinciden-tally, the more I helped others, the more it satisfied me. And that's what I've been doing."

He reported a step change in his life satisfaction: not just a quantitative change, like a higher Cantril rating, but something more fundamental, a change in what the concept of *quality of life* means to him. In his case, making that step change required a crisis. "I didn't know about the depth of happiness and satisfaction one could get from these other types of en-deavors. I didn't know there was a deeper level. It took something to tear apart those layers that were covering my core."

I had heard that word, *depth,* in one of the first interviews I conducted when I began exploring happiness and age. I was speaking with Karla, a friend who, at age fifty-four, seemed to have safely established herself on the happiness curve's upswing. When we spoke, Karla's life satisfaction was high and improving. In her fifties, she told me, she savored more than ever before the friendships she had nurtured over many years. She felt bet-ter organized, more efficient. She was doing more work with the neigh-borhood civic association, and had started volunteering in church. She reported uncovering an additional depth in life, an intangible dimension which had been beyond the ken of her twentysomething self. "It was al-ways striving and looking ahead then, as opposed to being in the now.

Now I feel grateful for the now. On a day-to-day basis I probably do the same things, but I *feel* different."

Just so: same life, yet it *feels* different. And so, of course, it is not the same life. The river alters the Voyager, not just the scenery. Although the world beyond the bend in the river looks less exciting without an overlay of unrealistic optimism, it does not look emptier or narrower. It looks richer and deeper. That is the beginning of wisdom.

8

HELPING OURSELVES

How to get through the U

A year after my first interview with Karl, whose case opens this book, we met for lunch. He was forty-six, and things were not better.

I didn't take notes. We were just sharing. My interviews for this book probe some intimate depths. They require a high degree of trust. In our first conversation, Karl had given me a window on feelings he had not been comfortable discussing even with his wife. After that, trust had blossomed into friendship. I was interested in his life, and he was interested in my book. I had filled him in on the happiness curve, and on the paradox of aging. I had shown him Hannes Schwandt's graph, the one explaining how, in midlife, years of cumulative disappointment about past years' life satisfaction combine with declining optimism about future life satisfaction to produce a nasty feedback loop. I had pointed out to Karl that he was at the bottom of the curve, statistically: a place where the undercurrent has fought contentment for years and seems as if it never will switch direction. I had also apprised him of the voluminous research showing that the undercurrent normally does switch, around the time you think it never will. I wondered whether any of this information about the happiness curve was helpful to someone grinding through a slump. Would knowledge provide reassurance or hope of a path forward? Or is it just abstract science on the printed page?

Not long after I showed him Hannes Schwandt's negative feedback loop, he emailed back: "Wow." He continued: "The *expectations gulf* = *despair/etc.* hypothesis makes sense in my case. My expectations for my marriage/career/etc. were not met by reality. Over the years, the disappointment piles up, and one eventually exclaims, 'I have failed. This is a dead end. What am I doing?'" Karl wrote of "illusions/dreams/imaginings not met, and the subsequent visceral response: denial, shocked/angry recognition of the reality, despair, and the fight-or-flight feeling. Does one bull one's way through, or does one run like hell from work, a relationship, one's home? Then there's the, 'Do I tell the spouse?' question.

"Time to feed the kiddos and make a martini. Alcohol is balm for anxiety, you know."

Well.

That did not sound good.

So we arranged to get together. Over Thai food, he reported that most days he still came home from work and felt trapped. He was still angry and disappointed with himself for feeling so disappointed, what with his manifold blessings. Learning about the happiness curve seemed to have somewhat placated the "rider," his thinking mind. But it did not seem to have calmed the elephant, which was still, as Karl had told me a year earlier, *confused, searching, scared*. Knowing that relief might be on the way in a few years was cold comfort.

Karl wonders: What can he do *now*?

Like a lot of people in their early sixties, Joshua Coleman has traversed the trough of the happiness curve and lived to tell about it. "Now that's kind of reversed," he said of the discontent he experienced in his forties. "I have a great deal of serenity about the things I don't like and have foregrounded the things I do." Coleman is unusually well positioned to share what he has learned: he is a practicing psychologist who works with individuals and families in San Francisco. In an average week, one or two of the patients he sees are experiencing some version of midlife trouble. By that, he means not midlife crisis, but rather the malaise I experienced myself in my forties, an accumulating drizzle of disappointment which can become self-sustaining but is quite unlike clinical depression or anxiety. Coleman said he doesn't think he has ever seen a midlife slump cause a full-fledged depression.

"It does seem that by the time people are in their forties, many people have achieved a lot of what they've hoped to achieve," he told me, "so there's this grand question of: *Now what? Is this it?* In the forties there seems to still be that great energy it takes to launch a career or family, but most of those things are in hand, so there's much bigger cause to compare yourself to other people. One of the things I see as a therapist is people constantly comparing their relationships and situations to other people. As they get into their sixties and seventies, they're much more accepting."

Recall, in this context, the hedonic treadmill. We expect success and accomplishment and status to bring satisfaction, but the goalposts keep receding, because our comparator group keeps moving up, and someone else will always have moved up faster. We do not feel ready or able to give up the competitive drive of youth, and we have yet to reap the rewards of the communitarian values of older age.

What to do, then? One answer is: *everything*. All the behaviors and attitudes that are good for you at all times of life are also good for you if you are caught in a midlife emotional trap. That is one reason why so much of the advice that comes up if you do an internet search on "midlife crisis" seems so anodyne. Here is something pretty typical, from the "midlife transition" page of Dr. Andrew Weil's website (DrWeil.com):

Explore and accept your feelings; allow yourself to reflect about your life on a regular basis; devote extra time to your partner or spouse to rekindle your relationship; set new goals; discover new hobbies; travel; volunteer; devote special time to your children; take care of your mental health—join a group or seek out a therapist if necessary. Exercise can help you take charge of your health and maintain the level of fitness necessary for an active, independent lifestyle.

All of DrWeil.com's advice is good, but it is generic, chicken-soupy stuff. Ditto the (also typical) advice on midlife career change at a website called AgCareers.com:

Identify your strengths and interests. Realize that work cannot make you a happy person. Create a financial plan for the lifestyle you want. Set realistic, achievable goals for your career. Tap and expand your professional networks. Be a lifelong learner for continued career success.

And so on. Summarizing the acres and acres of self-help literature for people navigating middle age is an Augean task, which I won't undertake here. Instead, I will narrow the focus. In conversations with Coleman and other psychologists, and in listening to the many people I interviewed, and also learning from my own period at the bottom of the happiness curve, I came across practices and advice that seem specifically applicable to the peculiar self-propelling dynamics of midlife slump. Though none is a panacea, all are based on solid science, all boast successful records, and all can help defeat the feedback cycle that works so hard to defeat us.

Normalize

That is therapeutic jargon for helping people see that their circumstances are not strange, alarming, or pathological. It is something psychologists say they focus on when counseling people for midlife dissatisfaction. "I do a lot of normalizing: helping them to see it's not a character flaw, that it's not evidence that they're inherently bad or inadequate," Joshua Coleman told me. "That there's a reason they're having their feelings that aren't evidence of a larger problem within them. That it's normal and expectable from a developmental perspective. And also that it's time-limited, given the research."

Think about Karl's use of the adjective *scared* to describe his forties' funk. He wonders, *Am I losing my mind?* Or Simon, whom we met in chapter 5, and who, in his mid-forties, has started to wonder if he will ever feel content, or if he even *can* feel content. "Maybe there's something deeply psychologically wrong with me," he frets. What Karl and Simon are feeling makes no sense to their rational selves, their "riders." So the rider puts a label on it: *abnormal.* But there is no pill, no medical quick fix, for this peculiar malaise— so maybe it is beyond help? At my own low point, I revised (downward) my opinion of myself. This ungrateful, dissatisfied, self-disparaging person: Was he the new *me*? Was this now my personality?

Psychologists say normalization works in several ways. Helping people understand, and internalize, that there is nothing unusual about midlife malaise can reduce the feelings of shame and isolation. Dan L. Jones, a psychologist and the director of the counseling center at East Tennessee State University, said he tries to emphasize that what people are going through is a transition rather than a crisis: a normal, albeit unpleasant, stage in adult development.

Besides de-pathologizing a midlife slump, normalizing it can help interrupt the negative feedback loop that gives midlife discontent its peculiar ability to amplify itself. People feel disappointed and discontented, but then, looking around and finding no adequate justification for their feelings, they feel disappointed and discontented *about* feeling disappointed and discontented. Negative feedback can take hold quite independently of objective life circumstances. In fact, the more successful you are objectively, the more disappointed you may be by your own failure to appreciate your success. One response is to try to be more appreciative: count your blessings, remind yourself of the good things in life, write thank-you letters. That is good advice, both because it can be therapeutic and because gratitude is a virtue. But, as we have seen, blessing counting can have self-defeating side effects: by reminding us of the privileged nature of our *objective* circumstances, it can make our *subjective* lack of gratitude seem all the more like a moral failing or emotional ailment. "People not uncommonly apologize to me that their complaints are 'first-world problems,' a perception or belief that only adds to their unhappiness," Coleman told me. In my case, the lift I got by counting my blessings also increased the bafflement and annoyance I felt about my inadequate gratitude. In Hannes Schwandt's jargon, counting my blessings raised my *satisfaction* curve temporarily, but any benefits I received were self-negating because I was also inadvertently raising my *expectation* curve.

Schwandt argues that the answer needs to include managing expectations directly, by making people more aware that optimistic forecasting errors are normal and therefore that disappointment is natural. In other words: *expect disappointment*. In fact, if in young adulthood you do *not* err on the optimistic side, you are probably depressed. When seen as a normal phenomenon, objectively unjustified malaise is not a character flaw, a pathology, or a dirty secret. It is a perfectly ordinary readjustment. You may be dissatisfied, but you don't need to be quite so dissatisfied about being dissatisfied!

"If they know that life satisfaction tends to be U-shaped in everyone and previous expectations don't match up with outcomes for most people, that could make people feel less unhappy about their life," Schwandt told me. Normalization, he believes, can have a double-whammy effect. "If you tell people there's a light at the end of the tunnel, this already helps you. And the second thing that helps you is maybe you can break the cycle of this vicious feedback effect. By knowing this is a normal developmental stage, you will also suffer less."

When my own fog of dissatisfaction began to lift, around the age of fifty, the change felt like something which was happening to me, not something which I was in charge of. I believe, though, that my discovery of the happiness curve during that time eased the process, by helping me normalize a slump which had previously seemed strange and culpable. This book, really, is an effort to share and spread the news that the happiness curve is normal, and in some ways beneficial—and that a frontal assault on it ("I'm NOT going to feel this way!") can be counterproductive.

So . . . count your blessings. But if counting your blessings leaves you feeling no less disappointed, there is nothing wrong with you. Gratitude is harder in the trough of the U, so cut yourself some slack.

Interrupt the Internal Critics

In my forties, as I have mentioned, I was beset by inner voices assuring me that I was wasting my life, accomplishing too little, falling behind my peers. That was nothing unusual. "One of the biggest causes of suffering is social comparison," Coleman said. "Status anxiety is a huge component of this kind of self-torture. Have I achieved enough? Am I a failure? Am I a success?" As we have seen, the race for ever more status, however genetically predetermined it may be, is self-defeating where happiness is concerned. That is the reason for the advice given by the economist Richard Layard which I quoted in chapter 2 and which bears repeating: "One secret of happiness is to ignore comparisons with people who are more successful than you are: always compare downwards, not upwards."

Easier said than done. We are wired, especially in the earlier part of life, to want more, more, more, and to look up, up, up. In youth, upward comparison gives us ambition as we make exciting plans and optimism as we imagine our future attainments and satisfaction. Two decades later, of course, our youthful ambition and optimism turn against us as we keep looking upward on the achievement ladder but realize we are running out of time to get there. In my case, what was especially disconcerting was that my compulsion for upward comparison sometimes ran amok, unmoored from my own values. I would feel envious of successful TV journalists or novelists, even though I never particularly wanted to do TV or write a novel.

Before my own penchant for compulsive self-criticism faded as I moved into my fifties, I learned I could obtain some relief by using a simple but surprisingly effective form of cognitive therapy. (Cognitive therapy teaches people to identify and disrupt immiserating and self-defeating thought patterns, and to replace them with more accurate and constructive ways of thinking.) Whenever I felt a social comparison coming on, I would jump in consciously and interrupt it, changing the mental subject to something constructive. After a while, I developed a two-word mantra for semi-automatic self-interruption: *No comparison!* ("Brent is so much more—NO COMPARISON!"; "I'm wasting my life because I should—NO COMPARISON!") Shouting "NO COMPARISON!" at myself was not a perfect stratagem, but it had the dual benefit of disrupting negative thought spirals and helping me feel that my rational side could exert some control.

For me, and I suspect for many others, the most insidious kind of upward comparison was comparison to myself, or rather to an idealized, out-of-reach version of myself. Why don't I ever do as much work as I should? Why isn't my latest article as good as the one I wrote a few months ago? Why didn't I say the right thing to my husband yesterday? We all err and fall short in all kinds of ways every day, and so I never lack grounds for self-criticism, and of course self-criticism is healthy, up to a point. In my forties, however, self-criticism took on a life of its own. Here, too, I eventually found a home-brew cognitive treatment: Throughout the day, when the internal critics started carping, I interjected the reminder, "I don't have to be perfect today." Just pulling myself up short and making that obvious statement to myself, when my mind began drifting to yet another checklist of all the things that were wrong with me or my life, helped interrupt and defang the relentless inner critics.

The self-interruptions I developed were effective for me because they were easy to use semiautomatically, and not because the phrases themselves possessed any inherently therapeutic power. My cognitive interventions may not work for you; you will want to experiment and discover your own. The larger point is that you might be surprised by how well cognitive interventions can work. Getting better control over the inner conversation is far from the whole battle, but it helps.

Stay Present

The trough of the happiness curve is a time trap. Life satisfaction in years past has not met expectations; life satisfaction in years to come seems likely only to decline. Disappointment about the past and pessimism about the future squeeze out fulfillment in the present.

Mindfulness—or *mindful presence*—refers to mentally occupying the present moment without judgment, instead of, for example, constantly letting our thoughts anticipate the future or reassess the past. *Be Here Now,* the title of a 1971 bestseller by Ram Dass, encapsulates the concept. Meditation, an ancient and widely practiced route to mindful presence, seeks to contain wandering thoughts and hush jabbering interior voices by fixing attention on something concrete and immediate like breathing; it has undergone extensive scientific scrutiny in recent decades, and it has emerged with flying colors. There is ample scientific evidence that meditation reduces anxiety and increases positive feelings. Corporations and even armed forces are adopting it. "The goal of meditation is to change automatic thought processes, thereby taming the elephant," writes the psychologist Jonathan Haidt. "Meditation done every day for several months can help you reduce substantially the frequency of fearful, negative, and grasping thoughts, thereby improving your affective style." Yoga, tai chi, and other present-minded disciplines can have the same effects. So, for that matter, can ordinary exercise.

During my lowest period, I didn't try meditation or yoga. I did use exercise and sessions listening to music in a darkened room. By trial and error, I also discovered another home-brew form of cognitive behavioral therapy. When my mind drifted away from the present to obsess about the past or future, I would try to intercept the drift and change the subject to the here and now. For example, I would listen to the breathing of my husband next to me in bed. In my interviews, some people dealing with midlife slumps report using meditation, apps, and mental exercises that build mindful presence. They, too, seem to get mildly but usefully helpful results.

Mindfulness, according to Coleman, can help quiet down the amygdala, a source within the brain of fear and anxiety. It can help us accept and manage difficult feelings and insoluble situations. "We can't always think our way through those," he told me. "A lot of the time we just have to develop serenity and acceptance and tolerance." And mindful presence can reduce the tendency to dwell on whatever dissatisfaction we may feel, interrupting and shushing negative feedback. So . . . *be here now.*

Share

Going it alone in times of hardship is never a good idea for *Homo sapiens,* hypersocial species that we are. We know instinctively to reach for support when hit with an external shock like a cancer diagnosis or unemployment, even if we prefer to share only with our nearest and dearest. The most insidious feature of a midlife feedback trap is that it turns our instinct for sociability against us. Our unhappiness is not justified by our objective circumstances; therefore it shows a character defect; therefore we are ashamed of our unhappiness; therefore we hide it. "People feel if they're not achieving all they could, they're inherently flawed," said Coleman. "Shame in general causes people to withdraw and shut down."

Moreover, dissatisfaction with status plays an important part in happiness-curve dynamics, and there is no better way, in modern life, to diminish one's status than to seem vulnerable or failing. For those coping with midlife dissatisfaction, Coleman said, "Exposing it to others means diminishing status by definition. The price of admission of what would be therapeutic or healing would be crossing a threshold which would increase status anxiety."

Karl, recall, had not discussed his malaise with his wife, for fear of triggering a "shitstorm." He had discussed it with only one friend. (Two, counting me.) Another mid-forties interviewee, Sterling, told his wife of his malaise, but after she hit the panic button he stopped sharing. "It's not something people generally talk about," he told me. "It's not something I'd go to my best friend with." When I asked Anthony, from chapter 5, how many people he had reached out to, he said, "Well, I think maybe zero." He guessed that his wife might know, but they had not discussed it. David, in chapter 7, was leading a start-up when he was at the bottom of his happiness curve, and he thought he couldn't afford to seem unsteady or despondent. Psychologists say women are more willing than men to seem vulnerable and to share their midlife complaints, but, if so, the gap may close as more women join the status race once reserved for men.

As we have seen, being caught in the trough is no small problem, and avoiding self-isolation, although no emotional panacea, can go a long way toward providing stability and preventing mistakes. Outreach can take the form of professional counseling or therapy, which you need not be sick or dysfunctional to do. "Going to counseling is like taking a class on yourself," Dan Jones, the East Tennessee State University psychologist, told me. "You're hiring a consultant on yourself. It makes people feel more self-aware. People feel listened to." But plain old friendship—social connectedness, in other words—has some of the same benefits.

Terry, forty-three, thinks talking to friends saved his marriage and may have held his life together. "When I hit forty and I had my second son, it dawned on me that the days of being a cool guy are pretty much over," he said. "I'm forty, I have two kids, I've got responsibility at work. Any footlooseness and fancy-freeness is gone. My life is changing diapers and being a dad. I love it, but it's just a total shift of identity for me, and an abrupt shift. I had some existential angst as a result. I didn't buy a convertible, but I started shopping a lot. I started buying clothes. Not extravagant, but everyone who knows me jokes about it. My external life has been steady, but my inner life was a real struggle, and in some ways continues to be, though it's lessened. Inside I was just thinking, *Man, is this what my long-term future looks like?*"

He started going to church with his wife, and there became friendly with, as he puts it, a bunch of guys. "In the past, I'd always say it's impossible for me to be friends with a guy who doesn't like sports; I'd have nothing to talk to him about. That has now proven to be false. I have intimate male friendships. A lot of these guys are in similar life phases."

The effect on his life satisfaction? "It's really huge. If it were just me and my wife trying to deal with this by myself, I don't think I'd be able to do it." His friends relieve his isolation, but even more important for Terry is that they invest in his wellbeing and hold him accountable, as he does for them. "I know I'm capable of doing something rash. I worry about that. I'm capable of crashing my marriage. The fact that I have these people whom I'm emotionally and spiritually accountable to really helps prevent that. I tell them what's going on in my life, and they tell me, and I feel like if I did something like that, I'd have to tell them. I don't want to have to show up and say, 'Yeah, I've had a fight with my wife and slept at the Holiday Inn.'"

In isolation, disappointment and discontent ferment and fester, which leads to shame, which feeds the urge for isolation. Breaking that cycle is job one. If you can, call a friend.

Step, Don't Leap

If the trough of the happiness curve feels like a trap, that is because it *is* a trap. Like one of those straw-tube puzzles that tighten when you try to pull your fingers out, it uses our own instincts against us. By pestering us with negative feedback and hedonic adaptation and those other perverse imps that block contentment, the happiness curve turns our objective accomplishments into subjective disappointments; by ratcheting down optimism, it converts our past hopes into gloom about the future; by subverting gratitude, it transmutes the blessings we count into sources of shame; by shaming and baffling us, it prompts us to hide when we most need to share.

Thus trapped, we react, naturally enough, with an impulse to flee: *Get me out of here!* Boiling up unbidden come fantasies of escape, schemes to bolt job or family, yearnings to occupy a whole different life. When I felt the urge to quit my job—*now! today!*—I knew, as I think most people feeling such urges know, that the flight instinct was not rational. But knowing it was irrational did not suppress it. I would earnestly tell my elephant that I had a good situation, that I was meeting my goals, and that it made no sense to walk into my boss's office and quit without a plan. The elephant's response: *get me out of here!*

Complicating the situation for me, and for many other people in a feedback trap, was that I really *was* getting stale professionally. At that point in my forties, I had made a deliberate choice to put money in the bank, even at some cost to personal growth. My profession, journalism, was undergoing upheavals which were tossing many midcareer journalists out in the cold—upheavals which I thought might reach me, as indeed eventually they did. My "rider" had worked through the options and decided that staying put and building reserves made sense. Looking back, I'm glad I didn't make a precipitous or impulsive move. By the time my job collapsed, I had figured out an idea for a start-up, and my bank account was flush enough to provide a safety net.

All of that, however, is clear only in hindsight. In real time, the price of standing pat through my forties was a seemingly interminable stretch of ennui and restlessness. Even had I known then everything I know now about the happiness curve, I still would have had no clear way to distinguish between change I needed to embrace and change I needed to shun. After all, sometimes we *should* change things up in midlife, even if change does *not* relieve restlessness or ennui. Karl had switched jobs in his early forties. The bad news was that his discontent followed him to the new job. But the good news was that his new job was better. He learned that the problem was in himself, not in his job; but he is still glad to have made the jump. By the same token, some people who leave marriages fail to fill an existential hole in their lives, but nonetheless do find a better match.

Another way to state this conundrum is to refer back to the happiness equation from chapter 4 . . .

$$H = S + C + V + T$$

. . . where H is your enduring level of happiness, S is your emotional set point, C stands for the circumstances of your life, V stands for factors under your voluntary control, and T stands for time's influence on life satisfaction. I wish the dissatisfaction I felt in my forties had come in a box plainly marked C or V or T. If C, I would have known to make a change in my life circumstances, for instance by changing jobs. If V, I would have known to work on my attitude or develop a hobby. If T, on the other hand, I would have known to prioritize patience and err on the side of caution. Unfortunately, in real life I had no way to know just how much of each element was in play.

Humans are not very good at understanding what makes them happy and what doesn't, even on a good day. In the midst of a multiyear funk, they are even more likely to misattribute the source of their troubles. How then, to distinguish signal from noise, and reaction from overreaction? Counseling can be particularly helpful here, because it provides a systematic way to disentangle confusions and sort through options, with the guidance of someone who knows where the common pitfalls are. Of course, people who experience something more like a fog than a hurricane, a persistent malaise rather than a full-on crisis, are less likely to seek professional help. That describes the majority of people in the trough of the U—which, remember, is a decrease but not a collapse in life satisfaction, and not usually an emergency. For noncritical cases, the best advice I have seen, and something of a consensus among professionals, is: *change is good, but keep it real.*

The *Get me out of here!* temptation is to throw everything away. The reality, however, is that change is less disruptive and more successful if we build on our accumulated skills, experience, and connections, taking them in new directions rather than starting over. Carlo Strenger and Arie Ruttenberg call midlife change an "existential necessity" for people with business careers, but they deplore what they call the myth of magical transformation. Writing in the *Harvard Business Review* in 2008, Strenger, a psychologist at Tel Aviv University, and Ruttenberg, the founder of a company that markets services to people in midlife, argue that the notion that we can become or do anything, if only we try hard enough, is self-defeating.

> We have seen hundreds of people come back from uplifting talks and intensive workshops believing that their lives were about to change forever. But the pattern is always the same: the magic lasts for several days, and within a couple of weeks the overwhelming majority of participants no longer understand why they thought the pep talks they heard would transform them. Subsequently, they feel confused—they don't quite know in which direction they would like to evolve, so they abandon their efforts to change. Paradoxically, therefore, the very doctrine that aims to encourage change in people serves to stifle it.

Instead, move laterally, incrementally, constructively, logically. That reduces the odds of impulsive mistakes and helps keep the downside manageable, making attribution errors less costly. Also, it works. Recall, as the psychologist Jonathan Haidt points out in chapter 5, how our inner incentive system rewards us with immediate but short-lived spurts of satisfaction for making progress *toward* a goal, whereas actual arrival delivers fleeting pleasure but soon becomes the new baseline. We may *feel* we need a great leap forward, but smaller steps toward attainable goals are not only more achievable but usually more satisfying. "Change doesn't have to be major to accomplish the goal of making you feel better," writes the psychologist Susan Krauss Whitbourne. "It might be a matter of altering your routine in some small way that gives you a different vantage point on the world. It may take longer, but even small adjustments can grow into truly innovative changes if you adopt the agile mind-set."

The point is not to avoid ever making a dramatic change or taking a big risk while navigating the bend in the curve. Rather, the point is that changes you make and risks you take should be *integrative,* not disruptive. Life adjustments should be respectful of your accumulated experience and your prior choices; they should be realistic about your values and obligations and opportunities. That said, integrative change can be big—very big.

I interviewed a fifty-five-year-old teacher named Barb whose midlife self-disruption provides a good example. In my survey, she described her fifties as *exciting, full, entertaining,* and rated her life satisfaction at nine, near the top of the Cantril scale—versus only a four for her forties, for which her descriptors were *struggle, stressful.* I rarely see turnarounds of that magnitude, so I tracked her down for an interview—via Skype to India, where she lives and works.

Barb was raised by a conservative family in Texas and never felt she fit in well. She used a lot of drugs and alcohol in her teens. In her twenties she met her husband and entered what turned out to be a successful marriage, but she struggled to figure out who she was. Her thirties brought children and a settled life teaching special education in an elementary school. Stability suited her. "I felt we had a good thing going." But the next decade brought turbulence. The kids, older, didn't need her as much. A move to an

Eastern state was hard: "I cried for two months." Teaching math, in middle school and then high school, had its rewards, and she felt intensely loyal to her students, but her background in special education brought her a lot of troubled kids to teach, and the relentless stress frazzled her. "It was really hard or really wonderful. There was hardly anything in between. It wasn't sustainable, but there wasn't anything else I was interested in doing. I felt really trapped. And my husband was not enjoying his job, either." Gradually, the aridity of their work lives desiccated their relationship. "Our marriage was never on the rocks, but it was hard to find the positive."

That was the state of things when they decided to move overseas. By then, Barb was fifty-one, and they had been toying with the idea of living abroad for a few years. When friends moved to Cairo, Barb went to visit and felt energized. That triggered the decision to begin a relaunch in earnest. "I had basically told my husband, 'We cannot go on with this. We have only so many working years left, and we can't spend them being miserable.'" Online, Barb found an international school in Cairo that needed a special education teacher with strength in math. "We did Skype interviews and the people at the school there were just great. You could tell it was going to be a good institution." Their kids were in their twenties. Her husband was retired. They felt ready.

How did the move go? "We loved it." Barb and her husband reveled in Egypt's rich history and culture. She learned some Arabic, made local friends, camped in the desert with a bedouin guide. Her husband got involved with the local schools. Then, when Barb's principal moved to a school in Chennai, Barb and her husband followed her. When I Skyped with her there, she described Chennai as amazing, a place where the people are gentle and the school absorbing.

Barb had once assumed she would live abroad for a few years and then return to the United States. "When we first did this, it was a given that at some point we'd go back to the States and I'd live out my old age there. But I don't know. I don't think I'll do that. I feel much more at home here than

I do when I'm at home." To the person who feels stuck at fortysomething, she had this to say: "Life is really short. You don't have to stay doing something that makes you miserable. But you have to be willing to take risks."

For the fortysomethings like Karl who yearn for freedom or escape, Barb's story may sound like an advertisement for bolting. Notice, though, that as dramatic as her story may be, the underlying theme is continuity. Barb found a professional berth that exploited her existing skills and experience, and she vetted it carefully. She didn't move to Cairo until the kids were independent and her husband was eligible for Social Security. With his pension, they knew they could get by on one job if necessary. They made sure they both felt ready and were on the same page. In her move to Chennai, Barb changed countries but kept her boss, maintaining an anchor relationship. Hers is a story of change, yes, but of change that was logically conceived, carefully timed, and methodically executed. It was integrative. Not disruptive.

My own self-disruption, the effort to launch a start-up in my early fifties, failed as a business proposition. But it did give me change and challenge, and it was a far cry from the impetuous flight I had imagined in my forties. My business plan exploited my experience and connections in journalism; I had enough severance pay and savings to make the gamble affordable; and I took care to preserve my relationships and options. I cannot claim the kind of professional and emotional home run that Barb scored. But I got my at-bat without ejecting myself from the game.

Wait

It gets better. This is the most important wisdom of all. And the hardest to use.

Lots of stratagems can help people who are languishing at the bottom of the U. Yet, at the end of the day, the currents we battle there run strong and deep, and, in real life, the countermeasures at our disposal can alleviate the dissatisfaction, but are unlikely to eliminate it. I am not even sure eliminating it is a good idea. Remember: the happiness curve, however unpleasant at its nadir, seems to be part of a healthy and important personal (and social) transition. If we could drink a potion and make it go away, we might find ourselves much the poorer later on in life. Perhaps, as Frost said, the best way out *is* through. For most people, a midlife slump is bothersome but not traumatic—especially if you are aware that it is common, it ends, and it is not catastrophic. Most people *can* wait, if they need to. For most, waiting will pay dividends.

In today's world of just-in-time everything, suggesting to people that patience and gradualism and soldiering on can help solve a pressing problem seems counterintuitive, if not countercultural. We prefer to think of time as our servant, something we use and fill, rather than as our master, shaping us in ways we may not control or even understand. So *wait* is difficult advice to take. Perhaps it helps to bear in mind that, in the context of the happiness curve and its peculiar feedback traps, waiting is not a passive strategy. It's not doing nothing. Waiting is a way of working with time and letting time work for us. Patience is not the whole answer for almost anyone, but it is a part of the answer for almost everyone. In the end, waiting was most of what I did in my forties. Of all the measures I used, it proved the most effective.

Thomas Cole's middle-aged Voyager, recall, is bereft of his tiller, bereft of oars. Reassurance, in the person of his guardian angel, hovers out of sight, even as the implacable hourglass remains ever in view. His hands clasped in fearful supplication, the Voyager looks to heaven for protection, placing his fate in the care of a higher power. To Cole, that higher power was God, yet the artist's imagery has a secular interpretation, too. In the Voyage of Life, you are a plaything of forces larger than yourself, borne upon a stream you cannot control. So *relinquish* control. Trust the river. Trust time.

And here is the thing about patience. It is easier to achieve—much easier—if you are not waiting alone.

HELPING EACH OTHER

Bringing midlife out of the closet

Self-help is valuable. Self-help is important. But none of what I just suggested is enough. Do everything right, and throw in exercise, diet, vitamins, and chicken soup. It still is not enough.

The more I researched this book, the more I came to see self-help, however necessary, as incomplete, and in some ways as missing the point. The larger, yet largely neglected, portion of the answer lies outside ourselves. My friend Karl and so many others like him are being asked to do too much on their own. They need social channels and a U-friendly environment. They need institutions and public norms that ease the way, instead of institutions that ignore the happiness curve and public norms that mock it. They need a story about what they are experiencing which assumes they are normal, not broken. Karl needs help from ashore.

So does Gary. It was he who first drew my attention to the happiness-curve closet.

Gary, like Karl, is a professional acquaintance who became a personal friend. Back when I first started thinking about the happiness curve and how to write about it, he was one of the people I brainstormed with. In his early fifties, when I interviewed him, he rated his life satisfaction only six, up from a bottom-scraping five a few years before.

"Whom," I asked, "do you discuss your discontent with?"

"I keep it contained within myself. I don't share it with many of my friends." He thinks of himself as a successful person, a strong person. "You like being in the success bubble and you don't want to share vulnerability and what feels like weakness," he said. Besides, he doesn't want to whine. "Even with my issues, I'm aware of the fact that I'm more successful and more comfortable than many of my friends. Complaining feels like what my kids call first-world problems."

I asked if he confides in his wife. "Yes, a little bit. Less so on the professional things. She's less professionally satisfied than I am."

Also, like so many others, he felt the standard templates—midlife crisis or depression—didn't fit. His brother-in-law had a classic midlife crisis, divorcing his wife, taking up with a younger woman, buying a motorcycle. "I guess I associate midlife crisis with a kind of acting out. Maybe I would have had more fun if I'd acted out, but I didn't." Medical treatment and depression also have not felt right. "I didn't feel I was clinically depressed or anything like that."

Everything I heard that day from Gary would, it turned out, be echoed in other interviews: the malaise and bafflement and shame, the silence, the belief that standard labels don't fit. Gary also said something that grew in significance as I learned more. "I wished I'd had in my life an older, wiser mentor type," he said. "Wouldn't it be great to have a safe space, and someone I could turn to and talk this through with?"

Safe space. A place for vulnerability. A place without secrecy and shame. And a *guide*. Those were what Gary needed, and what he could not give himself.

Gary was blocked by the two reigning social models for midlife discontent. One is medicalization. You need a doctor. Go get a prescription.

Take an antidepressant. Of course, mental illness is stigmatized, and so even people who are acutely depressed may resist appropriate treatment. But, recall, the bottom of the happiness curve is long but shallow. Most people do not experience acute depression. They experience chronic dissatisfaction, which is very different. Their values and their lives are in tension, and their achievement and fulfillment are out of sync, neither of which is a medical problem. They are therefore right to balk at the medical model. Gary, when I spoke to him, was successful at work, successful as a father and husband. The problem was not that he was failing or flailing or functioning poorly. Rather, he couldn't give himself emotional credit for *not* failing or flailing or functioning poorly. That's the feedback trap. Some people may need a pill to deal with it, but most need to feel normal and supported and not like disappointments to themselves and others.

Mockery, the other social model for what Gary is going through, is much worse than medicalization. Through no fault of its own, midlife crisis is the butt of a million jokes, as you can confirm online in a few seconds by doing an image search on *midlife crisis*. What comes up? Photo after photo of middle-aged men and red sports cars. Always sports cars, almost always red, frequently convertibles. A typical image shows a balding man in a red convertible speeding along a highway; below, the caption reads, "Is It Time for Your Midlife Crisis Yet?" Another shows a similar photo over the caption: "Midlife Crisis: Because Hot Young Ladies Love Fast Cars and Liver Spots!" A sports car guide calls itself "Midlife Crisis Cars." When I wrote about the happiness curve for *The Atlantic* magazine, the cover image showed, you guessed it, a sullen man in a red sports car. Though presumably not intended to be cruel, the sports-car meme has become the standard symbol of the materialism and self-indulgence and acting out that supposedly characterize middle-age discontent.

Also figuring prominently in midlife-crisis iconography are images of middle-aged men riding motorcycles. And images of middle-aged men surrounded by young women. And images of middle-aged men posing atop motorcycles while surrounded by young women. Those are the comparatively subtle images. Some turn the ridicule up to eleven, like the one showing a balding man holding a pistol to the head of stuffed bunny toy over the caption, "Midlife Crisis Begins with Baldness and Ends with Taking Your Common Sense." Women are not exempt, though their representation in the iconography is much skimpier. One cartoon image centers on a woman making a version of the frightened face in Edvard Munch's painting *The Scream,* amid sketches of the same woman being unable to cram herself into her clothes and looking with shock into a mirror. The horror! Sifting through midlife-crisis books, I came across one that helpfully includes a "bonus section" of midlife jokes. You'll need them, if you plan to discuss the subject.

No one wants to be a punch line or a cliché. No one wants to set off alarm bells about being on the edge of a second adolescence or a mental breakdown. So talking is risky. Gary tried. "It's a mixed bag," he said, when I asked how he had fared. "I've opened up to some people, and that has been very good. I've opened up to other people and they gossiped about it, and that felt way worse than the good of the good. The downside is much worse than the upside."

Few of us are deliberately cruel about malaise in midlife. It's just that we lack a box to put the problem in other than medicalization and mockery. As it happens, gay people in America once faced a version of this problem. Being open about homosexuality was apt to get you ridiculed and stereotyped, categorized as antisocial or psychologically ill, or all of the above. No, I am not suggesting that people like Gary face anything as severe as the discrimination and bigotry which gay and lesbian people once faced (and sometimes still do). Only that, in a couple of notable ways, the cases share a family resemblance. Lacking a social narrative in which homosexuality could be normal, gay people often internalized the story that there was something wrong with how they felt. Self-denigration fed shame and stress, which led to isolation, compounding the shame and stress: a negative feedback loop that became known, in the gay argot, as the closet. The fault lay not with gay people. It lay with society's misconceptions about what was going on.

What happens when society misunderstands entire age groups and shoehorns them into the wrong box? And how does that get fixed? American history provides an interesting example.

Imagine a world without adolescence. Not, that is, without teenagers. A world, rather, without the *concept* of adolescence. In that world, when young people pass through puberty and reach physical adulthood, society would assume they're ready for the workforce—and off to work they would go, instead of attending high school and sometimes college. Their competencies and social skills would be rudimentary, and they would bring the emotional resources of teenagers to the workplace, but usually their competence and maturity would be sufficient for the agricultural and artisanal duties they were expected to perform. They would marry young, too, and have children young.

As peculiar as that world seems, it was America about 150 years ago. The ancients, having had eyes in their heads, understood that the transition between the prepubescent years of childhood and full maturity was often turbulent. The ancient Greek historian Herodotus told of a Sumerian father who, around 1700 BC, deplored his son's insolent and indifferent behavior. Aristotle distinguished young manhood (puberty to about age twenty-one) from two earlier stages, infancy (until about age seven) and boyhood (seven until puberty), a formulation which matches pretty well with our own. Until recently, however, society had little need for the concept of a distinct stage of development between childhood and adulthood. School was for children, and then postpubescent teenagers entered the adult world. In Mark Twain's *Adventures of Huckleberry Finn,* no one seems dumbfounded to encounter a boy of thirteen or fourteen making his own way in the world, whereas today any such boy would be immediately handed over to Child Protective Services.

In the latter half of the nineteenth century, a combination of urbanization, industrialization, and compulsory mass education transformed the template for youth. As specialization and technology increased the workplace's need for skills and maturity, society responded by banning child labor, requiring school attendance, and keeping young people in school longer. High schools sprouted, and with them the expectation that teens belonged in the classroom, not the factory. Cities sprouted, too. In the pre–Industrial Age, teenagers had lived on farms and in small towns, with few other teens close by. Urbanization, however, created dense clusters of teens living cheek by jowl, attending schools together, and socializing together. As "teenager" became a group identity, a distinctive teen ethos and identity emerged; youth culture, as it became known, was born.

In 1904, the establishment of adolescence as a social category took a decisive turn. G. Stanley Hall, the first person in the United States to receive a professional degree in psychology, published an influential two-volume work titled, naturally, *Adolescence*. Hall posited that adolescence is a psychologically distinct time of conflicting and often extreme emotions. More important than the details of his theory is that he popularized a special term for what had until then been just an age. After Hall, the word "adolescence," almost unknown before 1900, entered the popular lexicon, where it remains. The concept of adolescence, today, is so firmly rooted that we can barely imagine life without it.

In a world where adolescence is an accepted fact, teens, instead of being hurled into adulthood, are enfolded in all kinds of institutions and norms that guide them through the transition from childhood to full maturity. High schools, colleges, community colleges; internships, summer jobs, apprenticeships, the military; counseling, helplines, specialist psychologists; a separate juvenile justice system. Still more important, we have a developmental narrative for adolescence: a story in which the challenges and difficulties of the teenage years are part of a normal transition. Although some teenagers may need medical attention for emotional problems, the vast majority need mentoring, a supportive environment, and preformed social pathways, like schools and jobs and dating, which guide them through challenges. Generally, we encourage teens to reach out if they feel confusion or emotional turmoil, and, if they do reach out, most of us have the good sense not to mock them.

Like adolescence, midlife reboot is an ordinary and predictable developmental pathway. Like adolescence, it is perfectly normal, and not at all pathological. Like adolescence, it is a period which some people breeze through, but which gives some people a lot of trouble. Like adolescence, it is something which many people would benefit from getting help with, even if they could manage to fight through it on their own. Like adolescence, it can be aggravated by isolation, confusion, and self-defeating thought patterns. Like adolescence, it is a risky and stressful period and can lead to crisis (especially if handled inappropriately), but it is not, in and of itself, a crisis. Rather, like adolescence, it is a transition, and, for those who have problems with it, it generally leads to a happier, more stable stage of life.

In short, although adolescence and the trough of the happiness curve are not at all the same biologically, emotionally, or socially, they are alike in that they are challenging and distinctive transitions which are commonplace, predictable, and nonpathological. But one of them has a supportive social environment, whereas the other has . . . red sports cars.

In chapter 4, I discussed how *time* is an absolute concept, whereas *aging* is a relative concept. Where we are on the happiness curve is determined to some extent by both. The clock and biology have a lot to say about our physical and mental condition, but society and culture have a lot to say about our expectations and emotions at any given age. Sometimes, time and aging can get out of sync. The situation of teenagers in the nineteenth century was an example. The problem got fixed when society added a box called *adolescence*. As it happens, another time-age asynchrony is happening right now. Fortunately, some smart people—such as Marc Freedman—are inventing a new box.

"I think what we're seeing," Freedman told me, when I interviewed him one summer day, "right in front of our nose, is the emergence of a new period of life."

Freedman is in his late fifties and lives and works in San Francisco. He is the founder and CEO of a nonprofit called Encore.org, which he describes as being in the "applied Laura Carstensen" business. He sees his job as developing and demonstrating ways to bring society's outdated model of aging into closer harmony with the modern reality. After growing up in Philadelphia, attending Swarthmore College, managing a modern-dance troupe, and receiving an MBA degree from Yale, he got interested in education and the power of mentoring. That led him to notice how much better kids do with older mentors in their lives, which got him interested in finding mentoring roles for older people, which led him to start Experience Corps, a nonprofit that organizes teams of people over age fifty-five to help inner-city schoolkids learn to read. That, finally, got him thinking about society's conventional model of aging, and how, within his own lifetime, it had been dramatically reinvented.

For many years, the model had basically two stages: education in childhood, then work in adulthood (which began young). If people became too old or disabled to work, there wasn't much for them to do, and they were likely to be poor, and they were unlikely to live long. When Social Security got started in the 1930s, few people were expected to survive to collect any benefits. But the longevity revolution unfolded much faster than anyone expected, and by the 1950s millions of people found themselves fitting into a new social box, called *retirement*. Retirement was mainly about not working, which seemed a lot like doing nothing. "There was a purpose gap that had opened up," Freedman said.

To create a story for the healthy elderly that seemed more appealing than, say, being put out to pasture, society came up with a new box, which Freedman has called the Golden Years. Digging a bit, he found that the Golden Years box dates to as recently as 1960, when an Arizona developer named Del Webb debuted Sun City, a so-called retirement community on the outskirts of Phoenix. The idea which Webb and, soon, many other marketers promoted was that retirement should be a long holiday, a time whose purpose is play and leisure. Underscoring the point, one of Webb's competitors was a chain of retirement communities called Leisure World. According to Freedman, "Older people were so rejected socially that the idea arose of building a community where everyone was old and so no one was old, and you could play shuffleboard and not be bothered by the presence of actual young people." So popular was the Golden Years idea that, when Sun City displayed its first six model homes, traffic backed up for miles to see them.

Lives continued to lengthen, however. Health and vitality in late adulthood continued to improve. Today, as we've seen, the sixth and seventh decades of life are no longer a short or infirm prelude to death; they are a time when most people are cognitively sharp and experientially skilled. They often are a time when people look for ways to give back to family and community and society.

Meanwhile, thirty-year careers and midlife stability are growing harder to come by. Between 2008 and 2013, one out of four Americans in their fifties lost a job (so did one in five people aged sixty to sixty-four). Many people are forced by economic need to relaunch or rebuild careers in midlife. Many others *choose* to relaunch, seeking renewed purpose or a more rewarding way of life. "Everything that used to seem rote, like moving in lockstep from high school or college into a job or industry that you would stay in for the rest of your life—that's all upended now," Phyllis Moen, a prominent sociologist at the University of Minnesota, told me. "Retirement is up-ended. Old age has been pushed back. You may have chronic problems, but you don't feel old. It opens everything up. It's like a second chance."

This new second-chance period does not yet have a name. It has been variously dubbed (in alphabetical order) *act IV, adulthood II, midcourse, middlescence, second adulthood, third age, third chapter,* and *young old.* If anyone deserves naming rights, it is probably Moen, who calls the new phase *encore adulthood,* in an important 2016 book of that name.

"Whatever the label ends up being," said Freedman, "they're all describing basically the same thing, which is a period of life that doesn't fit existing categories, a new stage of life between midlife and old age—and a population explosion of people flooding into it, yet an inability to exploit its possibilities."

Freedman cites Encore.org's survey research suggesting that something like 9 percent of Americans between fifty and seventy have already begun what he calls an encore career: a relaunch combining, as Freedman likes to put it, passion, a purpose, and often (though not always) a paycheck. As people in middle age and beyond seek more meaningful, socially positive missions, some, to be sure, turn to volunteer work, but many take commercial risks and enter new phases of their professional careers. Contrary to stereotype, people in late adulthood are avid entrepreneurs: figures compiled by the Ewing Marion Kauffman Foundation show that, in more than half of the years from 1996 to 2015, the rate of new entrepreneurship of people aged fifty-five to sixty-four matched or exceeded the rate of younger age brackets. (People aged forty-five to fifty-four were not far behind.) If Encore.org's survey is anything to judge by, something like 20 million Americans between fifty to seventy want to start an encore career. "That's two hundred and fifty million years of human and social capital that could be applied to areas like education, health, the elderly," Freedman remarked.

Baby boomers represent a human bow wave of social change. More than a third of Americans are fifty or older. Fewer and fewer of them stop working irreversibly; more and more dip in and out of the workforce, replacing the cliché of retirement on the golf course with customized hybrids of jobs, volunteering, caregiving, school, and leisure. "Retired but currently working"— not long ago an oxymoron—has already become the self-description of more than half of Americans age sixty-five to seventy-four who are in the workforce, and of a sixth of workers aged fifty-seven to sixty-four.

On the printed page, the idea of second acts and fresh starts in midlife sounds pretty glorious—but not so fast. In real life, nothing is harder than jumping out of the deep grooves we have carved for ourselves by our forties. What do I really want? Who wants me? How can I reinvent my life while meeting responsibilities and making ends meet? What are the options, and how can I sort through them all? What is achievable, and what is a daydream? What is the fallback if I fail? Those questions and many more clobber anyone who contemplates a relaunch. Relaunchers need guardrails to change course safely. They need institutions and programs and examples that provide support and structure. They need employers who will accommodate and hire mature workers who may want to work part-time, undertake not-so-big jobs, and apply old skills to new ventures. They need universities and financial aid geared to retooling in midlife; pensions and 401(k) plans flexible enough to cope with the "retired but working"; career counseling and job fairs and internships and gap years for graybeards in search of new missions and opportunities. They need society's permission to experiment and grow and err: permission which teens and twenty-somethings take for granted, but which adults in maturity often need just as much. And, of course, if they take a gap year or internship at age fifty-five, they need to be understood as doing something appropriate and natural, not as disrupting their lives or chasing their lost youth.

"So," I asked Marc Freedman, "how much social and cultural infrastructure exists right now for midlife repurposing?"

"None," came the blunt reply. "It's a do-it-yourself project." In his 2011 book *The Big Shift: Navigating the New Stage Beyond Midlife,* Freedman suggests that we talk about a midlife *chasm* instead of a midlife *crisis*: a gap between the substantial support people need in middle age and the meager support society gives them. "The intervening space is not just wide," Freedman writes, "it's confusing and chaotic, a mismatched mess of mixed signals, outdated norms, anachronistic institutions, and multiple misperceptions. A series of troubling features characterize this growing chasm—a void in individual identity, an absence of coherent institutions (and policies), and a lack of understanding about what's happening more broadly to the society." In our parents' time, Freedman continues, "individuals moving beyond midlife might have proceeded directly into the social institution called retirement— or, if that was delayed, tread water for a couple of years before ducking into that safe harbor of identity and security. Today, they are, for the most part, on their own, in uncharted waters, facing fundamental questions about what's next and what matters along with a society unprepared for them."

Freedman and others who are mapping encore adulthood imagine innovations like Individual Purpose Accounts, which would help people save up for gap years and adult education, or reforms allowing people to use a year's worth of Social Security benefits early, so they could go back to school or do an internship. There is no shortage of possibilities. But few have been realized as yet. The education system and the pension and retirement systems remain fixed on the three-stage model. Schooling is delivered in a lump on the front end; pensions and Medicare are delivered in a lump on the back end. As for people of "working age," they pay the bills for both lumps. Family responsibilities and fiscal burdens peak just as the happiness curve sags, so it is hardly a wonder if people at midlife feel squeezed.

Still, social change is coming. Indeed, it is happening already. "There's an adaptation that's going on in a lot of sectors," Freedman said. The adaptation is fragmented and improvisational and bottom-up rather than top-down, as organic social change very often is. Little by little, employers are adjusting to the priorities of baby boomers who seek to realign their work responsibilities instead of putting all their skills and experience on the shelf. In a recent study published in 2016 in *The Gerontologist,* Phyllis Moen, with coauthors Erik Kojola and Kate Schaefers, conducted in-depth interviews with twenty-three innovative organizations in the greater Minneapolis region, including private-sector companies, government agencies, and nonprofits. The organizations, they write, are "upending existing age-graded workplace norms and experimenting with new policies": providing flexible working hours; developing phased exits for employees who want to scale back gradually rather than retire all at once; hiring and re-hiring older workers and retirees; providing training and development to older as well as younger workers.

Communities and civic groups and social entrepreneurs are also inventing new templates. Freedman likes to tell the story of a group of rabbis who are creating a bar mitzvah ceremony for people in their sixties. Encore.org is itself an example of civic improvisation. Another sprang up spontaneously in 2000. Charlotte Frank and Christine Millen, friends and New Yorkers and veterans of the women's movement, found themselves leaving jobs but unready to retire. "As they talked to each other," Susan Collins recounted, when she told me their story, "they realized they couldn't be the only two women in New York facing this giant stretch of time and saying, 'Who the heck wants to retire?'"

Collins, who was in her early sixties when we met, is the executive director of The Transition Network. What began as a few small local gatherings has grown into a nonprofit with 2,200 members and chapters in 13 cities. That is small, as nonprofits go; but it is large enough to have proved its concept. For $100 a year, women in midlife and beyond can join a network of others who are in a reinvention stage or have passed through one. "You meet other people in the same type of situation and you realize you're not alone," Collins said.

Though the organization provides workshops and seminars and net-working opportunities, the heart of its model is what it calls *transition peer groups*. Those are monthly gatherings of eight to twelve women who explore preselected topics of their choice, topics like how to deal with adult children, and how to cope with stiffening bodies, and what brings content-ment, and how to forgive. The gathering is not group therapy or counsel-ing. "It's not here to resolve your psychological challenges," Collins told me. Nor is it group coaching. Nor is a place to solicit clients, hunt for a job, or pitch to investors. Rather, it is a conversation between peers about who they are and where they might be going and how to get there. The meetings are like book groups, except what's being read and discussed is the members' lives, and the mission is to plot the next chapter.

In Philadelphia one late summer morning, I sat in on a transition peer group. Eight women attended, most in their sixties, though one was eighty. In a small apartment living room decorated in warm beiges and tans, the women, all wearing business casual, sat on soft chairs arranged in a circle. Refreshments lay on a table nearby, but the group chose to launch straight into its two-hour session. The morning's topic, chosen by the host, was what to do about "baggage": physical clutter and emotional burdens. "What does it mean, what does it feel like," she asked the group, "when you let go of something that feels like a heavy weight on your shoulders?"

Gretchen, sitting on the sofa to my right, mentioned that she has trouble off-loading material things, such as her deceased husband's trea-sured necktie collection. Next to her, Heidi differed. "I found the Dump-ster easy. Physical things, I'm not attached to." Heidi's struggle was to get clear of emotional and personal attachments, and to figure out how to deal with the "overwhelming freedom" of retirement. Her husband had already planned out three years of travel and activities, but Heidi wasn't on board with all of that busyness. She noticed herself becoming more choosy about her investments of time and energy. "I feel there's only a fi-nite amount of time left, and I'm very aware of that."

Time emerged as a theme, which bounced from woman to woman like a beach ball. "I used to be friends with, my god, all these people," said Frances. "Now I'd rather be by myself than with some of them. I pick and choose where I spend my time."

Deb, across from me, agreed. "I do find now I don't spend time with people I find downers. That's been a new thing for me. I always did what I was supposed to do. If someone called to get together, I would not say no."

Several women remarked upon feeling less pressured even as they grew choosier. "I'm finding I don't have to fill things up," said Alice, immediately to my left. "You can have empty space around you. You can have free time. I'm finding that the less I do, the better I like it. To not feel the need to fill holes and spaces is the wisdom that's coming with my age."

Gretchen chimed in: "I don't know what's going to come. I don't care. I think it's because I've done everything I want to do, and everything else is a bonus."

From Elizabeth, a discordant note. She was eighty, not sixty-five, and she wanted to say that time was not as short as the others assumed. "You all sound like you think sixty-five is old because the world tells you sixty-five is old," she admonished. "As a few years go by, you'll realize sixty-five is pretty young."

The conversation flowed on, bending toward practical suggestions about volunteering and helping pack rats relinquish clutter. It was not an agenda-driven, goal-oriented discussion. "It's about being part of a community of women who are interested in the same things you are and who are building a life," Collins told me.

The Transition Network is interesting, and promising, partly because it is entirely a grassroots project. With the exception of director Collins and a couple of staff people, everyone is a volunteer. Membership is inexpensive. The group depends on local initiative to seed new chapters. Its communitarian model of mutual self-help is right out of the playbook of Alexis de Tocqueville, the nineteenth-century Frenchman who famously documented Americans' genius for forming voluntary groups and associations. But broader, more systematic adoption will require the involvement of bigger institutions that can move the social and cultural needle in a bigger way.

No large organization has yet stepped up on a large scale, but we have an early-stage prototype to look at. AARP is one of the largest membership organizations in the world, and one of the strongest lobbying organizations in the United States. In Washington, D.C., it is renowned for its clout on issues of interest to seniors. In recent years, however, it has faced the challenge of establishing its relevance to baby boomers who reject the Leisure World model of late adulthood and who are turned off by monikers like "American Association of Retired Persons" and "Modern Maturity," as AARP and its signature magazine were known until a rebranding a few years ago. In the early 2010s, searching for ventures that could introduce the organization to people in their forties and fifties, AARP kept encountering the phenomenon of midlife and post-midlife transitions. And so, in 2012, AARP launched a program it called Life Reimagined.

Life Reimagined took inspiration from a book of that name by the life coach Richard Leider and the journalist Alan M. Webber. Leider and Webber stress that big transitions aren't DIY projects and that, as Webber told me, isolation kills. "It's pretty lonesome inside your own head," Webber said, when I spoke with him about the project. "Everybody's life is an experiment of one, but nobody should have to go it alone." But change, never easy, is often especially threatening or scary or unsettling in midlife— not just to ourselves, but to our families and associates—and it requires a lot of information which few of us possess. Life Reimagined set out to provide a starting point. "It really is a personal guidance system for people who are in life transitions," AARP's John F. Wilson told me.

Unlike The Transition Network, Life Reimagined was not founded as a face-to-face community (though, as of this writing, it was laying plans to offer meetups). The concept was to provide online information and services. The website offered ebooks, quizzes, meditation guides, life-planning exercises and workbooks, and streaming courses about subjects like brain health, relationships, and finding purpose. Also, the site experimented with an online platform allowing users to shop for and schedule life coaching, at prices steeply discounted below prevailing market rates. AARP's Anne Marie Kilgallon told me the project's details were in flux as the organization sought to learn what midlife consumers want, but she said, "This commitment to transitions will not go away. I look at Life Reimagined as that best friend you can call to help you navigate whatever it is that you're dealing with. Our goal is to help everyone who's fifty-plus, not just our members."

And how might educational support look, if it comported with the U shape of reality? Here, too, we have early prototypes to look at.

In 2010, when Philip Pizzo, a pediatrician by training, was planning his own transition from being dean of Stanford University's medical school, he began pondering ways in which higher education could help mature people rethink their lives. "I've talked to hundreds of people, probably thousands, across the world," he told me. "It's amazing to see how many individuals are frustrated and disappointed by the time they hit their late forties and fifties. That seems to be much more normative than I would have predicted. Then the question becomes, what do people do? How do they realign themselves, and how can they do that?" He began to imagine university programs where midlifers could learn from and support each other, "and where they can utilize higher education to do what they did in the early phase of their life: re-explore, rethink, reconnect with people, and plan that next phase of their life. What takes place during adolescence is something that can take place again at midlife."

In January 2015, Stanford's Distinguished Careers Institute was born, under Pizzo's leadership. From applicants with several decades of life experience and a desire to recalibrate, the program chose about two dozen participants (called *fellows*). For a year, they would attend university courses, hear prominent guest speakers, and share their hopes and plans and know-how. "They're all in transition and often they don't have any-body to talk to about it," Pizzo told me. Fellows are high achievers, the kind of people who may be hesitant to share vulnerability; but by the second or third week, Pizzo said, participants often relate stories they may never have told anyone else.

As the institute's name implies (and as its mid-five-figure tuition affirms), the Distinguished Careers Institute was not for everyone. Pizzo compared it to the first Tesla roadster, a $100,000 electric car that used the purchas-ing power of early adopters to put electricity on the road and (Tesla hoped) seed a market for more affordable, utilitarian electric vehicles. "We started out with lots of bells and whistles to demonstrate proof of principle," Pizzo said. "I have no expectation or desire that the kind of program we've put together becomes the model. My hope is that there will be lots of seeds sown that will accomplish similar ends in a much more democratized way." Pizzo talks frequently with community colleges and universities about ways to build their own versions of programs supporting people who seek to re-boot. Some, such as Portland Community College and Pace University, already offer programs for encore careerists.

"There aren't really off-the-shelf solutions," Pizzo said, when I asked if there was any existing model for his efforts. With so little by way of prece-dent, pioneering efforts such as the Distinguished Careers Institute or Life Reimagined or The Transition Network tend to be small-scaled and wobbly. Still, prototypes have a lot to teach, so I went looking for another kind of prototype. How would a workplace look if it set out to abolish the midlife closet, creating a truly U-friendly environment? Somewhat to my surprise, one beautiful spring day I found myself in an advertising agency in downtown Chicago.

I was sitting with Danielle, an account executive, in a conference room in an office tower. The setting was very corporate. The conversation was not.

Danielle had been with Leo Burnett Worldwide for more than a decade. Leo Burnett is one of the world's biggest advertising agencies. Its clients had names like Coca-Cola, Kellogg's, and GM. The clients, the projects, and the deadlines were demanding, sometimes relentless. That was stressful for Danielle, plus she was a wife and mother of two, the elder of whom was entering his teens. As if that were not enough, at about the time when she turned forty, four years earlier, she had begun feeling malaise about her work. "I felt lack of inspiration. What is it at the end I was trying to achieve? Is it a promotion? Is it validation? Is it a great piece of work on TV? It kind of lost its meaning."

Advertising is not a career with an inherently high life-satisfaction quotient. If someone gets through an entire career devising thirty-second TV commercials *without* asking questions about meaning and purpose, there is probably something wrong with that person. (Not coincidentally, Kevin Spacey's depressed character in *American Beauty* is a middle-aged advertising executive.) The questions had caught up with Danielle. "Is life getting ahead of me? Am I getting left behind?"

One day, Danielle recalled, she encountered a senior executive who recommended Leo Burnett's in-house coaching program. He told her that coaching is a good way to improve leadership skills and locate blind spots. Around the same time, a friend in account planning also recommended the program. Danielle emailed a coach. The subject line: "Towards hope."

A lot of companies nowadays offer coaching, especially for top executives. Once viewed as a form of remediation, coaching has come to be seen in the business world as a way to bring out the best in high-potential employees. That was true of Leo Burnett. When I visited in 2015, Leo Burnett's stable of more than a dozen on-staff coaches had worked with hundreds of employees, and not just people at the top.

Nowadays, a lot of companies also claim that their employees are their most important asset. That, too, was true of Leo Burnett. "In our case," said Renetta McCann, the company's chief U.S. talent officer, "employees are our *only* asset. The ideas we have, the commercials that go on the air, the engagement with consumers, those all come directly out of our employees. The raw materials for what we produce come from within our employees. If today two thousand people left and a different two thousand people came in, we'd have a different product."

McCann is a short African American woman with a not at all diminutive personality. Bighearted and warm, with a worldly wise, empathetic manner that strikes me as more rabbinical than corporate, she likens midlife in the advertising business to the compactor scene from the 1977 *Star Wars* movie. "The floors are moving, the walls are moving, the ceiling is moving. What we've come to understand is that the people in the middle of the organization are the ones under the most pressure. At some time in that age zone, you wind up in the crunch. Getting the work out the door falls on you, and you've got to negotiate all these relationships. And God forbid you should have a life of your own: a spouse, partner, kids, whatever. Heaven help you."

Coaching, she said, was available for employees of all ages at Leo Burnett. "If you raise your hand, the company will find you a coach, it will find you the time to do the coaching, it will respect the confidentiality of that relationship, and the company will support you." The user base, though, was heavy on people in their late thirties and their forties: people wrestling with the values questions that Danielle found herself asking. McCann said, "Where in society are people given people to ask these questions to? At thirty-five and forty-five, that's when your values are probably most under pressure. You're still trying to fit in. You're still trying to be the kid your parents wanted. You're dealing with your spouse or partner. There's this incredible pressure to have The Answer. A lot of times, when you are pressed to have The Answer, people either stop asking questions or they don't ask high-quality questions."

McCann knew whereof she spoke, having traveled the happiness curve herself. Earlier in her career, she was global CEO of one of the company's business units. At fifty-two, she burned out, retired, went back to school, got a master's, then returned to the agency in a new role, now working with people. Along the way, she found answers to some of her questions. "One of the things I did was take a hard look at my own values. I found I had two different value sets, one set of values attached to my heart and one to my mind. One is about grace; the other is about curiosity." But she made the transition largely on her own. "It was a real internal struggle," she said. "I don't know if people knew I was struggling or not. If somebody else had asked those questions with me, I probably could have traveled the U faster. I might have had a very different shaped U."

In a business where burnout is common and costly, raising and confronting values questions before they reach the *American Beauty* point can be a profitable proposition. McCann said, "My hypothesis is that what prevents you from traveling the U is having your values more front and center." And so the agency encourages its employees to align their lives and their values, which is what coaching seeks to do.

Coaching does not assume you are broken and need to be fixed. Rather, it assumes you are well and whole, and it seeks to clarify your values and then help align your life with them. Coaching also is not the same as mentoring or consulting, because the coach's job is not to pass down advice or expertise. Instead, life coaches often refer to themselves as *allies*. They are trained to listen closely, to notice things, and to surface core questions about who we are and what we want and how to get there. "A lot of training for coaching is getting our own stuff out of the way so we can ask clear, powerful, often very basic questions," said Christopher McAuliffe, the founder of Accomplishment Coaching in San Diego. Unlike many forms of therapy, coaching looks forward, not backward, focusing on identifying and meeting life goals rather than diagnosing and solving emotional problems.

In some ways, though, coaching does resemble therapy. The conversation is strictly confidential. Coaching sessions typically last an hour. They might start with one session a week and then back off to one every few weeks. Also, life coaching is not just about career, even for professionals who are coached at work. As coaches often reminded me, the professional and personal sides of life are interwoven and cannot be separated. At Leo Burnett, a coaching intake form started this way: "Coaching addresses you as a whole person—your physical, emotional, spiritual, and intellectual self. In our coaching relationship we'll focus on both who you are 'being' and what you are doing in your life, and together (co-actively) we'll design the best way I can support you." The form continued with questions like: "What are your top five values?"; "If you had all the time and resources you wanted, what would you do?"; "How will I know when you're 'stuck'?"

In all of those respects, Leo Burnett's program, far from being unique, was characteristic of coaching's best practices. But here is what was unusual about it, and what attracted my attention. At Leo Burnett, coaching was *normal*. Coaches were fellow workers embedded within the company. They knew the players in the agency and the stresses of the job. Executives used and recommended the program as a matter of course. ("I want all my people to do it, and I've told them that," one boss said.) Coaching was part of everyday life in the company; people heard about it from colleagues in the elevator or coffee room, as Danielle did.

Leo Burnett had thus inverted the usual assumption that values questions belong in the closet, especially at work. "We've tried to take the stigma out of it," said Peter Diamond, a coach and former Leo Burnett executive who still practiced inside the company. "In three years, coaching went from something where I was very cautious to make sure that people weren't coming in and out at the same time, to being part of the fabric of the agency." People told me they would mention coaching in meetings, sometimes even with clients—a handily indirect way to express that no one is expected to be perfect or have all the answers.

I can't tell you, in a scientific way, the specific results of Leo Burnett's coaching program and, more important, of its coaching culture. When I asked if the company measured outcomes, a senior executive said, "We're intentionally not doing that." I can tell you that the program was popular, and many employees swore by it. "It keeps me sane," Sheri, a thirty-eight-year-old creative team manager, told me. "I rely on these meetings to help keep me grounded. It's easy to lose sight of your own goals when the universe's goals can be so demanding." Molly, a thirty-eight-year-old account director told me: "I think there must be more to life than answering emails at midnight and five in the morning. When you're able to talk out loud, it's amazing. It's just helpful for somebody to ask the right questions to get you thinking about things."

As for forty-four-year-old Danielle, she had uncovered the questions, but not yet the answers. "It hasn't resolved yet," she replied, when I ask about her efforts to find, in her words, "a goal, a path." So, I wondered, what did her coaching sessions accomplish? The words came pouring out. "With my coach, I don't always have to keep pretending that nothing fazes me. When I tell him all the bad stuff that's happening to me, he makes me feel I'm not the only one. He also gives me confidence. He has my back when he talks to me. He's not bullshitting me. He makes me think differently. He connects dots in a different manner than I do. And the objective evaluation he provides is just invaluable to me. He makes me more resilient, and he makes me more of a problem solver.

"It makes me at least feel that I'm normal."

Normal. That word again.

Society, not science, determines what is normal in the lives we lead, and *that,* right now, is the problem. The standard social templates for adult development and life satisfaction turn the happiness curve upside down, describing something more like a hill-shaped arc. In their book *Life Re-*

imagined: Discovering Your New Life Possibilities, Leider and Webber describe the conventional view this way:

> Each of us starts off fresh and new, ready to learn and grow and discover our individual potential. We arc upward as we go through our early years, and we continue to grow until about the time we hit middle age. At that point we've reached the apex of our lives, the top of the parabola. After that, as we pass middle age, we begin the process of decline that takes us into retirement, then old age, and eventually, death.

Within that outdated but still prevalent paradigm, the happiness curve is not normal. It is more like the opposite of normal. Sure, midlife crisis is a familiar phenomenon. But, as the very word *crisis* implies, it is extreme and extraordinary and bad. We avoid it if we can, and if we cannot avoid it, we hide it.

By telling a social story about normalcy that is at odds with reality, we manufacture dismay and shame about a perfectly normal transition. By expecting people to exhibit maximum mastery in midlife, we leave them to their own devices if they feel adrift and vulnerable. By leaving them to their own devices, we increase their isolation and therefore their unhappiness. By telling them that their best years are behind them at age fifty, we make them gloomy about the future. In all of those ways, by telling the wrong story about adult development, we bait and set the midlife trap.

The trap may never go away entirely. Some aspects of it appear to be hardwired. (Ask a chimp or a Barbary macaque.) Others, though, are products of social misalignment. I believe that the expectations gap—the difference between how satisfied we feel at age forty-five or fifty and how satisfied we believe we *should* feel—can and will narrow as word gets out about the happiness curve. Social support will come online as more people and institutions begin to understand the midlife transition for what it is: a healthy emotional reboot with a rich upside for individuals and also for society. Communities and companies and colleges, and eventually even the lethargic government, will provide resources and support for people making the midlife transition. Most important, the *story* we tell about aging and life satisfaction will comport with the lives we live. The happiness curve will be just as normal, just as thoroughly taken for granted and institutionalized, as adolescence. People will wonder why anyone was ever embarrassed about it. Maybe—we can hope—even the sports-car meme will be put to rest.

The prototypes and start-ups I have described in this book are, so far, trickles of change. But they are already carving new social channels. Improvisations like Leo Burnett's and Stanford's and AARP's and The Transition Network are emerging because people and organizations need them and are not waiting around. Already, it is possible to see how the essential pieces of a new support infrastructure can work together to ease us through our transitions. Researching The Transition Network, I interviewed Claire, a member of a chapter in New Jersey. In her forties, she felt growing discontent with her job as a corporate lawyer. In her fifties, "stressed, tired, needing change," she began doing research on nonprofit careers, only to encounter confusion. She was confident of her skills, but "How would I take them and make the transition to the not-for-profit sector? What's even out there? How do I get a foot in the door? There's no clear path here."

So far, so typical. But then she got lucky. An email led her to The Transition Network. "I saw that and I said, 'Wow, this sounds like a great kind of thing for me professionally and socially.' I didn't feel I was out on an island trying to do something without a map." Meanwhile, she received an email about Pace University's then-new program for life transitions, a class that armed her with information on how to repurpose skills and organize a relaunch. In the Pace class, she learned about Encore.org fellowships, which place career changers in yearlong positions with social-purpose organizations. Her fellowship introduced her to a nonprofit that assisted former inmates and their families with readjustment after incarceration. Her legal and administrative skills proved to be a good fit, and after the yearlong fellowship she accepted a part-time position as the organization's chief counsel.

More through serendipity than intent, Claire demonstrated how much more smoothly a transition can go, and how much less isolating it can be, when multiple social supports click into place. The Transition Network provided companions on the journey, Pace University provided a map, and Encore.org opened a pathway. When I asked her how she would have fared had she remained out there on her own, fishing for information online and trying to figure out where to begin, she replied that she might eventually have made a successful transition, but the process would have been difficult and demoralizing. "It would have been a much longer period of hit-and-miss."

When I asked how she felt about her transition, now that she had passed through it, she replied with a chuckle. "Both of my daughters say, 'Mom, you totally failed at retirement.' But I'm so much happier doing what I'm doing."

Such is the importance of social channels. Institutions and norms and precedents light our way through life and save us from always having to start from scratch. That is what I meant when I said that what Karl needs, even more than self-help, is help from ashore. Coping with the happiness curve requires the aid of voyagers omitted from Thomas Cole's paintings: the voyagers who have gone before. They can provide signs to mark the currents, beacons to indicate hazards, landings for respite amid rapids, and provisions for nourishment.

Social support is on the way. Its eventual arrival is assured by the clout of the baby boomer generation, required by the disintegration of endless-vacation retirement, and presaged by the eruptions of groups and programs and ideas of the kind I have discussed here. But creating adolescence—creating the social channels and stories that carved out a place between childhood and adulthood—was the work of several generations. Creating encore adulthood and a new normal for midlife could take as long. My friend Karl doesn't have a generation to wait. He needs relief now.

So here is something you and I can do for Karl. Right now.

Homosexuality stopped being abnormal in large part because little by little, one by one, gay people's relatives and friends and employers and colleagues became better informed and more supportive. Instead of laughing at us or telling us to get psychiatric treatment, the people in our lives accepted us and connected with us.

I have seen again and again, while researching this book, the relief people feel when they can have a nonjudgmental, fact-based conversation about midlife malaise. I see the surprise and smiles when they hear that the happiness curve is normal and seen around the world, even among apes. In fact, quite literally while I was working on this chapter I received an email from a stranger, a Canadian named Derek:

> I will make this short and sweet. I want to thank you very very much for your article on the U curve.
>
> I am a divorced forty-five-year-old with teenage kids and from the outside my life should be just peachy. Have a career etc. and things are generally good.
>
> I certainly don't feel that things are great and I feel like I am in the toughest part of my life. Was not sure why and was getting increasingly concerned about my mental well-being.

Thank you so much for your insight, work, and articles!!!
Happy to have come across you. You are making a difference
for people.

Of course, by *you,* the correspondent means not me, personally, but the message that the happiness curve is normal and nonpathological and even, in its own perverse way, constructive. Knowing this helps. What can help even more is if Derek's family and friends and neighbors and colleagues also knew it, and if they rallied around. As Terry, in the last chapter, attests, a "bunch of guys" can prevent each other from capsizing.

We can all be a bunch of guys to somebody. Wholesale social reform may require action by giant institutions, but retail reform requires only that each of us create a safe space for the people in our own lives. By retiring our clichés about midlife crisis and listening and empathizing and sharing our stories, every one of us can make someone's midlife transition less of a DIY project.

Each time we connect nonjudgmentally and positively with Karl or someone like him, we provide companionship to a voyager in turbulent waters. Indirectly, we help other voyagers, too. We make it safer for others to come out. We add our voice to a new social conversation. We realign normalcy just a bit. We place a marker on the shore.

The previous paragraph was where this chapter originally ended. As I was putting the finishing touches on it, however, an email arrived from Karl. By then, he and I had had a number of conversations about his life and the happiness curve, and I had given him the manuscript of the book to read. I had placed him under no obligation to give me a reaction and I wasn't expecting one; but his email, when it came, expressed, better than I could, what a difference social normalcy and personal connections can make. Karl launched this book's journey, so to let him conclude it seems only fitting.

He began by saying he was doing better. He wrote:

For one thing, it was a huge relief to know that I was not alone, and that this is probably something that is a hardwired part of life, almost like puberty. We should not hate ourselves for being awkward and pimply as teens; nor should we berate ourselves for being lost in midlife.

For another, I have always sorta understood that professional success does not make for personal bliss, but it was an insight that I had not fully accepted. Going through the midlife slump and learning that others who have achieved far bigger things have gotten trapped on the hedonic treadmill was the wake-up call I needed. Yes, I will keep trying to achieve more—I enjoy the challenge—but I now feel less emotionally invested in it, and now really get that I can't be happy by just producing more professional wins.

Which means I have begun looking for sources of joy elsewhere, and dialing back my career's presence in my mind. It is a small thing, but I now make a point of checking my work email less often, and have turned off many of the notifications that rattle my cell phone and distract me from being wherever it is that I am. I am trying to be more attentive to the moment and appreciative of where I am at. That's part of wisdom, right? Additionally, this past autumn I made time to phone family and friends more than I had before, and to develop an outdoor leisurely pursuit that was purely for my own edification. I'm not doing it to impress anyone—I just enjoy it and in the course of doing it I've made acquaintances with other folks who share this passion.

Finally, the evidence showing that emotionally things will turn up buoys me. So, too, does the idea of planning for a post-midlife second sailing, where I can find new work (if I so choose) and devote what time I have in life to the people and things that strike me as most worth doing.

Do I still need help from ashore? Sure. I'm still in the trough of the U curve.

But I no longer feel lost at sea, which is an immense relief.

EPILOGUE

Gratitude

Summer, 1990. A warm Tokyo evening. I am walking the streets of the Azabu Juban district with Donald Richie. He is the world's leading authority on Japanese cinema and an accomplished essayist and novelist. I have sought him out because now, at age thirty, I think I know what I want from life: to write something, someday, as good as *The Inland Sea*.

In the 1960s, Richie made a series of voyages through the islands of Japan's Seto Naikai, the narrow, strait-like sea that separates Japan's three main land masses. Today, the sea's islands and villages are succumbing to sterile modernity, but in the 1960s they remained backwaters, still connected to Japan's deep past and primordial values. "These islands are extraordinarily beautiful, and a part of their beauty is that it is passing," he wrote. "And so I want to go to the font of that humanity, to this still and backward place where people live better than anywhere else because they live according to their own natures." Richie chronicled encounters with priests and fishermen and lepers, schoolchildren and grandmothers and bureaucrats and barmaids, and then wove their lightly fictionalized stories together to produce a work of luminous prose and profound human insight. Published in 1971, when Richie was in his forties, the book quickly attained the stature of a classic. Meanwhile, Richie chronicled Japan's re-birth from postwar ashes, became the doyen of his field, befriended the artistic luminaries of three generations, wrote novels and newspaper columns and everything in between, lectured around the world, and received prizes and distinctions.

So, walking with him in Tokyo, I am startled when this extraordinarily accomplished man speaks of having experienced midlife crisis. Meaning what? "Midlife crisis begins sometime in your forties," he replies, "when you look at your life and think, *Is this all?* And it ends about ten years later, when you look at your life again and think, *Actually, this is pretty good.*"

Gratitude is healthy. Studies find it increases optimism, happiness, and physical wellbeing. It seems to reduce doctor visits and sleeplessness. You can make people feel and function better by getting them to write thank-you letters to those who have made a difference in their lives. If gratitude were a pill, every doctor would prescribe it.

Gratitude is also virtuous. Religions all over the world call upon their adherents to thank God for our blessings (and even for our misfortunes), and philosophers from ancient times have placed thankfulness at the foundation of ethics. "Gratitude is not only the greatest of virtues, but the parent of all the others," said the Roman philosopher Cicero.

Gratitude is also indispensable. Humans' success as a species depends on our ability to track and repay the help we receive from countless others, near and far. Our unique capacity for socially organized gratitude allows us to cooperate on a global scale, a feat no other animal comes close to matching. Without gratitude, human life would be nasty, brutish, and short.

When I was in the trough of the happiness curve, the bedevilment that troubled me most was chronic ingratitude. I knew I should be grateful, I tried to be grateful, if you had asked me I would have said *of course* I'm grateful; but I had trouble *feeling* grateful. My inner critics, who delighted in pestering me about what was wrong with me and my life, wouldn't be shooed away more than briefly by any blessing or admonition. My morale sank to its lowest when I feared that my gratitude deficit might be permanent.

My story would make a better screenplay if I had had an epiphany, discovered a new purpose, got religion, or found a breakthrough therapy, but I didn't. Nor did I quit my job, cheat on Michael, succumb to depression, or buy a red sports car. I mainly went with Plan A, also known as muddling through. Like most people at the bottom of the curve, I set my face and determined to slog forward and stay on track. In hindsight, it would have been a big relief to have known about the geography of the valley I was in, but I didn't know. I did, though, remember Richie's words, and they helped. If this extraordinary man could lose but then recover gratitude, then so could I!

He turned out to be exactly right. In my early fifties, the critics' voices faded. I don't recall any sudden change, but at some point I noticed that I was noticing them less. On more and more days, I woke up without hearing them. Each year, gradually but discernibly, I seem to be more content doing whatever I do that day, instead of beating up on myself for whatever it is I haven't done and might never do. Each year, just as the scholarship predicts, my attention seems more drawn to the positive. In Laura Carstensen's evocative phrase, I seem to be growing "more attuned to the sweetness of life than to its bitterness." I'm not sure if I am growing wiser, and I don't walk around in a state of bliss (and wouldn't want to), but I am confident that the undertow has turned. My boat may be battered and the hourglass is emptying, but the river is helping me now.

If I had to explain the upside of the U in just three words, the words I would use are these: *Gratitude comes easier.* That is the hidden gift of the happiness curve.

It is worth the wait.

AFTERWORD TO THE PAPERBACK EDITION

Aging proudly

I hadn't been fishing since I was eight. In my desert hometown of Phoenix, lakes and streams were not easy to come by, unless they were artificial, and my parents were migrants from New York City whose idea of aquatic wildlife was lox on an onion bagel. One day, though, in a piney town in northern Arizona, my father and a friend of his turned up with a rods and a tackle kit, and off we went to try our luck in Granite Basin Lake. Standing onshore, fumbling haplessly with hooks and bait and sinkers, we cast and reeled and cast and reeled. We caught nothing. For a long time, though, I remembered that day as a happy one, when the world seemed easy, and school and squabbles seemed distant.

In the fifty years that followed, fishing opportunities did not arise. I didn't seek them out. Even my leisure time was overbooked. But one day Karl emailed with an invitation. Would I like to join him on a fishing expedition in Washington, D.C.? An urbanite like me, he had won a fishing trip a few years back in a fundraising drive for his kids' school. Somebody's dad had picked him up and taken him out on the Potomac north of town, where the shad ran in numbers that awed him and the stream itself seemed alive. Transfixed, Karl acquired his own kit and took up fishing, but with a twist. Unable to snatch more than the odd hour or two between obligations to family and job, he prowled the city for urban fishing spots, places he could haunt before the kids got up and work started.

Thanks to the Clean Water Act and the Environmental Protection Agency, the local waterways, once toxic, today teem with aquatic life, much of it within a stone's throw of thoroughfares and office blocks. For the urban angler, the fish are sometimes the least of the challenges. Early one morning, when Karl was fishing by himself in a park beneath a bridge, a couple of bleary-eyed young guys hit him up for sex. (He declined.) Another day, at a spot near an expressway, three teenagers riding past on bicycles paused to taunt him: "You ain't gonna catch shit here!" Daring them to stay and watch, he gave them a fishing lesson. (Yes, they made a catch.)

And so it was that one fall morning before daylight I found street parking behind the Nationals' baseball stadium and made my way to a jetty. Amid a metropolis of more than six million souls, the place was deserted. Before me was the Anacostia River; behind me, a D.C. water-pumping station. From the bank, the opposite shore seemed surprisingly far away. My eight-year-old self seemed much farther. Karl was there with six rods, a Ziploc bag of chicken marinated in Kool-Aid and garlic, and a hushed predawn greeting. This time of day, he said, the catfish ought to be biting.

The late Donald Richie, a dedicatee of this book, had no children, but he used to say that his books were his children, because after he wrote them, they would make their own way in the world, and their doings always found ways to surprise him. In the time since *The Happiness Curve* was first published, I have had many opportunities to talk about it, and have heard from many people affected by it—often in ways that are gratifying, sometimes in ways that are surprising.

One of my main aspirations for this particular child—for this book—is to bring a measure of relief and reassurance to readers suffering through a mystifying midlife slump. Remember how Hannes Schwandt recognized that just knowing about the happiness curve can ameliorate its effects, by diminishing the feedback loop caused by self-reinforcing disappointment and worry? My mailbag supports Schwandt's finding. "Apparently, I am quite normal!" wrote one reader. "I'm not broken!" wrote another. Others, older, testify to the curve's upswing, even in the latest years. "My own 'happiness curve' is higher than it was at sixty or seventy," wrote an eighty-four-year-old woman. "It has me wondering what's next."

The mail I've received also reminds me that one curve does not fit all. I have taken pains to emphasize that everyone's mileage will vary, and although many people track the averages, as I have done so far, others wonder about their own less conventional courses. One writer told me that my description of unaccountable dissatisfaction and disappointment fit her to a T. "Here's the thing," she continued, "I'm not in my forties, or my thirties, I'm twenty-nine." Another writer told me he was experiencing his slump in his mid-sixties. In such cases, I wish I had pat answers. Remember, the U-shaped undercurrent, although pronounced, is never the only influence on happiness, and so no two voyagers experience the same journey. Time has its own agenda for our emotional wellbeing, but the patterns and interactions are many and complex.

Still, each year's research adds new texture. In particular, evidence continues to accumulate of serious problems in midlife, problems which too often remain unnoticed or under-noticed. For example, Andrew Oswald and the University of Pittsburgh economist Osea Giuntella have discovered what appears to be a sleep crisis in midlife. Using a large data set from nine industrialized countries (including longitudinal data, the best kind of data because it tracks individuals over time), they find that sleep declines to its lowest level around the age of fifty, and then rises steadily into older age. "A profound U shape existed in each nation," they found: a midlife sleep deficit which holds true across countries and people regardless of gender, employment, children, and marriage.

More worrisome is the fact that suicide, the most alarming of all indicators of existential unhappiness, is a distinctively age-related phenomenon, and, yes, midlife is a particular danger zone. If anything, the link between middle age and suicide appears to be growing stronger. "The over-seventy-fives have historically been most likely to kill themselves, especially if they are lonely or ill," reported *The Economist* in 2015. "But now it is the middle-aged who are most at risk. In 2012 the suicide rate for Americans aged forty-five to fifty-four was twenty per 100,000—the highest rate of any age group." In 2018, the U.S. Centers for Disease Control and Prevention issued data showing that suicide rates for middle-aged men and (especially) women had increased sharply between 2000 and 2016. "In most industrialized nations," Andrew Oswald wrote in 2018, "suicide is predominantly a risk among the middle-aged—and particularly among men in their late forties." The locus of midlife and suicide, he believes, bespeaks an urgent problem, one which cries out for laser-like attention, not benign neglect.

The social-science pendulum, having swung against the notion of midlife crisis, is swinging back. Elliott Jaques and pop culture may have gotten it wrong, but *something* is going on. Crisis or no, middle age is a time of significant and often misunderstood emotional vulnerability.

Of course, many people in their forties have tough lives. They are juggling jobs, young children, aging parents, school teams, scout troops, and condo boards. We all know that. But we tend to assume, as a society, that midlife is when our coping resources are at their peak, or at least should be. At midlife, we command the health of youth and the experience of age; we are strong and competent and at the top of our game! In any case, we are *expected* to be strong and competent and at the top of our game. Yet the truth, very commonly, is that we feel unmoored emotionally but dare not give voice to our doubts. And so we bull through in isolation and shame, thereby, of course, deepening the misery.

After this book was published, John Helliwell—the economist who, in chapter 2, introduced himself as Aristotle's research assistant—published a paper which indirectly highlights the high emotional cost of isolation in midlife. Using data from a variety of countries, he and several coauthors (Max B. Norton, Haifang Huang, and Shun Wang) investigated how social relationships interact with each other and with age to affect subjective wellbeing over time. Specifically, they looked at the effects of having a supportive, partner-like boss; having a supportive, best-friend spouse; and having stable, long-lasting community roots. Their finding: strong, trusting ties to boss, spouse, and community can mitigate and in some cases completely counteract the effect of the midlife U.

I have emphasized throughout this book that social connectedness is the most important of all the variables which contribute to a sense of wellbeing in life. And that is true at any age. What Helliwell and his colleagues are telling us, however, is that connectedness can make an especially large difference in middle age. We are each other's safety nets. The sooner we can relinquish the myth that middle age is a time of maximum mastery, and that showing vulnerability or discontent indicates some sort of abnormal and alarming "crisis," the more support, for ourselves and each other, we will be able to provide. As the suicide statistics suggest, lives depend on it.

In addition to being a time of natural (if often surreptitious) vulnerability, midlife, as we have seen, is also a time of natural (if often disconcerting) transition. Our expectations become more realistic, our values become more other-directed, and our brains shift toward positivity. As I discussed in chapter 9, moving through this transition should not be a DIY project. Midlifers need pathways and signposts toward lifestyle changes that accommodate their changing values. I mentioned the importance of resources like coaching, support networks, education, and flexible employers and pensions. I also emphasized the immense, indeed unprecedented, bounty which individuals and society will reap when encore careers become the norm. In the time since this book was first published, however, I have come to think that I did not adequately acknowledge the real-world obstacles to reinvention in middle age and late adulthood. More specifically, I didn't reckon adequately with the false stereotypes that grip and throttle our imaginations about aging.

Let's face it. Older workers are less productive, less engaged, less motivated. They are resistant to change, less able to learn, and at sea with new technology. Because they are less healthy, they are less reliable and have shorter tenures. They aren't as sharp, as energetic, or as adaptable as younger people. As Mark Zuckerberg famously said, when he was twenty-two years old, "Young people are just smarter."

Sorry, Mark. Every one of the claims in the preceding paragraph is false. In his recent book, *Wisdom@Work*, Chip Conley summarizes the evidence, which is not controversial among experts on aging. Not only are older workers just as productive as younger ones, they make workers around them more productive, possibly as a result of their experience navigating conflicts and problems. Perhaps for that reason, age-diverse teams perform better, outperforming national industry averages. Older workers are just as engaged and motivated as younger ones. "In fact," writes Conley, "no other age group has as high a level of engagement as older workers." Older workers also are not hard to train or resistant to adaptation, though they may respond better to different training techniques. It is true that raw cognitive firepower tends to decline with age, but older people compensate by employing and synchronizing more regions of their brain ("all-wheel drive," as this phenomenon has been called). Older teams may be slower, but they also make fewer mistakes. As for health, "Older and younger workers are equally healthy (both physically and psychologically), at least day to day," writes Conley. "And, in fact, on average, older workers take less time off than younger workers." On balance, older empty nesters may cost their companies less to insure than do younger workers with families on the health plan. And they are less likely to quit and job-shop than are younger workers, and so their tenure on the job is comparable.

It is also a myth that older people lose their creativity and ingenuity. The peak age for new patents is in the late forties, but innovation continues: Inventors remain highly productive in the latter half of their careers, and, as Pagan Kennedy reported in a 2017 *New York Times* article (headline: "To Be a Genius, Think Like a Ninety-Four-Year-Old"), the highest-value patents often come from inventors over fifty-five.

"Every aspect of job performance gets better as we age," Peter Cappelli, a management professor at Wharton business school and the author of *Managing the Older Worker: How to Prepare for the New Organizational Order*, told *AARP Magazine* in 2015. He added, "I thought the picture might be more mixed, but it isn't. The juxtaposition between the superior performance of older workers and the discrimination against them in the workplace just really makes no sense." One could generalize his point even further: There may be no other area in modern life where expert consensus and public perception are so entirely at odds.

Between myth and reality is the chasm of ageism. In Europe, according to the psychologists Liat Ayalon and Clemens Tesch-Römer (writing in the *European Journal of Aging* in 2017), ageism is the most prevalent form of discrimination, reported by more than a third of study participants over age eighteen. Other estimates, including in the United States, range much higher, with two-thirds and more of respondents reporting having seen or experienced age discrimination. Health-care providers give older patients less information, are less likely to offer them innovative treatments, and speak to them condescendingly or talk past them altogether. (I often experienced this phenomenon with my ailing father. Though he was sitting next to me, health-care workers and social-service providers would direct their comments and questions to me, or speak to him as if he were a child, despite his blade-sharp mind and Yale law degree. Treating older people like children is not only demeaning, it harms their care and their health.)

In the workplace, prejudice is even more rife. "Employers perceive older workers as costly and less productive," write Ayalon and Tesch-Römer. "Not surprisingly, older adults have a hard time finding a job, and they are most likely to be the first to be laid off due to economic considerations." When testers send out job applications which are carefully matched on every dimension except age, older applicants consistently receive fewer interviews and callbacks. (The disparity seems especially acute among women.) Older people are more likely to experience long-term unemployment. And so on, and so on. In sum, ageism is possibly the most common and least questioned of all forms of discrimination.

Generally speaking, the problem is not animus. The problem is ignorance. In fact, according to Chip Conley, "older adults actually endorse these ageist stereotypes more than younger adults." Evidence suggests that children form negative attitudes toward aging as early as fourth grade, and not just in the United States but in countries and cultures around the world. Those implanted stereotypes are carried with us like rotten seeds, sprouting decades later into deprecatory self-images and comments. When we act on the stereotypes, and transmit them to others, we make them self-fulfilling. Experiencing an ordinary memory glitch, we think nothing of saying, "Sorry, I had a senior moment." We act ashamed of our age and talk as if birthdays are bad news. During my travels after the book came out, I checked into a hotel where I was greeted by a seventy-something desk clerk. I was jolted to see an "old man" giving me service usually provided by someone young enough to be my offspring, and when I saw him work efficiently and walk me briskly to the elevator, my knee-jerk reaction was, "Wow, pretty good, for a guy his age." Only then did I receive a second jolt, when I realized that the only thing wrong with the picture was my attitude: an attitude I would have denied possessing until it cropped up that evening.

The stereotypes which devalue late adulthood are bad in all kinds of ways. Most obviously, they place obstacles in the path of people who, in their fifties and beyond, seek to change careers or reenter the workforce. As is always the case with discrimination and stereotyping, the result is to underutilize and misallocate precious talent and experience. Moreover, internalized stereotypes are damaging to both mental and physical health. (Just ask a gay or lesbian person who has struggled with self-hate.) In 2018, four researchers—Becca Levy, Martin Slade, and Robert Pietrzak of Yale University, plus Luigi Ferrucci of the National Institute on Aging— found that holding positive attitudes about aging significantly reduces the likelihood of dementia among people over sixty. Other research associates age-positivity with longer lifespan.

Fortunately, word is getting out. "Ageism is percolating into the public consciousness in all kinds of permutations," Ashton Applewhite, the author of the anti-ageism manifesto *This Chair Rocks*, told me. Little by little, awareness is spreading that Mark Zuckerberg was wrong. (He himself repudiated his claim that young people are just smarter.) Still, there is an aspect of ageism which I think has yet to be recognized. As harmful as ageism is in late adulthood, it may be just as harmful in middle age.

Why do so many people imagine that if they are not satisfied with their lives in midlife, they never will be? Why do they believe that time is growing short at age fifty, and so they had better make some radical change *right now* (sometimes, in the process, making a radical mistake)? Why, looking ahead, do they see a future of decline? Very largely because the stereotypes about late adulthood backflow into middle age. Suppose it were general knowledge that satisfaction with life tends to increase right through old age; that our span of healthy, happy years, far from growing short at age fifty, stretches out for decades (and that century-long lives beckon to unprecedented numbers of people); that our values change faster than our bodies, and that the losses brought by aging are paired with compensating gains; that late adulthood is a natural time for renewal and repurposing, rather than a time of banishment to idleness and of preparation for death. Imagine how different life would look at fifty!

The happiness curve arcs through the whole of life. No part is distinct from the rest. At every age, our expected future shapes our emotional present. Change the way we view the later decades, and we change the way we experience the younger ones. All the way back to fourth grade.

When I asked what should be done about ageism, Applewhite had no difficulty listing good ideas. Furnish school curricula with a more complete, and thus more positive, view of aging. Teach managers how to cultivate an age-diverse workforce, and include age in companies' diversity guidelines. Endeavor to publicize the facts about aging, and treat ageism as a public-health issue.

I am for all of that, and more. Yet I have come to believe that the most powerful force for change is inside our heads. Hannes Schwandt's feedback loop within individuals, in which expectations and disappointment chase each other to create misery in midlife, is mirrored by another, analogous feedback loop within society as a whole. The story we tell ourselves about aging and emotional development—the story of youthful emotional turbulence (true), of midlife emotional mastery (not reliably true), and of late-life emotional decline (not at all true)—distorts our expectations at every point in the cycle, leading us to make midlife more difficult and late adulthood less productive than either needs to be. To put the case more bluntly: Most of what people think they know about happiness and aging is wrong, and what they don't know is hurting them.

In the main text of this book, I emphasize the importance of replacing stereotypes with supportiveness where midlife is concerned. Without demoting that priority a whit, let me add something to it. Ageism is immiserating for people of *all* ages. And there is a great deal each of us can do about it, simply by knowing the facts and then by conveying them and acting upon them. As Applewhite told me, "If you don't look at your own attitudes toward aging, we're never going to have systemic change."

Fifty-eight, as it turns out, is not too old to take up fishing. And despite having last cast a line at age eight, I managed to arc my baited hook out over the river. Not much happened at first. Something seemed to be discouraging the fish that chilly morning, so Karl and I had plenty of time to talk. Our conversation, that day, was not about his midlife wellbeing, or my own. It was about the fish, and about just being there, and we felt fine.

Something people regularly ask me when I talk about the *The Happiness Curve* is how researching and writing it has changed my own life. The answer is that when I look ahead, I see the world differently. Sunset years? Bah! Between my knees and my shoulders, I have had to abandon exercise routines that I used to love. I have become aware of physical decline, more now than even two or three years ago. But the creaking of the joints and the ticking of the clock no longer seem so ominous or life-defining. I look forward to birthdays more than I have done since childhood. I proudly tell my age: no mock-serious shame! (And yes, feel free to ask.) I look at people older than myself with more respect and optimism, and less fear and pity. I have not entirely relinquished the burden of ambition: the competitive, comparative, status-conscious part of myself. Nor do I want to. But the days of the noisy morning demons, obnoxiously scorning me for wasting my life and accomplishing nothing, are past.

In one respect, I have changed too little. Writing this book has shown me how much further I have to go in thinking first of others, and also how worthwhile that goal truly is. I hope the quest to learn generosity will define my remaining decades. On the positive side, I have plenty of room for improvement.

When conflicts and dilemmas and difficulties arise, and they often do, they still bring anger and worry and stress. Less so, though. As Laura Carstensen predicted, late adulthood seems to help me focus on the people and pursuits that matter most. And on the fish. The fish matter, too.

It didn't take very long, after all. A rod jumped to life, a bell tinkled, and Karl fought the reel. The haul was a slippery foot-long catfish. Karl held it for my inspection as he removed the hook from its lip. The creature gaped and gawped. I stared back. Can one see wisdom in the face of a catfish? That day, I thought I could.

We threw it back in and rebaited the hook. I was fishing again. Fifty years had disappeared.

Acknowledgments

Time matters. Writing a book like this one requires asking dozens of strangers, usually strangers with impressive titles and hectic schedules, for hours of their time. The scholars, therapists, life coaches, advertising executives, social entrepreneurs, and assorted experts and innovators I interviewed were selflessly responsive to my inquiries and generous with their knowledge. I would thank them all by name if doing so didn't entail listing everyone in the book. So I will economize: all, without exception, have my gratitude.

My even greater debt is to the dozens of people who entrusted me with personal stories. To say that the happiness curve is, scientifically speaking, a statistic is really to say that it represents the intersection of millions of data points, each one of which is a human biography. At first, when I started work on this book, I wondered if more than a handful of people would share their Voyage of Life. Instead, so many were so forthcoming that I felt I might possess some kind of magical key that unlocked diaries. I was not able to include all of the biographies I collected, but every story contributed insight, and every narrator has my profoundest thanks.

Sources and Methods

In researching this book, I interviewed dozens of people about the trajectories of their lives. In doing so, my approach was reportorial, not scientific. Unlike the big-data researchers whose research is described here, I neither attempted nor desired to assemble what social scientists call a representative or random sample of the population. Rather, I sought people who had illustrative stories to tell or insightful perspectives to offer—and who were willing to share them in considerable detail.

Because my interviews delved into intimate matters and sometimes explored feelings shared with few if any others, a high degree of trust was required. Understandably, strangers tended to be guarded or unresponsive when confronted with a journalist inquiring about their inner lives, and so I found myself relying disproportionately— although by no means entirely—on people in my social circles and people with whom I had a personal connection. My interview population is thus skewed toward professionals and high achievers: a limitation which readers should bear in mind and which I hope to improve upon in future work. Where I could do so without compromising confidentially (which is generally), I have indicated when people I interviewed were personal friends or acquaintances.

Except in a couple of cases where identity is an element of the story, and then only with interviewees' consent, I have used pseudonyms for my life-trajectory interviewees. Here and there, I change details that might reveal identity. Any such changes preserve social and demographic context.

To avoid scholarly apparatus, I have provided source references in the text where doing so is not too cumbersome. Following are additional notes and details on sources.

1. The Voyage of Life

The 1916 quotation calling for Thomas Cole's *Voyage of Life* to be restored and displayed in New York or Washington is from an anonymous article ("Thomas Cole's Voyage of Life") in *The Art World,* October 1916. On Cole, I also draw upon Earl A. Powell's *Thomas Cole* (Harry Abrams, 1990); Joy Kasson's "The Voyage of Life: Thomas Cole and Romantic Disillusionment," in *American Quarterly* 27 (1975); *The Correspondence of Thomas Cole and Daniel Wadsworth* (Connecticut Historical Society, 1983); and the National Gallery's exhibition history of its set of the Cole quadriptych. Thanks to researcher Matthew Quallen for his help with Cole.

2. What Makes Us Happy (and Doesn't)

An essential resource, providing a wealth of data and multiple analytical perspectives, is the *World Happiness Report,* which has been published almost annually since 2012. The economists John Helliwell, Richard Layard, and Jeffrey Sachs have made *WHR* a touchstone in the realm of happiness research. All editions can be downloaded at worldhappiness.report.

Also foundational for this book are the many articles and several books by Carol Graham and her various collaborators. I cite most in the main text. In addition, I draw on Graham's "Adaptation Amidst Prosperity and Adversity: Insights from Happiness Studies from Around the World" (*World Bank Research Observer,* 2010). I can't thank Carol enough for the many discussions, emails, and data analyses she provided.

The study of life-satisfaction duration by Bartolini and Sarracino is "Happy for How Long? How Social Capital and GDP Relate to Happiness Over Time," in *Ecological Economics* 108 (2014).

The study of windfall winners in Kenya, by Haushofer et al., is a working paper accessed via Haushofer's Princeton website, www.princeton.edu/haushofer/.

My source for the dollar-value equivalent of marital breakup and unemployment is David G. Blanchflower and Andrew J. Oswald, "Wellbeing over Time in Britain and the USA," in the *Journal of Public Economics* 88 (2004).

The paper by Deaton and Stone on emotional parents' life satisfaction is "Evaluative and Hedonic Wellbeing Among Those With and Without Children at Home," in *Proceedings of the National Academy of Sciences* (*PNAS*) 111:4 (2014).

The German study of life satisfaction among new parents is Rachel Margolis and Mikko Myrskyla, "Parental Wellbeing Surrounding First Birth as a Determinant of Further Parity Progression," in *Demography* 52 (2015).

3. A Timely Discovery

The writings of David Blanchflower and Andrew Oswald on life satisfaction are voluminous, indispensable, and fascinating. In addition to their many articles discussed in the text, I consulted "The U-Shape Without Controls: A Response to Glenn," in *Social Science & Medicine* 69 (2009) and "International Happiness" (National Bureau of Economic Research working paper, January 2011). Their findings on age and antidepressant prescriptions are from their working papers "Antidepressants and Age in 27 European Countries: Evidence of a U-Shape in Human Wellbeing Through Life" (March 2012) and "The Midlife Crisis: Is There Evidence?" (July 2013). Both papers are available on their websites.

The finding by Powdthavee, Oswald, and Cheng that the U curve occurs in individuals over time is reported in their paper "Longitudinal Evidence for a Midlife Nadir in Human Wellbeing: Results from Four Data Sets," in *The Economic Journal* (October 15, 2015).

"A Snapshot of the Age Distribution of Psychological Wellbeing in the United States" by Stone et al. was published in *PNAS* 107:22 (2010).

The article by Weiss, Enns, and King on the heritability of personality and wellbeing in chimps and humans is "Subjective Wellbeing Is Heritable and Genetically Correlated with Dominance in Chimpanzees," in *Journal of Personality and Social Psychology* 83:5 (2002). The article by Weiss and King on chimp and human personality development is "Great Ape Origins of Personality Maturation and Sex Differences: A Study of Orangutans and Chimpanzees," in *Personality and Social Psychology* 108:4 (2014). I also draw upon Weiss's chapter on parallels between chimp and human wellbeing, "The Genetics and Evolution of Covitality," coauthored with Michelle Luciano, in *Genetics of Psychological Wellbeing: The Role of Heritability and Genetics in Positive Psychology,* ed. Michael Pluess (Oxford University Press, 2015), pp. 146–60. Oswald's and Weiss's coauthors on "Evidence for a Midlife Crisis in Great Apes Consistent with the U-Shape in Human Wellbeing" are the psychologist James E. King and the primatologists Miho Inoue-Murayama and Tetsuro Matsuzawa.

4. The Shape of the River

The Susan Krauss Whitbourne quotation is from "Worried About a Midlife Crisis? Don't. There's No Such Thing," at *Psychology Today*'s website (www.psychologytoday .com, 2015). The study of vegetable consumption and happiness, by Oswald, Blanchflower, and Stewart-Brown, is "Is Psychological Wellbeing Linked to the Consumption of Fruit and Vegetables?" (National Bureau of Economic Research, 2012). The finding by Graham and Ruiz Pozuelo that higher levels of happiness are associated with earlier U-curve turning points are in "Happiness and Age: People, Place, and Happy Life Years," in the *Journal of Population Economics* (2016). See also the notes above to chapter 3.

5. The Expectations Trap

For a comprehensive and comprehensible overview of the psychology of happiness, Jonathan Haidt's 2006 book *The Happiness Hypothesis: Finding Modern Truth in Ancient Wisdom* (Basic Books) can't be beat. Quotations are from page 143 and various locations in chapter 5.

Also foundational is the work of Martin E. P. Seligman, whose 2002 book *Authentic Happiness: Using the New Positive Psychology to Realize Your Potential for Lasting Fulfillment* (Atria Books) provides much insight, as well as the useful happiness formula which I adapted.

The 1990 experiment by Kahneman, Knetsch, and Thaler on endowment bias is reported in "Anomalies: The Endowment Effect, Loss Aversion, and Status Quo Bias," published in the *Journal of Economic Perspectives* 5:1 (1991).

Tali Sharot and various collaborators have published extensively on optimism bias. Sharot lays out her findings concisely and readably in her ebook *The Science of Optimism*. Other Sharot work I consulted includes "The Optimism Bias" in *Current Biology* 21:23 (2011); "Neural Mechanisms Mediating Optimism Bias," coauthored with Alison Riccardi, Candace Raio, and Elizabeth Phelps, in *Nature* 450 (2007); "Selectively Altering Belief Formation in the Human Brain," coauthored with Ryota Kanai, David Marston, Christoph W. Korn, Geraint Rees, and Raymond J. Dolan, in *PNAS* 109:42 (2012); "The Optimism Bias," in *Time* magazine (May 28, 2011); "Optimistic Update Bias Increases in Older Age," coauthored with R. Chowdhury, T. Wolfe, E. Düzel, and R. J. Dolan, in *Psychological Medicine* 44:9 (2013); "Human Development of the Ability to Learn from Bad News," with Christina Moutsiana, Neil Garrett, Richard C. Clarke, R. Beau Lotto, and Sarah-Jayne Blakemore, in *PNAS* 110:41 (2013); and "How Unrealistic Optimism Is Maintained in the Face of Reality," with Christoph W. Korn and Raymond J. Dolan, in *Nature Neuroscience* 14 (2011).

6. The Paradox of Aging

Laura Carstensen's astonishingly rich and multifaceted research provides the backbone of this chapter, and her relevant articles are too numerous to list. Exploration should begin with her seminal article, coauthored with Derek M. Isaacowitz and Susan T. Charles, "Taking Time Seriously: A Theory of Socioemotional Selectivity," in

American Psychologist 54:3 (1999); and with her book *A Long Bright Future: Happiness, Health, and Financial Security in an Age of Increased Longevity* (PublicAffairs, 2009). For engaging summaries, see Carstensen's April 2012 TED talk, "Older People Are Happier" (www.ted.com/talks/laura_carstensen_older_people_are_happier), and her 2015 Aspen Ideas Festival talk, "Long Life in the 21st Century" (www.aspenideas.org /session/aspen-lecture-long-life-21st-century). Other Carstensen contributions I consulted include "Emotional Behavior in Long-Term Marriage," with John M. Gottman and Robert W. Levenson, in *Psychology and Aging* 10:1 (1995); and "Aging, Emotion, and Evolution: The Bigger Picture," with Corinna E. Löckenhoff, in *Annals of the New York Academy of Sciences* 1000 (2003). I owe Carstensen a deep debt of gratitude for her help with this book.

Brassen's coauthors on "Don't Look Back in Anger!" are Christian Büchel, Matthias Gamer, Sebastian Gluth, and Jan Peters.

Blazer's article on depression among the elderly is "Depression in Late Life: Review and Commentary," in *The Journals of Gerontology, Series A: Biological Sciences and Medical Sciences* 58:3 (2008).

Yang's quotation, "With age comes happiness," comes from her article "Social Inequalities in Happiness in the United States, 1972 to 2004: An Age-Period-Cohort Analysis," in *American Sociological Review* 73:2 (2008).

Comparing the effects on life satisfaction of aging and education, Sutin writes with Antonio Terracciano, Yuri Milaneschi, Yang An, Luigi Ferruci, and Alan B. Zonderman, in "The Effect of Birth Cohort on Wellbeing: The Legacy of Economic Hard Times," in *Psychological Science* 24:3 (2013).

Gana's findings on aging and life satisfaction in France are in "Does Life Satisfaction Change in Old Age? Results from an 8-Year Longitudinal Study," coauthored with Nathalie Bailly, Yaël Saada, Michèle Joulain, and Daniel Alaphilippe, in *The Journals of Gerontology, Series B: Psychological Sciences and Social Sciences* 68:4 (2013).

The remark by Carstensen et al. that emotional life may not peak until well into the seventh decade is from "Emotional Experience Improves with Age: Evidence Based on over Ten Years of Experience Sampling," coauthored with Susan Scheibe, Hal Ersner-Hershfield, Kathryn P. Brooks, Bulent Turan, Nilam Ram, Gregory R. Samanez-Larken, and John R. Nesselroade, in *Psychology and Aging* 26:1 (2011).

The study by Lacey, Smith, and Ubel on misunderstandings about age and happiness are from "Hope I Die Before I Get Old: Mispredicting Happiness Across the Adult Lifespan," in *Journal of Happiness Studies* 7 (2006). More evidence that happy older people believe that other older people are unhappy is in Laura Carstensen and Susan Scheibe, "Emotional Aging: Recent Findings and Future Trends," in *The Journals of Gerontology, Series B: Psychological Sciences and Social Sciences* 65B:2 (2010).

Cooney's piquant quotation about old age and bad luck is from the manuscript of *No Country for Old Women,* provided to me by the author.

Jeste's findings on successful aging can be found in "Correlates of Self-Rated Successful Aging Among Community-Dwelling Older Adults," coauthored with L. P. Montross, C. Depp, J. Daly, J. Reichstadt, S. Golshan, D. Moore, and D. Sitzer, in *The American Journal of Geriatric Psychiatry* 14:1 (2006); and in "Association Between Older Age and More Successful Aging: Critical Role of Resilience and Depression," coauthored with Gauri N. Salva, Wesley K. Thompson, Ipsit V. Vahia, Danielle K. Glorioso, A'verria Sirkin Martin, Barton W. Palmer, David Rock, Shahrokh Golshan, Helena C. Kraemer, and Colin A. Depp, in the 2013 *American Journal of Psychiatry* article discussed in the main text. In 2016, Jeste, along with Michael L. Thomas, Christopher N. Kaufmann, Barton W. Palmer, Colin A. Depp, A'verria Sirkin Martin, Danielle K. Glorioso, and Wesley K. Thompson, published further findings that mental health improves with aging ("Paradoxical Trend for Improvement in Mental Health with Aging: A Community-Based Study of 1,546 Adults Aged 21–100 Years," in *The Journal of Clinical Psychiatry* 77:8).

The finding by Kunzmann, Little, and Smith that aging confers protection from psychological distress owing to declining health is from "Is Age-Related Stability of Subjective Wellbeing a Paradox? Cross-Sectional and Longitudinal Evidence from the Berlin Aging Study," *Psychology and Aging* 15:3 (2000).

Mather's paper on processing emotions in old age is in "The Emotion Paradox in the Aging Brain," *Annals of the New York Academy of Sciences* 1251:1 (2012).

For a useful review of evidence that older people are more attentive and responsive to positive stimuli, see Susan Turk Charles and Laura L. Carstensen, "Emotion Regulation and Aging," chapter 15 of *Handbook of Emotion Regulation,* ed. James J. Gross (Guilford Press, 2007). Also good on aging and positivity: Raeanne C. Moore, Lisa T. Eyler, Paul J. Mills, Ruth M. O'Hara, Katherine Wachmann, and Helen Lavretsky, "Biology of Positive Psychiatry," in *Positive Psychiatry: A Clinical Handbook,* eds. Dilip V. Jeste and Baton W. Palmer (American Psychiatric Publishing, 2015); and Laura L. Carstensen, "The Influence of a Sense of Time on Human Development," *Science,* June 30, 2006.

The research on emotional selectivity among macaque monkeys is in Laura

Almeling, Kurt Hammerschmidt, Holger Sennhenn-Reulen, Alexandra M. Freund, and Julia Fischer, "Motivational Shifts in Aging Monkeys and the Origins of Social Selectivity," *Current Biology* 26 (2016).

7. Crossing Toward Wisdom

The literature on the emerging science of wisdom is fragmented and awaits the publication of a major synthesizing works that puts the various pieces together. Still, taken together, the articles of Dilip Jeste, Monika Ardelt, and Igor Grossmann cover most of the fundamentals. An ideal place to begin exploring the contemporary science of wisdom is Katherine J. Bangen, Thomas W. Meeks, and Dilip Jeste, "Defining and Assessing Wisdom: A Review of the Literature," in the *The American Journal of Geriatric Psychiatry* 22:4 (2014).

Jeste's and Vahia's comparison of the *Bhagavad Gita* with modern wisdom science is "Comparison of the Conceptualization of Wisdom in Ancient Indian Literature with Modern Views: Focus on the *Bhagavad Gita*," in *Psychiatry* 71:3 (2008).

The finding that wise thinking and behavior vary within individuals is in Igor Grossmann, Tanja M. Gerlach, and Jaap J. A. Denissen, "Wise Reasoning in the Face of Everyday Life Challenges," in *Social Psychological and Personality Science* 7:7 (2016). Grossmann's experimental finding that wise reasoning can be induced is in his paper, coauthored with Ethan Kross, "Boosting Wisdom: Distance from the Self Enhances Wise Reasoning, Attitudes, and Behavior," *Journal of Experimental Psychology: General* 141:1 (2011).

On intelligence and wisdom, Grossmann's finding of no reliable association between them is in "A Route to Wellbeing: Intelligence vs. Wise Reasoning," coauthored with Jinkyung Na, Michael E. W. Varnum, Shinobu Kitayama, and Richard E. Nisbett, in *Journal of Experimental Psychology: General* 142:3 (2013). Intriguingly, Dilip Jeste and Thomas Meeks's report that intelligence and wisdom implicate different brain regions; see "Neurobiology of Wisdom: A Literature Overview," in *Archives of General Psychiatry,* April 2009, a splendidly comprehensive article. Other valuable research on the distinction between wisdom and intelligence is Dan Blazer, Helena C. Kraemer, George Vaillant, and Thomas W. Meeks, "Expert Consensus on Characteristics of Wisdom: A Delphi Method Study," in *The Gerontologist,* March 2010; and Monika Ardelt, "Intellectual Versus Wisdom-Related Knowledge: The Case for a Different Kind of Learning in the Later Years of Life," in *Educational Gerontology* 26 (2000).

The research by Bluck and Glück on the lesson-teaching, transformative characteristics of wisdom situations is in "Making Things Better and Learning a

Lesson: Experiencing Wisdom Across the Lifespan," in *Journal of Personality* 72:3 (2004).

The quotation from Jeste, Bangen, and Meeks on the active component of wisdom is from their article "Defining and Assessing Wisdom," cited above.

On wisdom's physical and emotional benefits, I consulted a variety of sources.

Ardelt finds wisdom has a strong effect on life satisfaction, in "Wisdom and Life Satisfaction in Old Age," *The Journals of Gerontology, Series B: Psychological Sciences and Social Sciences* 52:1 (1997). A useful summary of research on wisdom and health, by Jeste, Katherine Bangen, and Michael Thomas, is "Development of a 12-Item Abbreviated Three-Dimensional Wisdom Scale (3D-WS-12): Item Selection and Psychometric Properties," in *Assessment,* July 24, 2015. Grossmann's finding of multiple health benefits from wise reasoning is from the article coauthored with Jinkyung Na et al., cited above. Jeste and James C. Harris find that wisdom can compensate for physical decline, in "Wisdom—A Neuroscience Perspective," *Journal of the American Medical Association,* October 13, 2010.

Grossmann's examination of time diaries, finding more positivity when people are in wise-reasoning mode, is coauthored with Tanja M. Gelach, and Jaap J. A. Denissen, and can be found in "Wise Reasoning in the Face of Everyday Life Challenges," cited above.

The statement by Jeste and Meeks that promotion of the common good is a consistent component of wisdom is from "The Neurobiology of Wisdom," cited above.

Blankenhorn's profile of William Winter is "In Defense of the Practical Politician," *The American Interest,* May 24, 2016.

The 2013 paper by Grossmann et al. reporting an association between wisdom and age is "A Route to Wellbeing," cited above. Grossmann's and Ethan Kross's paper finding no meaningful difference in wise reasoning by older and younger adults is "Exploring Solomon's Paradox: Self-Distancing Eliminates the Self-Other Asymmetry in Wise Reasoning About Close Relationships in Younger and Older Adults," in *Psychological Science* 1:10 (2014). Grossmann's paper on wisdom and age in the United States and Japan is "Aging and Wisdom: Culture Matters," coauthored with Mayumi Karasawa, Satoko Izumi, Jinkyung Na, Michael E. W. Varnum, Shinobu Kitayama, and Richard E. Nisbett, in *Psychological Science* 23:10 (2012). See also Grossmann's article "Reasoning About Social Conflicts Improves into Old Age," coauthored with Jinkyung Na, Michael E. W. Varnum, Denise C. Park, Shinobu Kitayama, and Richard E. Nisbett, is in *PNAS* 107:16 (2010).

I took Monika Ardelt's thirty-nine-question wisdom test via *The New York Times* website, at www.nytimes.com/packages/flash/multimedia/20070430_WISDOM/index.html.

8. Helping Ourselves

One reason I haven't tried to summarize the best thinking on self-help and reinvention in middle age—besides the sheer impossibility of doing so—is that I could not improve on Barbara Bradley Hagerty's *Life Reimagined: The Science, Art, and Opportunity of Midlife* (Riverhead, 2016). Her engaging book is chock-full of good advice and solid science.

Haidt's discussion of meditation is in *The Happiness Hypothesis,* cited above and in the text. On the medical value of mindfulness-based techniques, I draw upon Samantha Boardman and P. Murali Doraiswamy, "Integrating Positive Psychiatry into Clinical Practice," in *Positive Psychiatry: A Clinical Handbook,* cited above.

The Strenger and Ruttenberg quotation is from their article "The Existential Necessity of Midlife Change," *Harvard Business Review,* February 2008.

The Whitbourne quotation about the value of incremental steps is from "Four Surefire Ways to Change Your Life for the Better," *Huffington Post,* February 16, 2015.

9. Helping Each Other

Three books are invaluable in charting the new territory of encore adulthood. For a wide-ranging, well written survey, see Marc Freedman's *The Big Shift: Navigating the New Stage Beyond Midlife* (PublicAffairs, 2011). For pathbreaking thinking on the social implications of this new phase of life, see Phyllis Moen's *Encore Adulthood: Boomers on the Edge of Risk, Renewal, and Purpose* (Oxford, 2016). For self-help, see Richard J. Leider and Alan M. Webber, *Life Reimagined: Discovering Your New Life Possibilities* (Berrett-Koehler, 2013).

On the invention of adolescence, I draw upon Greg Hamilton, "Mapping a History of Adolescence and Literature for Adolescents," in *The ALAN Review* (the peer-reviewed journal of the Assembly on Literature for Adolescents of the National Council of Teachers of English), Winter 2002; David Bakan, "Adolescence in America: From Idea to Social Fact," *Daedalus* 100:4 (1971); John Demos and Virginia Demos, "Adolescence in Historical Perspective," *Journal of Marriage and Family* 31:4 (1969); and Marc Freedman's book *The Big Shift,* cited above.

Encore.org's polling on prevalence of encore careers is from "Encore Careers: The Persistence of Purpose," at Encore.org. This fact sheet reports on an online survey of 1,694 adults ages fifty to seventy, conducted by Penn Schoen Berland in 2014.

The figures on age demographics of start-up entrepreneurs are from *The 2016 Kauffman Index of Startup Activity* (Table 5).

The figures on people who describe themselves as "retired but not working" are from Phyllis Moen's *Encore Adulthood,* cited above.

Index